W9-BGL-520

WITHDRAWN

Blood Ties

LIFE AND VIOLENCE IN RURAL MEXICO

James B. Greenberg

THE UNIVERSITY OF ARIZONA PRESS   TUCSON

Publication of this book is made possible in part by a grant from the
Provost's Author Support Fund of the University of Arizona.

THE UNIVERSITY OF ARIZONA PRESS
Copyright © 1989
The Arizona Board of Regents
All Rights Reserved

This book was set in 9/12 Joanna.
Manufactured in the United States of America.
♾ This book is printed on acid-free, archival-quality paper.
93   92   91   90   89   5   4   3   2   1

Library of Congress Cataloging-in-Publication Data

Greenberg, James B.
    Blood ties: life and violence in rural Mexico / James B.
  Greenberg.
        p.   cm.
      Bibliography: p.
      Includes index.
      ISBN 0-8165-1091-1 (alk. paper)
        1. Chatino Indians–Social conditions.   2. Chatino Indians–
Biography.   3. Vendetta–Mexico–Oaxaca. 4. Santa Catarina Juquila
(Oaxaca, Mexico)–Social conditions.   5. Indians of Mexico–Oaxaca–
Social conditions.   6. Villages–Mexico–Oaxaca.   7. Indians of
Mexico–Oaxaca–Biography.   I. Title.
F1221.C47G72 1989
305.8'97–dc 19   88-29538
                                                          CIP

British Library Cataloguing in Publication data are available.

A survival manual for my wife, Eva, her family, and our children, Henry and Erica

Contents

Maps

Preface

In many ways this is a very personal book based on the life of a Chatino man, Don Fortino, who was a good friend. However, it is not simply his life story. It is a means of exploring a topic of great personal concern: the violence endemic to this region. I say personal concern because it is not simply a matter of intellectual curiosity. The bloodshed in the region has cost the lives of many of my wife's kinsmen and *compadres*, and of many of my friends. It continues to threaten their lives and to affect my own.

My introduction to the violence of the region began in 1973, when I first visited the district of Juquila looking for a village in which to do fieldwork. On the way into the district I kept hearing stories about people being hacked to death with machetes. My first encounter with violence came almost immediately after I arrived. I had gone to Yaitepec to see if I could do a study there. As I was talking to the town's officials, the town's *topiles*, or constables, brought in two young men for a murder. I asked if someone could put me up for the night. My host had a machete scar running from his eye to his lip. He had another on his hand where his thumb had almost been severed. I soon noticed that many men bore such scars. As my fieldwork proceeded, I began to put numbers to these first impressions.

The homicide rates were astounding. From 1930 to 1949 the homicide rate in Yaitepec had averaged 120 per 100,000 population. The introduction of coffee as a cash crop in 1950 split the village into feuding factions, and the rate soared to 480 per 100,000 through the 1950s and 440 per 100,000 through the 1960s (Greenberg 1981:182). Between 1973 and 1977 homicide rates in Yaitepec averaged 511 per 100,000 (Bartolomé and Barabas 1982:74). Yaitepec does not stand alone. Homicide rates of from sixteen to twenty-nine times the national average occur throughout the district.[1] In the town of Juquila from 1973 to 1975, the average rate per 100,000 was 284, in Ixtapan it was

408, and in Panixtlahuaca 450 per 100,000. In 1977 the rate in seven Chatino villages averaged 300 per 100,000 (Bartolomé and Barabas 1982:221, 74).

These rates, however, are somewhat deceptive. Since more than 95 percent of the victims are men, the rates understate the case. A rate of 450 per 100,000 is really a rate for men of 900 per 100,000. Moreover, about 80 percent of these deaths are of men aged from 15 to 50. In other words, there is a better than 30 percent chance that a man will be killed before he turns fifty.

During the fifteen months I was in Yaitepec, I witnessed two murders, four shootings, two machete fights, and many fistfights, yet no one would talk to me about these matters. Even my best informants clammed up the moment I asked, however obliquely, about conflicts. I began to understand why they were so reluctant to talk about these things when a young man was shot in front of me during the fiesta of Santa Cruz. A man charged up to the victim with a .22-caliber pistol and fired one shot, putting a bullet between his eyes. The victim fell but was still alive. The authorities carried him back to his mother's house. People expected him to die, but he hung on. Two days later he was still alive. I asked if anyone had gone to get a doctor and was told that no one would go. I tried unsuccessfully to persuade the town officials to send a topil to Juquila to fetch the doctor. Finally, I went myself.

The doctor said that if the victim survived the night, he would go the next morning. I arranged for my assistant to come to Juquila and inform me of the man's status the next morning. About 5:00 A.M. my assistant's mother knocked on my door. She had come to ask me not stop at their house when I brought the doctor but to go directly to the victim's house. She didn't want anyone to think she was involved.

As it turned out, the bullet had not penetrated the skull, and the man survived. The lesson, however, was clear: even the appearance of being involved was dangerous. As an outsider, I could help anybody as long as I helped everybody, but for the villagers such actions are interpreted as taking sides. The same fear made them mute whenever I brought up the subject of conflict. In a small community, with its complex patterns of intermarriage, its tangled web of friendship and compadrazgo, it is hard to trust anyone to keep a confidence except one's immediate family. Such talk is dangerous; it could cost people their lives.

My access to information about conflict changed when I married a woman from Juquila. Since a careless word to the wrong person could not only be dangerous to me but could compromise them, my wife, her family, and their close compadres began to tell me about the various conflicts. They warned me about certain people and tried to explain the Byzantine workings of local politics. I was told how to answer even the most seemingly innocent questions. My brother-in-law put it to me frankly and bluntly:

Don't be so trusting. In America you might be able to, but not here. I don't even trust my own shadow. Look, we have our enemies. Who knows what they might be capable of? If someone asks you, "When are you leaving?" or, "How long are you staying?" if you are leaving on Monday, you say that you are going on Thursday. If they ask you where I've gone, if I am in Yaitepec, you tell them that I went to Panixtlahuaca. Don't trust anyone.

I soon realized that it was important for me to understand local politics. I had to learn how to evaluate the social consequences of various feuds. To do this I had to know not only who the principals were but also who their friends, relatives, and compadres were. I needed to learn how to evaluate what every killing, every incident, meant for their social relations and how these social ties might affect my wife's family. Since such networks extend to villages throughout the region, sorting out the pertinent facts required a knowledge of social relations and local politics not just in Juquila but across the entire region.

Though my wife and her mother, father, brothers, and sisters helped to teach me the basics, it was my compadre, Don Fortino, who really taught me about the region's conflicts and politics. Though not an educated man, more than anyone else I had met during my fieldwork he understood both my personal and intellectual interests in these topics and volunteered to help me with my work. After hundreds of hours of conversation between 1973 and 1978, I suggested we write a book based on his life history. I explained the risks that it might involve, and he agreed, provided that I change the names of local people and disguise their identities as far as possible. Over several weeks, we taped twenty-eight hours of interviews. Since then, he has gone through the tape and has suggested the deletion of materials he felt were potentially too dangerous to publish. Part I of this book is the product of this work.

In many ways Don Fortino was a highly unusual and gifted man, comfortable in both the Chatino and the mestizo worlds. Even though his mestizo father abandoned his Chatino mother before he was born, Fortino grew up among both mestizo and Chatino relatives. He spoke both Chatino and Spanish fluently. Although the Mexican Revolution forced him to leave school in the third grade, he had taught himself to read and write. He was a man of natural curiosity. He was also a particularly astute political observer, as attested by the fact of his survival into old age. In a sense, he was a political observer all his life. He lived through the Revolution in Juquila. He witnessed the local events of the War of the Cristeros, which was brought on when President Calles attempted to bring the Church under state control. He participated in local politics and observed the evolution of conflicts and feuds in the region from their beginnings. As a shopkeeper and barber, he knew people from throughout the region. They came into his shop every day. He used the opportunity to cross-check their stories, or as he put it, "to dig out the truth about things."

What impressed me from the first about Don Fortino as an informant was his amazing memory for detail. In a district of 40,000 people, he could recount a person's genealogy if given simply the father's name. His skill as a storyteller was no less remarkable. His recounting of incidents was often replete with uncannily accurate dialogue. More than once I was witness to an exchange or incident that I later heard him recount with almost the fidelity of a tape recording. This is not to say that the dialogue in his narrative is always a faithful reproduction of what was said. As a storyteller he often used dialogue as a device to give a story immediacy, reconstructing exchanges as a native who knows what must have been said under the circumstances.

It is, of course, no less interesting to know what a native believes must have been said in these circumstances. Don Fortino made every effort in the interviews to answer my questions as completely and honestly as possible, telling me when he did not know certain things. Inevitably, however, some of his account is self-serving. Much of it represents an ideological interpretation of events from the point of view of the faction in the community to which his family and my wife's family belong. So his reconstructions of dialogue, and to some extent of events, are best viewed as normative statements, which is to say that Don Fortino's narrative, although extremely rich, cannot be taken at face value. To reveal its full richness requires a careful exegesis.

In an attempt to provide the critical analysis that Don Fortino's narrative deserves, I have divided this book into two parts. Following the introduction, which furnishes the essential ethnological background on the regional economy and its violence, there is Don Fortino's narrative, which weaves his account of regional politics and violence into the events of his own life. I have prepared introductions to groups of chapters in Don Fortino's narrative to provide a context for the events he describes. The book concludes with four chapters of analysis. These explore the various aspects of conflict and violence raised in Don Fortino's narrative. The first chapter in this section compares Don Fortino's explanations of violence with those provided by social scientists who have studied rural Mexico. This chapter is followed by a historical chapter, which traces the roots of conflict in the region, and a chapter on the ideology of violence, its meaning to participants and victims, and the defensive strategies people use to avoid conflict or to deal with it. The final chapter addresses patterns of conflict and the process of dispute expansion or resolution. As well, it speaks to the effects of violence on social relations and the fabric of society.

Acknowledgments

In preparing this manuscript, I amassed a debt of gratitude to many people, and first among them is my wife, Eva, who patiently transcribed the tapes. I am also indebted to Carlos Vélez-Ibáñez, director of the Bureau of Applied Research in Anthropology at the University of Arizona for his support for and belief in this project, and to several of our research assistants who have translated portions of Don Fortino's narrative: Sandra Sáenz de Tejada, Pamela Bartholomew, and Laura Cummings. In addition, Barent Gjelsness deserves credit for his help in editing the manuscript, as does my compadre Professor Roberto Molina Rendón for preparing an initial draft of the map of the town of Juquila. This book also has been greatly improved by the suggestions and comments offered by Gerardo Bernache, Mel Firestone, Salomón Nahmad, and Henry Selby. Barbara Montgomery prepared the maps for the book.

Blood Ties

Introduction

My first impression of Juquila was that it was a sleepy mountain village of adobe houses with red tile roofs. Nothing in its appearance suggested that it was beset by deep-rooted conflicts and violence. It seemed a jewel set in an emerald-green mountain valley. Cornfields like green postage stamps dotted the pine-covered peaks that rose above the village. Since there was no bus to Juquila, I had come by truck from Oaxaca perched atop cases of Pepsi Cola. It was a long and arduous journey, taking eight hours to go 140 miles.

As the truck negotiated the narrow road into town, I noted that Juquila sprawled over several hills. Its houses stood amid cornfields and gardens surrounded by coffee, mango, guayaba, avocado, lemon, and banana trees. As we pulled into the heart of the town, we left the rural village and entered a decidedly urban, typically mestizo, colonial town. An impressive colonial church and a *palacio municipal*, or town hall, dominated its central plaza. The symbols of the state's presence could hardly be missed. Juquila is the seat of the district. The palacio on the plaza housed, in addition to the office of the *presidente*, the district court, the office of the public prosecutor, a state police post, an army barracks, a prison, and the state tax collector's office. As well, the plaza boasted telegraph and post offices, a municipal market, shops, stores, restaurants, and even a hotel. Nothing in my initial impression suggested that this place was particularly violent.

The truck stopped in front of the store of a coffee buyer. It was Saturday, a market day. The plaza was crowded with Indians wearing brightly colored costumes, selling fruit, vegetables, pottery, straw mats, and the other goods that the surrounding villages specialize in making.

As few Americans ever came to the village, my arrival was something of a sensation. A group of curious villagers gathered round. A tall, well-built man in his seventies pushed through the crowd and asked if I needed any help. This was Don Fortino. I asked him where I might get something to eat. He

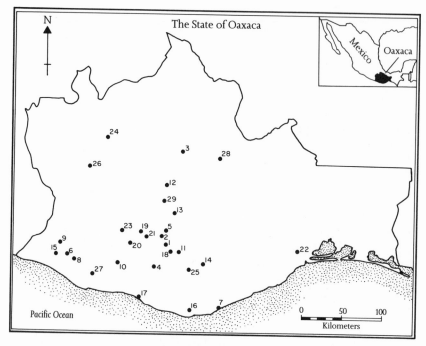

N

The State of Oaxaca

Oaxaca

Pacific Ocean

0   50   100
Kilometers

1 Almolongas	11 Miahuatlán	21 Sola de Vega
2 Amatengo	12 Oaxaca	22 Tehuantepec
3 Anulco	13 Ocotlán	23 Teojomulco
4 Coatlán	14 Ozolotepec	24 Teposcolula
5 Ejutla	15 Pinotepa	25 Titiquipa
6 Huaspaltepec	16 Pochutla	26 Tlaxiaco
7 Huatulco	17 Puerto Escondido	27 Tututepec
8 Jamiltepec	18 Santa Ana de Cuixtla	28 Villa Alta
9 Jiyacán	19 Santa María	29 Zimatlán
10 Juquila	20 Santiago Minas	

pointed to one of several restaurants on the plaza. "It's not much, but it's as good as you'll find here," he said. I ambled across the plaza, followed by a gaggle of kids laughing and yelling "Gringo! Gringo!" and entered the nearly empty, fly-infested restaurant.

Several men, Don Fortino among them, soon came in and invited me to join them. They asked if I would like a beer. When I accepted, they concluded I was not a missionary. Questions. Where was I from? Did I know Guillermo Upson, the Prides, and several other missionaries that had worked in the district over the past thirty years? I told them I was an anthropologist. I was affiliated with the Instituto Nacional de Antropología e Historia (INAH) and had come to the district to study the Chatino language and culture. I added that I was interested in the civil and religious offices and the system of fiestas that organized Chatino communities.

The other men at the table, it turned out, were relatives of Don Fortino—the small society of Juquila—Fortino's son, Nico Santiago, his half brother, Don Timoteo, Timoteo's son Diego, and Don Fortino's nephew Anselmo Valentín. The Santiagos were all local merchants and coffee buyers. In addition to small stores, they owned hotels, plantations, and cantinas, and they dominated the politics and commerce of the village. I soon realized that although others may hold office, these were the men who called the shots. They ran the local chapter of the Partido Revolucionario Institucional (PRI), the national ruling party. My answers to their questions apparently satisfied them, but it was my letters of introduction from INAH, the state governor, and the military that impressed them. They promised to help me in any way they could.

When I expressed interest in visiting Santiago Yaitepec, they expressed concern for my safety. Don Timoteo tried to dissuade me. "It's dangerous," he said. "They are ignorant savages who would as soon murder you as look at you." Don Fortino disagreed: "They're no worse than anyone else, and better than some." He told me that if I wanted to go, he would contact his half sister, Chica. She lived in Yaitepec, and I could probably live with her.

The next day, Don Fortino introduced me to his sister's stepson, Salomón, who would take me to Yaitepec. Although Yaitepec is only an hour's walk from Juquila, it was all that I could do to keep up with Salomón, who strode barefoot ahead of me up the steep, rocky mountain trail. At last the village came into view. Few houses could be seen, as most were hidden by trees. Fortino's sister's one-room house stood on a hill in a compound with several other similar houses. Chica, a woman in her middle fifties, met me at the gate and introduced me to her husband, Emiliano, who turned out to be Fortino's compadre. A man in his early sixties, he had a machete scar running across his face from his left eye to his lip. Nevertheless, despite his terrible visage, he was warm and unassuming. They were friendly and polite, asking me to sit down and offering me a Pepsi. I told them that I wanted to live in Yaitepec and learn their language and customs. Their questions seemed simple. Was America across the sea? What did Americans eat? Later I would learn that what they were really asking was: Are you from the land of the dead that is across the sea? and Do you eat little children? as folklore has it that gringos do? Did I have a wife or children? Because I was unmarried, there was a long discussion over where I could stay. They finally decided that, since Fortino would not have sent me if I could not be trusted, I could live in a house that had belonged to his father but that now stood empty.

Learning About Village Conflicts

I arranged for Chica to cook for me and to teach me Chatino. I also hired Salomón as my assistant. I began to attend the daily meetings of the town council. I asked for permission to examine the town's archives. No one cared. The archives consisted of bundles of termite-chewed papers thrown into a corner of the town hall, but they proved to be a rich source of information.

As I sorted through the archives, I soon realized that Yaitepec was rife with violence. There were volumes of depositions describing murders, and although they furnished some details of a case—such as time, place, manner of death, and often the name of the accused—they gave precious little indication of motive.

At first this carnage seemed the result of a senseless series of drunken fights and revenge killings rooted in ancient personal animosities. Gradually, however, I began to see that this explanation was too simple. The village had fought long and bitter battles over boundaries with Yolotepec, Temaxcaltepec, and Juquila, not only in the courts but also in the field. In a series of homicides, the authorities of one village or another were accused of murdering people in these disputed zones. It was also clear that litigation was an expensive affair that regularly pumped money out of the poor Indian communities without ever resolving their disputes (Dennis 1976: 175–184). In addition, following the introduction of coffee to communal lands in about 1950, changes in land tenure sparked a brutal series of blood feuds that pitted family against family. Ultimately these feuds divided the village's two barrios against each other. At least a third of the households in the village had been involved in homicides. The village was in a state of civil war (Greenberg 1981: 171–182).

Yaitepec was also embroiled in a prolonged conflict with the Valencias, the owners of a coffee plantation called La Constancia. Their father, a priest from Juquila, had leased the land from the village at the end of the last century, but the Valencias had long claimed title to it. The village had petitioned for the restitution of these lands since 1935 but to no avail. Again, there was a series of homicides related to the dispute. The Valencias were accused of shooting villagers who invaded their land, and the villagers had on more than one occasion killed members of the Valencia family. It was also apparent from the archives that to thwart attempts to recover these lands, the Valencias had formed an alliance with one of the village factions. By providing the members of the faction with political protection and refuge on La Constancia, they had built a private army, which continued to raid the village and kill members of the other faction.

Factionalism and Violence

Although this paper trail of past bloodshed and political intrigue afforded some insight into the region's problems, it was not something that the Indians would talk about. I soon discovered, however, that mestizo society is every bit as violent, as I learned at firsthand through Don Fortino. I had only been in Yaitepec a couple of months when there was an attempt to ambush Don Fortino's son, Nico. Nico and his wife had gone to Panixtlahuaca in their Volkswagen Beetle to buy some coffee. On their way back to Juquila, assassins opened fire on their car. It was riddled with bullets, but they escaped uninjured. Nico and his family fled to Oaxaca, leaving his store in his sister's care.

Because of my relationship with Chica and Emiliano, Don Fortino confided in me as he quietly went about investigating who was behind the attempt on his son's life. Nico, he explained, had several enemies. His uncle Timoteo had involved Nico in his dispute with the Muñoz family, and Nico had gotten into a fistfight with one of them. When this man was killed, the Muñoz held Nico responsible. It did not matter that Nico denied it. Nor did it matter that the public prosecutor found no evidence to implicate him. Nico was not being tried by a court but by public opinion, rumor, and gossip.

Fortino looked for the same kind of evidence in his own investigations. The key question was: Who had a motive? Don Fortino soon concluded that the local priest and his mistress, Sabina, who were allies of the Muñoz family, were behind the attempt. On the afternoon of the ambush, Fortino's daughter had overheard one of Sabina's maids say to another maid, presumably referring to Nico's fate: "The barbecue will be here soon, right?" The other maid told her to shut up. As for a motive, the priest and his mistress were the Santiagos' principal economic and political competition. The priest had set up Sabina as a coffee buyer and was himself something of a *cacique*, or political boss, in his position as the leader of the local chapter of the Partido de la Auténtico Revolución Mexicana (PARM), which opposed the Santiago-controlled PRI. He had the support not only of the local communal lands organization but also of Indians in surrounding villages.

Although there were those among Fortino's in-laws who were ready to take revenge, Fortino discouraged them, fearing a bloodbath. Instead, the Santiagos sought to use their patrons to get the archbishop to apply political pressure to put the priest on notice that if anything happened to Nico, he would be held responsible. Although it took almost a year, the archbishop finally intervened, and the way was clear for Nico to return to Juquila.

Interethnic Violence

Less than two months after the attempt on Nico's life, I witnessed the murder of Don León Valentín, Fortino's brother-in-law. Although I had already seen an attempted murder during the fiesta of Santa Cruz and three shootings just the day before, this murder affected me deeply, as I knew and liked both León and his son Anselmo.

Don León and Anselmo had come to Yaitepec in their truck to buy some hides and to attend the fiesta of Santiago. They were loading the hides on their truck when I saw them. I had just met and begun to court my wife, Eva, and I asked for a ride to Juquila. Don León, however, was a little drunk and first wanted to watch the horse races—a bloody little event in which horsemen galloping under live chickens hung from a rope stretched across the road try to pull their heads off. I accompanied them up to the little store that overlooked the road, where a crowd of Chatino spectators had assembled on the patio.

Don León bought a bottle of mescal and began to drink. Anselmo kept insisting that they should go. Don León answered, "Just as soon as I finish my drink." He was soon roaring drunk. Suddenly he pulled a gun out of his jacket and, reeling, began to fire shots in the air. A villager behind him pulled a knife and stabbed him in the back. The blade penetrated his lung and Don León collapsed, drowning in his own blood. Anselmo lunged at the man, who slashed at him, missing him by inches. Before Anselmo could act again, knife-wielding villagers surrounded him and allowed the killer to escape.

This was a public act of murder. Unlike an ambush, this public act was an appeal to the witnesses for vindication. The crowd showed by their actions that they tacitly approved of the murder. Don León was not only a mestizo from a village with which they had a long history of conflict, but more to the point, he had endangered their lives. As far as many villagers were concerned, it had been a justifiable homicide. The killing had been in defense of the public and was perhaps even a laudable act. Despite warrants issued by the district court in Juquila for the perpetrator's arrest, village authorities made no effort to arrest him, and he went about the village as if nothing had happened.

Factionalism, Violence, and the Politics of Patronage

Grief-stricken over his father's murder, Anselmo went into a deep depression. He started to drink heavily. When I came to Juquila on the weekend to attend the market and see Eva, I would invariably find Anselmo drunk.

Although amiable when sober, he was a classic angry drunk, and his wife often bore the bruises to prove it.

Anselmo's drunken behavior soon occasioned an incident that was to teach me even more about the Byzantine politics of patronage in Juquila. About two months after his father's death, Anselmo went into the store of his comadre to drink. Women can say things that would get a man killed. Because of this, they are instrumental in spreading the gossip, rumors, and lies that are the lifeblood of local politics. Anselmo's comadre began to berate him. She declared that if he were a man, he would have avenged his father, not let the man who killed him walk around free, and she called him a drunken sot who could only beat up women. Anselmo reacted violently. He grabbed a machete and began flailing away, cutting his comadre on her arm and scalp, slashing her husband's arm, and even cutting his own leg in the process. I was standing on the plaza talking to Eva and her mother when Anselmo stumbled out of the store, machete in hand. They began to scream, and he dropped the machete and took off running. He cut through the church, where a mass was in progress, ran down the steps beside the palacio, and took off into the hills.

I went into the store to see what had happened. The army nurse had been summoned and was sewing up wounds. A crowd had gathered. The husband was the presidente of the communal lands committee and a leader of the PARM faction. He was also an ally of the priest, who opposed the PRI faction, including Fortino's family. The men, all PARM supporters, were enraged by the attack. In their anger they dredged up old memories. Anselmo's brother had murdered his wife with a knife and fled the village, but this one was not going to get away; they were going to lynch him when they got their hands on him.

I felt compelled by my friendship with Fortino to warn him about what was being said. His attitude surprised me—"If they catch him, he has it coming"—but it should not have. Anselmo's actions were not only indefensible, but given the already tense situation between Fortino's family and the priest, this incident could easily spark a bloodbath, something Fortino was trying to avoid.

That night Anselmo tried to sneak back into town and was spotted in front of the house where I was staying. A shoot-out ensued. Someone had taken cover in the doorway and was firing what sounded like a .45 automatic. I huddled in a corner out of the line of fire. Bullets came through the door. Although the house was less than two hundred yards from the state police post and army barracks, no one came. As suddenly as it had begun, it was over. Anselmo had escaped and no one had been shot.

The next day, the judge of the district court summoned relatives of the principals involved in the dispute. Village factionalism often is a fairly stable, enduring form of conflict. As long as the status quo does not change too much, it remains in a dynamic equilibrium, and the level of violence accompanying it remains low. The attempt on Nico's life, followed by Anselmo's attack on his comadre and her husband, however, threatened this equilibrium and increased tensions between the factions. Because the principals were closely tied to the leadership of the two factions, this conflict had the potential of escalating into a nasty feud, pitting PRI and PARM supporters against one another. The judge's only concern was to defuse the situation before it went any further. If they promised that there would be no more violence, he would not apply the letter of the law but instead would drop the charges against both parties. But if there were any more violence, he would throw them all in jail for five years.

The judge's ruling, however, did not end the conflict, nor did it lessen by one iota the underlying competition and hatred between the two factions. Since his comadre's husband was the head of the communal lands committee, he soon sought revenge in other ways. He persuaded the town that its municipal market needed to be enlarged by tearing down the concrete stalls there, beginning with the stall that belonged to Anselmo and his wife.

Since the fiesta for the Virgin of Juquila was drawing near, Anselmo had gone to Oaxaca to buy supplies. When he returned he found that a hole had been knocked in one wall of his stall. He went to the presidente to complain, but the presidente, a PARM supporter, refused to act. He claimed that he was powerless to do anything because the market came under the communal lands committee's jurisdiction. Anselmo went off to drink and returned to the palacio drunk. He pulled a pistol, pointed it at the presidente's head, and pulled the trigger. The gun misfired. He threw the pistol onto the floor and it went off. The presidente called the police. Anselmo was arrested and charged with attempted homicide. This time, I figured, Anselmo would go to prison. But events soon took the case in a different direction, and I learned yet another lesson about the politics of patronage.

Since many pilgrims flew in from Oaxaca during the fiesta of the Virgin, the presidente decided that he could make some money by assessing a landing fee on planes using the town's dirt runway. The first plane that landed paid the fee and took off to pick up another load, but the second pilot to land refused and took off without paying. The presidente ordered that a log be placed across the runway. When the first plane returned, it hit the log, flipped, and crashed into a ravine, injuring fifteen passengers and wrecking the plane.

The presidente was in such hot water that just to stay out of prison he needed all the political help he could muster, so he turned to the Santiagos. In return for their help, he dropped the charges against Anselmo and gave his assurance that they would not tear down Anselmo's stall in the market.

Nevertheless, as a result of this incident the presidente was forced out of office. Ironically, Anselmo was later elected presidente.

The Politics of Consensus vs. the Politics of Patronage

The politics of patronage, though important, are only half of village politics. The other half is the politics of consensus, typically manifested in mass demonstrations or land invasions. I was soon to learn that although elites try to mold a consensus through patronage, the underground currents of consensus are not easily controlled and often run counter to the elite's wishes.

Shortly after the incidents during the fiesta, the authorities in Juquila signed a twenty-five-year lease with a lumber company, Etla S.A. The lease gave the company the right to cut timber on a tract along the road to Yolotepec. When the authorities in Yaitepec learned of this, they were more than a little upset. They believed that the tract in question was on Yaitepec's lands. Although factionalism and feuding racked Yaitepec, a threat to its communal lands was one issue that could unite the community, and the villagers threatened violence if any of their trees were cut.

A meeting was arranged with a representative of the company, ostensibly to show him the boundaries in question. This meeting had almost sacred overtones for the village, so the whole town council hiked up the mountain to meet the company's man at a point he could reach by jeep. Emiliano, as head of the communal lands committee, showed him a map from 1862, which the villagers preserve as a precious possession. He pointed out the mountaintops and river alignments that bounded the tract that Yaitepec claimed. The Etla representative was not impressed. Their map, he told them, had no notary marks and would be worthless in court. He wanted to cut the timber now, but because of the possibility of violence he agreed to delay cutting along this tract until the boundary dispute between Juquila and Yaitepec could be resolved. He suggested that the villagers take their case to the Instituto Nacional Indigenista (INI), which had just opened a center in Juquila. For now, the company would wait, but he warned them that if the dispute were still unsettled in five years, the company lawyers would persuade the federal government to nationalize the land. Etla would then obtain the lumber rights from the government, in which case neither community would get anything.

Returning to Yaitepec, the town council held a meeting to discuss the matter. Since the INI was a government agency, the local authorities understandably viewed it with suspicion. Long experience had taught them to be wary of the government's mestizo-dominated institutions and political parties. The alliance of businessmen and property owners in Juquila, for example, had

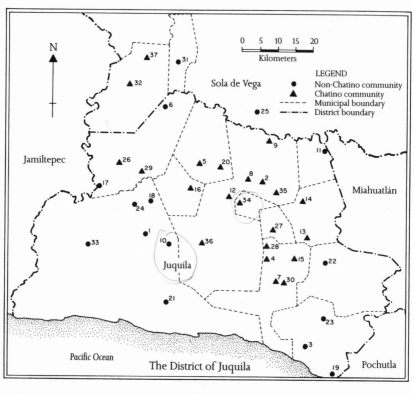

The District of Juquila

1 Acatepec
2 Amialtepec
3 Bajos de Chila
4 Cerro del Aire
5 Cieneguilla
6 Cinco Cerros
7 Cuixtla
8 Ixpantepec
9 Ixtapan
10 Jocotepec
11 Juchatengo
12 Juquila
13 Lachao Nuevo

14 Lachao Viejo
15 Nopala
16 Panixtlahuaca
17 Paso de la Reina
18 Peñas Negras
19 Puerto Escondido
20 Quiahije
21 Río Grande
22 San Gabriel Mixtepec
23 San Pedro Mixtepec
24 Santa Cruz Tututepec
25 Santiago Minas
26 Tataltepec

27 Temaxcaltepec
28 Teotepec
29 Tepenixtlahuaca
30 Tiltepec
31 Tlacotepec
32 Tlapanalquiahuitl
33 Tututepec
34 Yaitepec
35 Yolotepec
36 Zacatepec
37 Zenzontepec

used the PRI to claim this very tract of land. The PARM was no better. When they began building a new church, the priest, acting as a contractor, had overcharged them for labor, materials, and transportation. In doing so he had depleted their funds and had left the church unfinished. Emiliano suggested that they go to his compadre Don Fortino for advice.

The following day Emiliano, the presidente, the *síndico*, and I went to

Juquila to see Don Fortino at his store. There Emiliano, as if reciting a morality play, recounted the whole saga of Yaitepec's battles not just with Juquila but also with Yolotepec, Temaxcaltepec, and the Valencias. Don Fortino told us that the only way to resolve the problem was to take their case to the Departamento de Asuntos Agrarios in Mexico City. He also suggested that they should go to see the INI's director because the INI had lawyers to help Indian communities with such matters. "Show them your titles," he urged and went on to lecture them: "Even though Don Arnulfo Valencia is my compadre, it pains me to see how these people have taken advantage of you, to say 'This is mine' when it isn't." But he continued, "This is something that must be handled legally, not the way you've been going about it for the past forty years—you shooting them, them shooting you. And what results have you had? Nothing has been settled. They still have the land, and you continue to fight with Yolotepec and Temaxcaltepec."

We went to see the director of the INI center in Juquila, a young man who had just finished his bachelor's degree in anthropology the year before. Juquila was his first posting. Emiliano again recited the saga of Yaitepec's battles and showed the director the village's land titles. The titles turned out to be copies of notarized copies made in 1926 of titles issued in 1863, which had been altered by unknown persons to conform to Yaitepec's claims. In short, they were worthless. The original titles, Emiliano explained, had been stolen by the Valencias in collusion with a former presidente.

The director gave Emiliano a letter of introduction to the INI's lawyers in Mexico City but told him that he had to go there before the end of the month or it would be too late. Later that day when I went to the town hall the authorities asked me in the most formal and polite Chatino to accompany Emiliano and the members of the communal lands committee to Mexico City. They needed a guide. Only Emiliano had been to Mexico City, and he only once. He did not know his way around the city. Frankly, I told them, I could not afford to go, because my stipend had not arrived. When they offered to lend me the money to go with them, I reluctantly agreed.

The trip to Mexico City was much more than simply a matter of business, it was a sacred mission, so before we could set out, we had to tell the patron saint of the village of our mission and seek his blessing. When we got to Mexico City we went to see an INI lawyer. He told us that according to the information he had obtained from the Departamento de Asuntos Agrarios, there was no conflict between Juquila and Yaitepec. The INI opinion, moreover, favored not only Juquila but also Yolotepec and Temaxcaltepec. The lawyer was pessimistic about Yaitepec's chance of winning the boundary dispute but encouraged the delegation by saying that there might be a chance to win a fight for the Valencias' land. When the INI failed to champion their cause fully, Emiliano, who had been to Mexico City before, decided to seek aid from the Confederación Nacional Campesina (CNC). Even though the CNC has advocates to help peasants through the Departamento de Asuntos Agrarios' bureaucratic maze, its labyrinth is designed to empty peasants' pockets with delays and enrich an army of officials, solicitors, and lawyers.

When Emiliano tried to explain the saga of Yaitepec's problems to the advocate, he became impatient. He wrote a letter that was full of inaccuracies. He told us to come back tomorrow and he would take us to the Departamento de Asuntos Agrarios. Emiliano panicked. The letter implied that they had titles, which they did not. It misstated the number of pueblos invading their lands. It said nothing about their conflict with the Valencia plantation. The next day, however, the advocate's attitude seemed to have changed. I suspect he thought I might have some political influence. He corrected the problems in the letter, but since it was already too late to go the departamento, he arranged to meet us there the next day.

Even with the CNC advocate's help, the Departamento de Asuntos Agrarios was a bureaucratic nightmare. Officials had little time or patience for Indians. We were shunted between offices, enduring endless waits to see someone else. We filled out forms and filed petitions, only to be told that we had the wrong form and needed to go back to the other office. It took the advocate two weeks to obtain copies of the land titles and maps. Finally he made an appointment to see the director of the Office of Communal Lands. The director reviewed Yaitepec's file. The file was complete. His office could proceed. It was his opinion that the titles did not support Yaitepec's dispute with Juquila. Since in the INI's opinion the problem of municipal boundaries should take precedence over conflicts with small landowners, the director scheduled a meeting in his office for representatives from Yaitepec, Yolotepec, and Temaxcaltepec for the following month. If they could not settle the matter among themselves at that meeting, he told them, then the Departamento de Asuntos Agrarios would make the decision. As we were leaving, the director took Emiliano aside. He apparently suggested to him that if they made it worth his while, he would see what he could do to help them.

Upon our return, Emiliano gave a full report to the town council at a town meeting at which almost all the male heads of families in the village were present. A lively discussion followed over what should be done. It came out that Juquila had bribed the director in 1970 with 25,000 pesos ($2,000) to obtain a presidential resolution that gave Juquila the tract of land Yaitepec claimed. Yaitepec could do the same. Emiliano argued that they needed money to bribe the director of the Communal Lands Office, to "give force" to their petition. All agreed and a collection was taken up. All the contributions were carefully recorded, and 15,000 pesos were raised for the bribe. Each contribution was more than simply another addition to the bribe. It was a vote of confidence giving weight to the village's consensus.

The meeting also had a very political aspect, and one in which faction-alism showed its monstrous face. By bringing back valid titles and maps, Emiliano's prestige and political influence in the community increased con-siderably. As the ritual drinking progressed, Emiliano became drunk. He began to denounce first the municipal secretary, charging that he was cheat-ing the pueblo, and then the presidente, accusing him of being in the pay of the Valencias, of being their compadre. Emiliano insinuated that they had given him a piece of land to work on their plantation for services rendered. Drunk and abusive, Emiliano insisted that he was the "father of the pueblo" and that the presidente and the municipal secretary should resign. Some of the calmer voices on the council tried to reconcile the two parties, arguing, "We shouldn't fight among ourselves. How can we hope to win our battles with other pueblos if we fight among ourselves?" The matter, however, was not laid to rest. The next day the presidente and the municipal secretary filed a complaint against Emiliano with the public prosecutor in Juquila, accusing him of public defamation and of having threatened to kill the presidente.

Next month, Emiliano and the other members of the communal lands committee set off for Mexico City to keep their appointment in the Office of Communal Lands. This time I did not accompany them, as I was too involved in other matters: I was getting married.

Upon their return I learned from Emiliano that he had gone with the CNC advocate to see the director of the Communal Lands Office. The advocate dis-couraged Emiliano from offering the director a bribe, saying it was unneces-sary. It seems that the representatives from Temaxcaltepec and Yolotepec had not shown up. Since they failed to come to the appointment, the matter of their boundaries was turned over to a special studies unit for a decision. I also gathered that they reached some sort of agreement with the advocate and the director at this meeting concerning the lands of La Constancia. Apparently, the two men advised them to invade the plantation and told them that if there were any problems with the public prosecutor in Juquila, they should come back to them. I asked Emiliano if any of this had been put into writing. He said no. One can only speculate that the director and the advocate figured that since possession is nine points of the law, if the peasants invaded the plantation, administratively the matter would be easier to handle.

The next morning when Emiliano presented his report to the town coun-cil, a heated argument followed. The presidente and the municipal secretary opposed the invasion on firm legal grounds—they had no written permis-sion. Emiliano accused the presidente and the secretary of being traitors to the pueblo. He charged the presidente with dragging his feet because he was a compadre of the Valencias and had fields on their plantation. The secretary was not only cheating the pueblo; worse than that, he was the head of the communal lands committee in one of the villages that Yaitepec claimed had taken its lands. The question was finally put in God's hands. At the end of the meeting, the council decided that the village elders would go to Juquila and ask the priest to come and say five special masses. This decision was a vote of no confidence in the presidente and the secretary. It was a vote to bypass their authority and make the decision by community consensus.

Next day, the masses were well attended. The presidente and the secretary, however, were conspicuously absent. The special masses, in this context, not only measure the degree of consensus in the community (both through attendance and through contributions to pay for them) but also give such a consensus sanctity. After the masses, the money was counted publicly on the church plaza by the authorities, who then declared, "There is force now." The money was then taken to the priest, who tried in vain to dissuade the village from invading the plantation. After the priest left, a town meeting was held on the church plaza. All the elders, as well as most of the other men of the village, were present. Emiliano argued, "There is force in the pueblo now. Don't be afraid to enter! Our patron saint, Santiago, will give us his sword!" Again he insisted that the presidente and the secretary were traitors to the pueblo and must be removed from office. After some debate, the men of the village voted to oust them and to invade the plantation the following morning.

That afternoon, Eva and I went down the mountain to Juquila to see her parents. As I crossed the plaza the next morning, I ran into the presidente and the secretary from Yaitepec. I asked the secretary what was going on. He told me they were swearing out another complaint against Emiliano. As we were talking, a messenger arrived with the news that the pueblo had invaded the plantation and a Valencia had been killed.

From the various accounts given me, the villagers had cut the fences and were clearing the fields to plant corn when one of the Valencias came out of the forest firing a pistol at them. He was gunned down. In panic the men returned to the village. Emiliano and the communal lands committee immediately set off for Mexico City to report to the director of the Communal Lands Office and to the CNC advocate.

This tragic turn of events troubled me deeply, and I turned to Don Fortino for advice. He suggested that I leave Yaitepec and move in with my wife's family in Juquila. His compadre Emiliano, even if he were innocent, had been compromised. The Valencias would blame him for the murder. The bad blood that existed between Emiliano and the presidente forebode no good, and my close association with Emiliano could only put me in danger. I followed his advice.

Emiliano's lot was much as Fortino had predicted. In an obvious attempt to cripple the movement against their lands, the Valencias accused Emiliano and the other members of the communal lands committee of the "assassination." The charges, however, were never proved. Because the priest had said masses in Yaitepec, the PRI in Juquila blamed him for the invasion as well. To prove that he had tried to prevent the invasion, the priest convinced Juquila's PARM-controlled communal lands committee to refuse to rent communal lands to the people of Yaitepec. Since almost half of Yaitepec needed to rent lands from Juquila, this act of retaliation was particularly brutal.

Things went from bad to worse. In Mexico City, Emiliano apparently obtained written permission to take the plantation's lands from the director of the Communal Lands Office. Upon his return, the villagers again decided to invade the plantation. In the meantime, however, the Valencias had obtained an injunction that prohibited the villagers from taking possession of their lands until the case was settled in court. So when the second invasion took place, the Valencias called in the state police, who opened fire on the villagers as they fled. Many were wounded as they fled, and others were arrested.

After the second invasion, the village consensus evaporated. Although Emiliano continued to have considerable support in the village, many blamed him for what had happened—not only the former presidente but also all those whose kinsmen had been arrested or wounded. In Juquila, among the reactions to the second invasion was a political attempt to gain greater control over Yaitepec by demoting it from a county to one of Juquila's townships. When things simmered down, however, the pressure to degrade Yaitepec's status dissipated too.

Although Yaitepec's land problems were still mired in the bureaucracy (where they had been pending since 1935), when I left the field to return to the United States, Emiliano was still hopeful. I returned to Oaxaca two years later, and things had not changed. No progress had been made to settle Yaitepec's land disputes, and factionalism in the village was still rife.

Factionalism in Yaitepec

After the ouster of the presidente, Emiliano had expropriated the official seal and set himself up as a cacique. In effect, this gave him a veto over the town council, since he could refuse to stamp any document that he did not like. When I saw him he bragged, "I'm the father of the pueblo. If you need anything, just come to me. I have the presidente's seal." Unlike his mestizo counterparts, whose extensive social and economic networks link them to powerful patrons at the state and national level, Emiliano's power base lay solely in Yaitepec. While things went well, this was well enough, but when they began to go badly it meant that Emiliano had nowhere to turn for help or protection. And they soon went badly.

Emiliano's seizure of the official seal did not sit well with everyone, particularly Saúl Amado, the new presidente, who bore an old grudge against Emiliano anyway. Emiliano had bought a piece of land that Saúl believed by right of inheritance should have come to him from his uncle's widow. Trouble soon followed. As presidente, Saúl Amado began to stir up the people against Emiliano. He accused him of being a cacique and blamed him for the troubles they were having with Juquila, the Valencias, and the police. To teach Saúl a lesson, two of Emiliano's compadres pushed him off a cliff, breaking his tailbone. Not deterred by this, the presidente continued his campaign against Emiliano. His words hit a responsive chord. An angry mob from Yaitepec's Barrio Abajo attacked Emiliano's house, hoping to kill him, but he was at his rancho. In defense, Emiliano armed a small army of his sons and supporters and threatened to kill the presidente.

Blood Feuds

Not long after this, Emiliano's son Siriaco was killed during the fiesta of Santa Cruz in a fight with one of his own cousins. In the month that followed, a slaughter ensued; two or three men from the Barrio Abajo were killed. The death of his son was a compromiso, or difficulty, which made Emiliano a marked man. He had two choices. He could live the life of a *valiente* and seek revenge or his own death, or he could flee. Since Siriaco's murder had compromised his son Valeriano as well, Emiliano sent him to Veracruz to keep him out of harm's way. Emiliano then fled the village, going first to Juquila and then to Zacatepec, a Chatino village nearby. Only his eldest son, Salomón (a son by a previous marriage), who had never become involved in his father's politics, remained in Yaitepec.

Life in Zacatepec was difficult, however. Chica later told me that Emiliano prayed constantly and paid for numerous masses to protect his family from harm. Since all his property was in Yaitepec, Emiliano began to go back and forth from Zacatepec to Yaitepec. When the trouble appeared to have passed, Emiliano moved back to Yaitepec, despite Don Fortino's warnings. He was lighting a candle at the gate to his house to protect it when he was shot and killed. Valeriano returned from Veracruz to avenge his father and brother. Like one whose fate was sealed, Valeriano went looking for death. He chose to live the life of a valiente. With some fifteen followers, he went on a brazen killing spree that so terrorized the villagers that they hid in their houses. At last, he found his death. It was, according to Chica, his own friends who betrayed him. They murdered him and to mock his brave heart, cut it out and stuffed it in his mouth.

Like so much of the violence in the district, although the passions that led to the tragic death of Emiliano and his sons were bound up with local issues, their deaths were not simply the result of a local blood feud. Instead, they were the consequence of conflicts and social processes that went far beyond the village. Like billiard balls bouncing off the banks and crashing into one another, these outside forces propel blood feuds. In this game, factionalism and blood feuds serve as mechanisms of social control to undermine the effectiveness of consensual politics. To extend the metaphor, the game of factional and consensual politics is not played on a level table but on a table whose institutional contours are the historical product of the game itself, a game in which some of the balls have greater political and economic weight than others. Emiliano and his family, like the other casualties of blood feuds, were not merely victims of their enemies but were pawns in a much bigger game, a class struggle whose rules they were hardly aware of.

This book is in many ways a personal one. It looks at the lives, feelings, and problems of many people I know and love. Since each letter I receive from Juquila and each visit I make there brings news of political battles or the murder of friends, it is my way of coming to terms with the violence that surrounds and often engulfs them. It is my attempt to see the larger whole in the microcosm of their lives and to try to understand their view of the world. My purpose is threefold. First, to present, through Don Fortino's eyes, a testimony of the history, politics, social relations, and violence in the region. Second, to show how conflicts at the regional and national levels shape individual lives and affect social relations in the village. Finally, to examine, through Don Fortino's perception of these processes, the ideology that underlies conflict and to answer such questions of human concern as What are the issues people fight over? and How do they view and explain violence? Although this book is an examination of one man's life, one man's testimony, the social processes and conflicts that have shaped Don Fortino's life are much larger than one man or one region. The social realities reflected in his narrative are not limited to Juquila, or even to the state of Oaxaca, but instead are local reflections of Mexico's legacy of colonialism and of its development within a modern capitalist world system.

Part I

DON FORTINO'S LIFE

AND TESTIMONY

The Revolution

AN INTRODUCTION TO

CHAPTERS 1 AND 2

The circumstances surrounding Fortino's birth are almost an allegory for the clash between the capitalist world and the Indian communities that led to the Mexican Revolution. Fortino's father was an educated mestizo. He had come to Juquila to establish a large plantation in the midst of the scramble for Indian lands during the dictatorship of Porfirio Díaz (president, 1876–1911). Fortino's mother was a simple Chatino woman. When, shortly before Fortino's birth, she discovered that her husband was spending the money she had saved on other women, she threw him out in a rage. Not only was this act an analog of the passions and angers expressed in the Revolution, but the contrast between his father's wealth and the poverty into which Fortino was born is also symbolic of the unbalanced economic development fostered during the Porfiriato.

During the Porfiriato a liberal ideology of laissez-faire capitalism held sway. According to its tenets, Mexico's road to becoming a progressive industrial country depended on its attracting foreign capital to develop and exploit its physical resources. Liberal ideology preached that development rested on private property. The large amount of land that Indian communities and the Church held as corporate property was viewed as a remnant of colonialism blocking this development.

As early as 1856, reform laws had been passed to convert corporate forms of property to private ownership. Although initially these laws were applied to Church lands, during the Porfiriato large landowners used them to methodically strip Indian communities of their lands as well. At the time, Indian communities included almost half of Mexico's population. As these communities lost their lands, landless peasants had little recourse but debt slavery on large haciendas and plantations.

While these policies did indeed provide Mexico with electric power plants, light and heavy industry, railroads, and telegraph and telephone lines—and even public schools in remote villages like Juquila—they did so at great cost to the countryside. By 1910 some 3,000 families had come to own more than half the land in the country, while 90 percent of Mexico's population had become landless peasants living in miserable peonage.

Although Chatino communities lost only 10 percent of their communal lands to plantations during the Porfiriato, they reacted violently to the mestizos who had come to take their lands. In 1896 the Chatino rose in rebellion. In a revolt known as the "War of the Pants," they tried to kill all the mestizos, who wore pants rather than the native garb. Although this rebellion was quickly and brutally suppressed, it was symptomatic of the pressure that burst forth later in the Revolution of 1910.

When Francisco I. Madero spearheaded a revolt against the political tyranny of the Porfiriato in 1910, he unleashed pent-up passions and forces that ultimately he was unable to control. In Oaxaca the Revolution initially pitted local caudillos (strongmen) who backed Díaz against those who favored the Maderistas and later against those who supported the constitutionalism of Venustiano Carranza. In this later battle, Díaz's backers tried to declare Oaxaca an independent state and withdraw from the Revolution. They even flirted with the Zapatistas to defend the state. By 1915, however, the battle had become primarily one between the Zapatistas and the Carranzistas.

During the Revolution a succession of forces seized the village. First came the Serranos, a militia the governor organized to defend the state against the Carranzistas. After the Carranzistas captured Juquila, the village became the site of repeated battles between government troops and Zapatistas, and endured depredations at the hands of both. Cattle were stolen, and crops were requisitioned. The troops of the opposing armies raped women and burned large areas of the village. Each invasion sent villagers fleeing to the hills to hide.

The conflict between the Carranzistas and the Zapatistas, however, was more than a struggle between rival factions or even between classes; it was a confrontation of different historical trajectories. The Carranzistas' constitutionalist vision was of a progressive, modern, homogeneous nation-state. The Zapatistas were fighting to recover their lands and to restore a past in which independent Indian and peasant communities governed their own affairs according to their own traditions.

Even though Don Fortino was just a boy when the Revolution began, his vivid account of its often-quirky violence and strange turns provides some insight into how it affected the lives of ordinary people.

Chapter 1

MY EARLY YEARS

My mother was a native of Juquila. Her parents were León Aguilar Suárez and Sofía González. My grandmother died in 1898, three years before I was born. My grandfather died in 1915. My aunts say he was over a hundred years old and died spent, of old age. My grandfather, León Aguilar Suárez, was from Sola de Vega. My grandparents had five children together. The oldest was Modesta Aguilar, then came Dominga, then there was my mother, my uncle Sabino, and finally my aunt Martina Aguilar González.

My father was Don Berto Santiago, a native of Miahuatlán. He came to Juquila in 1890 when he was twenty-six years old. There he met my mother, and they had four children together. The first, Serafina, was born in 1896, the year of the War of the Pants, when the Indians of Juquila, San Juan Quiahije, and Panixtlahuaca rose up and attempted to kill all the rich mestizos, whom they identified because they wore pants. My sister Serafina, unfortunately, died at the age of four. Then my sister Magdalena was born. She was the first to survive. She died in 1959. Then Teófilo was born, then myself. I was born May 19, 1901.[1] These were the children my parents had together. My father already had three children from before. In all, he had some eighteen children by different women.

Just before I was born, my mother left my father because he had gone off with my brother Timoteo's mother, but I was already tucked away. My father had women everywhere. That's why my mother told him, "No, no, no! Get out!" If he gave her money to save, my mother would lay it away, like my children all do. Then he would come and take it from her and give

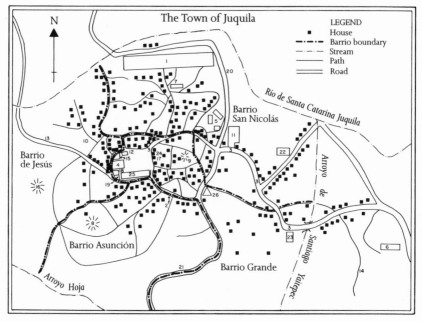

1 Airfield
2 Avenida Union 84
3 Calle Principal (road to
   Oaxaca)
4 Catholic church
5 Benito Juarez and Sor
   Juana Ines de la Cruz
   elementary schools
6 Instituto Nacional
   Indigenista center
7 Quetzalcoatl kindergarten
8 Loma Rajada

9 Lomo del Torro
10 Monument to the
   Revolution
11 Municipal cemetery
12 Municipal market
13 Path to San Miguel
   Panixtlahuaca
14 Path to Yaitepec
15 Pilgrim guest house
16 Portillo de la Luna
17 Post office
18 Public restrooms

19 Public library
20 Road to San Miguel
   Panixtlahuaca
21 Road to Zacatepec
22 Rural health clinic
23 Technical secondary
   school
24 Telegraph office
25 Town hall (palacio
   municipal)
26 Water works

it to another woman. My mother threw my father out because he took the
money that they had earned together and gave it to other women. This is
what disgusted my mother. No, this didn't suit her.

"No," she said, and took off her earrings, her rings, and out of rage threw
them in the garbage, far away. Because she couldn't stand my father's actions,
she threw his things out in the street. She threw him and his things out. "I'm
in my house," she said. "This is the house of my father. And you are here
in my house. You go off to amuse yourself! Go on, get out of here. I'm in
my house, and you look for a place to live with your other women; not here
anymore." She threw his stuff outside. My father left.

My father wasn't a drunk, but he liked women. His father was the same way. My grandfather Don Andrés Santiago had some forty-five children by different women.

My mother then had to support us alone by sewing people's clothes. They would give her shirts to sew and the white trousers that they used then. That is how she supported us, the poor woman: sewing for people.

After my father left my mother he went to Tututepec. There he obtained a piece of land near Santa Cruz Tututepec. It was a beautiful piece of land. He established a sugar plantation there. Of the walls of his house and the dikes he built to irrigate his land, all that remains now is a large plain. The plantation was destroyed by the Revolution.

My father was a businessman. He was very bright, very intelligent. The only vice he had was women—wasting his money on women. He was a hard worker and very quick with figures and everything. I'm not well educated, but he was well prepared. He went to school.

When I was old enough to comprehend things, I was angry at my father for everything and anything. He would say, "Leave your mother and come with me." And I would say, "That's all right for you, since you don't need anything. What, we should leave our mother, who with work, with hard work, raised us, with so much struggle gave us food, schooling, and clothes? Here, in the house of Papa Che, of my grandfather, is where I'm going to stay."[2]

Nevertheless, my father would still come to visit us. He would buy us some clothes—a hat, a jacket, a blanket, whatever—then leave again. Six months or a year later he would return. He couldn't leave his workers to themselves, because one who has workers must pay them. If they said, "I worked," even if they didn't, one has to pay them anyway. And if they have an agreement with the foreman, well, there is the problem. So he came when he could.

Living with the Priest

Because we were so desperately poor, when I was eight or ten years old my mother delivered me into the hands of the priest, Rosalino Soreano, that I might get some education. The father received me with pleasure, and I lived in the curato with him for many years. At first, I just assisted him at mass and returned home each day. That's how it went for several years. After I learned how to manage the church—how to arrange the ornaments according to the colors in the Latin Manual—I lived in the church with him.

Padre Soreano was my padrino de evangelio and was very respected. Certainly, according to the Catholic religion one must respect one's padrino de evange-lio, and I had great respect for him. When he was priest, the faithful had great respect for the Church. It's true he transgressed slightly. He became involved with a woman and had a daughter by her, Aurelia Vásquez. Padre Soreano

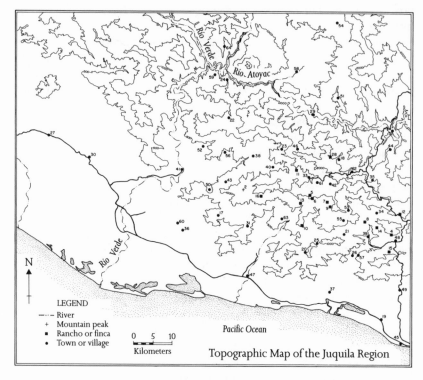

N

LEGEND
—··— River
+ Mountain peak
■ Rancho or finca
● Town or village

Pacific Ocean

0   5   10
Kilometers

Topographic Map of the Juquila Region

Mountain Peaks		
1 Cerro de la Neblina	19 Bajos de Chila	42 Las Placitas
2 Cerro del Tigre	20 Barranca Honda	43 Peñas Negras
3 Cerro Grande	21 Cerro del Aire	44 Plan de Minas
	22 Cerro Flor	45 Puerto Escondido
Ranchos and Fincas	23 Cieneguilla	46 Quiahije
4 La Aurora	24 Cinco Cerros	47 Río Grande
5 El Borrego	25 Cinco Negritos	48 San Gabriel Mixtepec
6 El Camalote	26 Cuixtla	49 San Pedro Mixtepec
7 La Constancia	27 Huaspaltepec	50 Santa Cruz Tututepec
8 Las Delicias	28 Ixpantepec	51 Santiago Minas
9 La Esmeralda	29 Ixtapan	52 Tataltepec
10 El Plantanar	30 Jamiltepec	53 Temaxcaltepec
11 Rancho Viejo	31 Jocotepec	54 Teojomulco
12 San Rafael	32 Juchatengo	55 Teotepec
13 Santa Rita	33 Juquila	56 Tepenixtlahuaca
14 El Sinaí	34 Lachao Nuevo	57 Tiltepec
15 La Soledad	35 Lachao Viejo	58 Tlacotepec
16 Yerba Buena	36 La Luz	59 Tlapanalquiahuitl
	37 Manialtepec	60 Tututepec
Towns and Villages	38 Masaquesla	61 Yaitepec
17 Acatepec	39 Nopala	62 Yolotepec
18 Amialtepec	40 Panixtlahuaca	63 Zacatepec
	41 Paso de la Reina	64 Zenzontepec

always treated me well. He had the goodness to help me and gave us his love. When he saw that they mistreated me, he would call me at bedtime to give me the hot chocolate they served him. "You drink it," he would say to me.

"No, Padrino, how can I drink this? It wasn't intended for me. They brought it for you. You drink it."

"Look, son, drink it," he would beg me, at times shouting that I should drink it. He would beg endlessly. It was too much. It vexed me at times. I wouldn't drink it. I said to myself, If it wasn't meant for me, why should I drink it? No, I don't deserve it.

School

When I was seven or eight years old, I began to go to school. We were going to school in 1910 when the Revolution of Don Francisco I. Madero against the dictatorship of Don Porfirio Díaz began. In 1911, I was still going to school, but in fear. At times we would go, and at times we wouldn't. In 1913, shortly after General Victoriano Huerta killed Don Francisco I. Madero, Don Venustiano Carranza began to govern. By 1913 the Revolution was in full swing and I was forced to leave school. I left in the third grade. I didn't go any further. I no longer went, because of the shooting day and night. Fear was the only thing one knew. We were constantly having to run and hide, first from one group, then another. Every so often the Zapatistas would hold the town for a while and then flee when they ran out of ammunition. The Carranzistas would also flee. They had a lot of ammo, but they didn't have the discipline to fight. We constantly had to flee, constantly hide in fear.

In 1914 the authorities were able to exert a little control, and there were teachers again. We wanted to resume our musical studies in the school of music, but some local citizens killed my music teacher. He was a good man, but they killed him anyway.[3] So we didn't go any further with it. The ones who learned something were Saúl León Villanueva and my brother Timoteo, but I didn't go any further with it.

A Nicolás Vásquez of Juquila was one of those who assumed the post of teacher. He was the first-grade teacher. He was very strict, horribly so. He would hit one over the head with a ruler until blood flowed. He would hit one on the legs with a meter stick, leaving big, bloody bruises, for the slightest thing.

One time, I couldn't stand it anymore and I said to my mother, "No, Mama, I'm not going to school, the teacher ... Look! Really! How many blows in the head he gave me, until blood was running! It hurts me too much to go to school. With all the beatings he's given me, he continues to beat me more."

"This isn't possible," she said, and went to lodge a complaint with Don

Federico Jijón, the *jefe político*, the political chief of the district. She asked him if he would do her a favor and remedy the way this teacher treated children. She told him that Don Nicolás treated children with such cruelty that he would split open the skin on their heads from so many blows with rulers and meter sticks.

This so enraged Don Federico Jijón that he ordered the police to bring in Don Nicolás. He said to him, "What excuse do you have for beating this child so cruelly?"

"No," he replied, "I haven't beaten him."

"Let's see. Show him his head so he can see his work," he said. "Look at these five big lumps right here, and all the little ones all over. You should know, that you have no authorization to punish the children in this manner. There are many ways to punish them without beating them. For now, I'm going to forgive you, but the next time you do this to this child or any other child, and they come to complain, I'll send you to jail. I'll consign you there so that you'll learn that you shouldn't mistreat children."[4]

"Well, señora," Don Nicolás said, "it's that he doesn't understand. He's so mule-headed," and this and that.

"Enough," said Don Federico Jijón. "Do you have any children?"

"No," he replied.

"That's why you don't know how troublesome they can be, but the day that you have a son," he said, "you'll see."

Thus it was that this teacher stopped punishing me so cruelly. Afterward, Leonigildo Vásquez, Don Nicolás Vásquez's brother, became the teacher. He taught first and second grade. Don Bartolo Núñez was the third- and fourth-grade teacher, but as I've said, I was able to finish only the third grade.

Soon after, the government broke down and stopped paying this teacher his salary. The poor teacher went about selling bread in the pueblos—in Zacatepec, in Yaitepec. The poor man would go there to sell the bread made by his wife, Virginia Ramírez of Juquila. Finally, he got sick of it and went to Oaxaca. So it was that I was only able to finish the third grade. I left school in 1913 and never went again.

Economic Plight

To tell the truth, the beginning of my life was filled with misery, pain, and sadness. We were desperately poor. Before I went to school, I had to go bring firewood and to fetch water. I would go bring firewood with a Señor Nicolás Ríos and Darío Barrades. They would say to me, "Let's go bring firewood."

"Let's go," I would say. At times I would go with another man, the son of Don Nicolás Ríos.

"Let's go bring some firewood, Tino," they would say.

"Let's go," I would say, "but I can't cut any firewood. My machete doesn't have an edge."

"That's all right. Let's go."

So I began to go to bring firewood. "Come on," they would say, "We'll cut the wood and bind it. You just have to carry it." Well, we would go to a place they call the Tierra Colorada. There we would go to cut firewood. They would cut it for me, bind it up, and I would carry it back. They took me with them two or three times like this, at first. When I was a little older I would go alone or with a group of friends, each with his machete, to cut wood.

A month before Todos los Santos, about October 2 or 3, we would begin to cut and stack great quantities of wood so it would be dry for the Day of the Dead.[5] Then we had to trundle it down the mountain to the pueblo on our backs. Well, someone started to steal the wood we had stacked. An old man who was directing us told us, "They've stolen your wood, now you steal theirs." So we went to steal firewood too. Badly done. Very unjust. If I had reflected on it at the time, I would not have done it.

Anyway, when I left school I began to help my mother. I began to work to help support the family. I began going to weed cornfields. Considerate people would say to me, "Come on. Come help me weed my field and I'll pay you six centavos." If they were good people, they would give me two or three tortillas. My mother was a seamstress and a baker. She made sweet pastries and I would go out and sell them.

My grandfather, Aguilar, still had some cattle then, but as God would have it, his cattle died, all of them. He had moved his ranch from a place they call El Borrego to Rancho Viejo. My uncle Sabino didn't take good care of the cattle there, so he began to lose more.

My uncle grabbed the land my grandfather had there. Afterward he sold it, and we lost out. We got nothing. Part of it he sold to Contreras Robles. Another piece he sold to Anselmo's grandfather, Darío Valentín. My cousin Erasmo got most of it. He was a hard worker. He was the son of a North American named Jerónimo Worman.[6]

The Revolution in Juquila

The fighting first reached Juquila when Governor José Luis Dávila wanted to make Oaxaca a state independent of the Revolution of 1910. He wished to make Oaxaca a free state so it would not become involved in the Revolution. So throughout the state he placed troops armed with old muskets, the kind they loaded with powder and caps. There were a few men who had good arms, but they were the officers—the rest, well, no, they didn't have good weapons. So when things got tough in Oaxaca, in the capital of the state, the armed troops that were stationed in Juquila, guarding the plaza, left.

In 1913 the last of the jefes políticos was still in Juquila. He organized a command in Juquila made up just of elements of the pueblo. He gave them the rank of captain, lieutenant, sublieutenant, sergeant, and simple soldier. At that time the Maderistas came and went. They said they were coming and that they weren't coming. "Francisco Madero's men are coming from Pinotepa now. They are just over there," they said. The people thought that even the rocks that one sees on the other side of the pueblo were Madero's men in position to take Juquila. At the time, they held a large, crowded market during Semana Santa [Holy Week], but just of fruit. Everyone ran, scattering their fruit; people lost their things, but it wasn't true that Madero's men were coming. People were so frightened that they took sick. It affected the heart of my aunt Martina Aguilar González. That is how frightened they were when they said that the Maderistas were coming from the coast. Well, nothing happened. The division made up of elements of the pueblo remained in Juquila.

Around 1915 the Serranos arrived to reinforce the zone, to prevent the Carranzistas from entering Juquila. The Serranos were soldiers of the state. They had good arms. They said that the Carranzistas were coming from San Pedro Mixtepec. The Serranos went out to find them. On the other side of Nopala, in the direction of Cerro Grande, they were ambushed. They lost some soldiers, and the colonel of the Serranos was killed. They retreated, and reconcentrated in Oaxaca. The Carranzistas took Juquila.

Later we learned that two of our countrymen had told Captain Acuña that it would be very easy to enter Juquila. They told him there were only some provisional soldiers that the government had left to defend the plaza there. They didn't have powder. They didn't have guts. They didn't have anything. That's how it was that they let them come. The Carranzistas set fire to the Loma del Toro, burning its houses.

In Juquila there was an Arnulfo Valencia, who had gone to the military college and had left with the rank of sublieutenant. He didn't continue in the military, because he left to take care of his father's finca in Yaitepec. They named Arnulfo the comandante of the Serranos in Juquila. Urbano Núñez and his brother Alfonso were also appointed officers of the division. Other members were Señor Concepción Ramírez, Señor Enrique Ramírez, a cornet player named Malaquías Rojas—well, many people. When the Carranzistas took the plaza, these friends took off and went to Rancho Viejo to take refuge. I don't know who it was who denounced them, but the Carranzistas went to Rancho Viejo and grabbed them.

They said they were going to shoot the Serranos. However, when they went before Colonel Gustavo Labastida, who asked them how it was that they had become involved, how they had conspired against the Revolution of Don Venustiano Carranza, they claimed they had been forced. They had been conscripted by the government and were not there voluntarily. They had no reason to fight with anyone. "Nevertheless, when the government orders, it orders, and we have only to obey, just as now when you come here to govern, we must obey. If another comes to take the plaza, we must obey them." Thus it was that with these declarations they let them all go except Urbano Núñez. This one was very *macho*. He was not so pliant.

"If you want to kill me," he said, "do what you want with me. In the end of everything, I acted in the defense of the pueblo. I was fulfilling an obligation given me. I didn't go because I was a volunteer, I went because it was an obligation. But if you want to kill me, it doesn't matter."

Because he spoke like that, and just for that, Don Gustavo Labastida was going to shoot him. Then Alfonso Núñez approached Doña Rosalba de Palacios, a close relative of the colonel. He said to her, "Aunt Rosalba," because she was his aunt, "we don't have anyone else who can help us here but you, to free my brother Urbano. They say they are going to kill him tomorrow."

"Let's go," she said, and she went running.

"Listen, Gustavo, I've come to visit you."

"Very good, Aunt. How have you been?"

"Very well, thank you. How's it going with our countrymen here?" she asked. "Well, I know it's been very difficult. According to the way it looks, you're going to shoot the men."

"No, we've turned many of them loose, but the one who has given us some opposition is Señor Núñez."

"Urbano! Ah, the poor man is my nephew," she said. "He's one of our relatives, yet."

"What? He didn't say anything to me."

"Well, he doesn't know. Don't be mean. Do me the charity of releasing him," she said. "He's a hard worker. He only got involved in this because he was conscripted, not because he had any desire to go fight. You've seen the poor weapons you've taken from them: muskets, two or three thirty-thirtys, a shotgun, two or three forty-fours, an automatic that the comandante had."

"Well, all right, Aunt."

"Be careful that nothing happens," she said.

"We are going to detain him until tomorrow, then I'll release him."

"Let that be the truth, not that tomorrow I'll learn that you've killed my nephew, son."

"No, it's all right. No, Aunt, you can be sure I'm going to release him. Free. Well, Aunt, I'll take into consideration that what he has done has been only an act he was forced to do, because they conscripted him. He didn't become involved in this of his own free will. Myself, I'm lending my services of my own free will. They didn't conscript me like they forced them. It's all right."[7]

"Then I'll give you my thanks, son. I'll be leaving now, with your permission."

"Yes, Aunt. Farewell."

She left and told Alfonso that it was arranged. Right away he went to ask the comandante's permission to see his brother, because he had been held incommunicado. Then he went to the jail and told them, "I have the comandante's permission to see my brother."

"They said to be careful now that things have been arranged," he said to Urbano. "Aunt Rosalba fixed it with Colonel Gustavo Labastida, our relative, so nothing is going to happen to you now."

"That's good."

They were happy there in the jail. The next day, early, they released him. "We are going to let you go completely free," they said. "You have to promise that you will not become involved in this business again. You must swear you are not going to take up arms, because then there will be no escape."

"But, señor, there's nothing here," he replied. "What we did was only to appear to comply with some orders that they gave us. Without artillery, without rifles, what resistance could we offer? You have brought three cannons and good arms. We don't have anything ourselves."

Mark you, that is why they let go the division of Serranos that the government had left in Juquila up until that time.

After the Serranos were routed, the Carranzistas began to govern. They spread along the whole coast. In Pinotepa, General Juan José Baños set up his headquarters. He was there with his general staff. In the entire sector of Juquila, Pochutla, and the rest, he stationed his paymasters, colonels, and captains, who were charged to keep vigil over the troop movements of the enemy. They were to note what pueblos and what kinds of pueblos were frequented by the Zapatistas, in order to penetrate the Zapatistas' camps.

At the time, General Juan Rodríguez, a native of Teojomulco, led the Zapatistas in the district. Don Juan Rodríguez took possession of Juquila by force of arms several times. Many times he was not able to take the plaza, but there was this one time that he marched in and cut the Carranzistas to pieces.

The night the Zapatistas were going to take Juquila, it was May 3, Cirilo Armadillo—they called him that because he liked to drink and was always rolling in the mud—said to me, "Give me some money for a drink, brother. Don't be stingy."

As I had some twenty centavos, I gave him ten centavos. A quart of mescal went for twenty centavos then. With the ten centavos I gave him he could buy a half quart of mescal—that would be a good drink.

"Go to bed early, friend," he told me.

"Why?" I asked.

"Because in a little while the Zapatistas are coming. They've been on the path from San Juan Quiahije for a while now. I just came from there."

"And what were you doing there?" I asked out of curiosity. "What did you do there?"

"I'm with them," he said. "I'm a Zapatista. I only came here because I have many relatives here. Just be dumb." That was the way he spoke—be dumb, by which he meant that one should shut one's mouth and say nothing.

"Now, brother," I said, "thanks a lot. I'm going right now." I went for another little turn around the plaza, and then I went to our house. When I got home I said nothing. I didn't want to frighten my poor mother, who already had suffered so much in this revolution. Even though I was a young man then, and strong, I knew what death was. I said to myself, Even though the fight isn't with me, a stray bullet, or an abuse, and they might easily kill me. No, I didn't say anything to anyone. Silent.[8]

About four in the morning I heard in the direction of the Loma del Toro, Bang! Bang! and fffsss, a bullet, the bullets through space. Then in the direction of the plaza, shots rang out. Others came up from the ravine, as down there was the Arroyo de Abajo. Down there, there were no soldiers, except some that were off to one side.

The captain of the Carranzistas had taken the parsonage as his quarters, because it had pillars and was defensible. So from down there they crept up the ravine and attacked the Carranzistas' quarters. Cirilo cut through one of the doors of the church with an ax. Then they went up into the church tower and began to shoot down from the tower. They killed Captain Calderón. Manuel Calderón he was called.

I said to myself, Now this is serious. The only thing one could hear were shots, the barking and howling of dogs, and the squawking of chickens. The frightened people were quiet. There was heavy fire from the Loma del Toro, from the Loma de la Rajada, from the Portillo de la Luna, in the center, and from the house of Nicolás Vásquez. There were one, two, three, four, five detachments of Zapatistas that attacked the plaza.

They set fire to the Loma del Toro to drive the Carranzista troops out. The Carranzistas were undisciplined. They were soldiers only because they were men and had valor, but they didn't have the discipline for a fight. Men who are prepared don't fight that way. They don't deliver themselves up the way these poor men delivered themselves up. No, they couldn't defend themselves from the fire set against them.

The only detachment that came out clean was in the Portillo de la Luna. It consisted of some twelve men who had come with Señor Rodrigo Ayuzo from the finca Santa Rita. He is the brother of Don Genaro Ayuzo. These men had left the finca so they wouldn't be alone out there, where they could be killed. They sought protection in Juquila from the jefe of the Carranzistas. They stayed there for many years. In fact, to date these soldiers are still there with their sons and grandsons. There was Fernando Ríos; his brothers Rodolfo, Nicolás and Patricio; and a Margarito Ríos. Well, these came out clean. Not a one was killed, nor did they kill anyone.

I suppose they had some sort of agreement: If you don't attack us, we won't fire a shot. I suppose that is what they said, but I never learned the essentials, because they couldn't say anything. It is a lack of discipline or civil courage to perform the duty of a soldier and to say to the other: "Don't shoot me and I won't shoot you. We're friends." In full revolution? I don't believe there is room for that. "Kill me, and I will do the same if I can." Right? But, no, this is how it went.[9]

When their friends saw that the others had lost everything and that the column of Zapatistas was slipping down to grab them, they told them, "Women, this way. Run down that ravine there. Wait for us."

"All right."

They took their things—babies, everything—and went running down there. Nothing happened to them. Then these friends sneaked the men out two or three at a time, running from there to rejoin the others. The men retreated firing, but firing from a distance, as they went. From Juquila they went to Santa Cruz Tututepec, where they stayed with my father, Don Berto Santiago, a few days. He fed them and took care of them. Then they said, "We're going to join the detachment that's in San Pedro Tututepec." They joined this detachment, but they returned to Juquila later because the Zapatistas didn't stay.

The Zapatistas took the plaza, made a mockery of the Carranzistas, but didn't stay. They weren't going to resist a charge from all the fierce troops that were there. No, it wasn't possible. The Carranzistas returned to take charge of the plaza, and there they stayed. And so it went, every so often.[10]

Once during the Revolution I was going around with my friends—strolling, playing the guitar—when Melquiades Ramírez, the brother of the comandante Leonardo Ramírez, and a couple of other bad types came up to us. My friends, out of fear, took off, leaving me with them by myself. I couldn't see how I could excuse myself, since the fiesta would end if I were to go, because I was the one who was playing the guitar. What they wanted was for me to sing and play. They wanted to sing too. Even with my modest abilities, their singing didn't sound good to me. So I became obstinate and said to myself, That's enough, I'm not going around with them anymore.

"Well," I said to them, "I'm going to go."

"No, you're coming with us."

"And why should I if I don't feel like it? I'm sleepy and want to go to bed."

"No, no, you're coming with us willingly or die," said Melquiades, pulling out his knife. I ducked aside and ran. They were looking the other way, and I snuck between their legs and took off with my guitar and everything. I ran toward the house of Nicolás Vásquez. Near it was a thicket of sacamanteca bushes, so when I turned the corner I crouched in them.

"He went this way!"

They went running up the hill toward the house of Héctor. After I saw that they had passed, I stood up, and going by way of the house of Nicolás Vásquez, I climbed the hill. I took a little path that went up to the house of Lázaro Flores. From there I grabbed the path that went up to the house of Maximilliano Salinas and from there to our house. At that time we lived on the corner in my mother's house, but before going home I yelled from up there on the hill: "Here I am! Come and get me!"

"Wait there!" he yelled back.

"All right!" I said.

The next day Melquiades saw me. "No," I told him, "you, by yourself, you're worthless, even if you are carrying a knife." I was really very quick. I was standing here, and when he saw me I was over there. His knife just slashed the air. He wasn't able to do anything to me. Really, I was very quick. That is why I'm here to tell it.

Once, during the Fiesta of the Virgin, December 8, the Zapatistas wanted to take the plaza in Juquila. We knew they were going to try it. Suddenly, we saw people from Miahuatlán, the Cuerudos of Miahuatlán, coming down the path. The Cuerudos were Zapatistas. Among them I saw a first cousin of mine, Concepción Santiago. That was his name, but they called him Concho Biche. He was the right-hand man of Don Genaro Ramos. Don Genaro was the commander. He caused trouble—and then some—around Miahuatlán until 1945, when the government finally got rid of him. He gave himself the rank of general because he had many captains and so his men would respect him more.

Well, this time the Carranzistas were prepared. They threw them back. The men from Santa Rita had returned: Fernando, Rodolfo, his brother Nicolás, and their sergeant, Margarito Ríos. They came out into the open and over-threw the Zapatistas, who were stretched out along one side. They went after them unarmed, very bravely. The attack was heaviest on the other side. There the Carranzistas were firing at them from the hill where the monument to the flag is now. They laid down heavy fire, since they had lots of ammo. They had piles of it, boxes of ammunition, loads had arrived. They beat them back. They were unable to enter Juquila. Many of these Cuerudos died in Yaitepec too.

My cousin came out of it without a scratch. After the Revolution he remained with General Genaro as his second in command. As I said, Don

Genaro was committing all sorts of crimes. One time he ordered my cousin to kill someone, and he asked, "Why should I kill them? They haven't done anything."

"I order you to," he said.

"You may order," he replied, "but I'm not going to obey."

He didn't go. About a week later Don Genaro sent two of the killers he kept to kill my cousin. They spotted him standing in the doorway of a pool hall with his hands on the two sides of the door, like on a cross, and there in the doorway of the pool hall they shot and killed him from the street. That's how my cousin died: not in the Revolution, not in combat, but by betrayal by this man.[11]

After all these events, a Colonel Israel del Castillo came to finish off the Zapatistas who were still spread around. He came to Juquila in 1923 or 1924. He brought close to a hundred well-armed men with him. The Indians of Panixtlahuaca were Zapatistas. After the Zapatistas burned out the Carranzista soldiers in Juquila on May 3, 1918, the Carranzistas went to Panixtlahuaca and set fire to the town. Since the houses were made of thatch and bamboo, the whole town burned to the ground.

Anyway, Jaime Flores, Lauro Pérez, and Saúl Pérez, who had gone around with the Zapatistas, told this colonel that there were still some Zapatistas in Panixtlahuaca. Erasto Flores had his encampment there. In Panixtlahuaca, a townsman of ours, Wilfredo Aguilar, was going around with the Zapatistas. A compadre of the Zapatista José Próspero named Antonio Mendoza was also living in Panixtlahuaca. So this Israel del Castillo wrote to Antonio Mendoza, "You're pardoned. Come. This letter will give you safe passage. Nothing will happen to you here. The people of Juquila know you very well and have given you excellent references."

He came. "Now," said this colonel, "we're going to find Erasto. You're going to guide us, because you know well where he is. And so that they will pardon you, we're going to bring your services to the attention of the government, so they'll acknowledge your value. Now that you're acting as a guide for the soldiers of the government, all charges against you will be dropped."

"All right," Antonio said.

"All right," said the colonel, and Antonio Mendoza went off with them by way of Cerro de la Neblina toward Cinco Cerros. It was getting late, and they decided to make camp at the Cerro Flor. "Let's camp here," said Antonio Mendoza, "so we can arrive there before dawn."

"All right," said the rest of Israel del Castillo's soldiers. Antonio Mendoza, however, had already planned an ambush. As soon as Castillo's men stacked their arms in a tent, the Zapatistas would rush the tent, take Don Israel del

Castillo's soldiers' arms, and kill everyone. That's how it went; they killed them.

From Cerro Flor the Zapatistas went to Cinco Cerros. There my father, Don Berto Santiago, had his finca and houses with laminated tin roofs. They took all the barbed wire from his corrals. The lands there were communal, but my father had no difficulties with the people. They respected him a great deal. He built them a town hall. In a time in which everything was scarce, he built them a good school. He gave work on his plantation to all these poor men. He helped them a great deal. After the Revolution, the old authorities of Santa Cruz Tututepec begged us to come back. They begged us to work the lands that my father had left, because they weren't able to. Well, we didn't want to go, because of the way they had treated my father. I said to my brother Timoteo, "Why should we go there, so suddenly they can do the same to us. No, we'll stay in our pueblo, working what little we can."

Well, my father's foreman, Cornelio González, was the man who injured him most. He was his hired hand, his foreman. When my father was the presidente of the village of Santa Cruz, he made him his secretary. When his term was up, he said, "Now you're going to be presidente," and that is what happened. He became presidente and continued working on the plantation as foreman. When the Zapatistas began to come and go there, Cornelio came to an agreement to go with them. They gave him the rank of captain and he turned on my father. He sent word two or three times that he was going to kill him. My father sent word back: "So this is how you're going to repay all the services and all the favors I've done for you! I'm very grateful to you for warning me. You can come to the finca whenever you want. I'll be waiting for you." In reality, my father was ready to wait for him there, because a mozo, a servant, for whom he had done so many favors, had rebelled against him.[12]

My father would have killed Cornelio if he had come, but as luck would have it, others beat him to it. After the federales stopped coming and before Don Israel del Castillo came to Juquila, Cornelio and Lázaro González and a Colonel Cervin had a detachment in Juquila. They lived there as comandantes. I don't know exactly why, but they had a difference among themselves, and they killed Colonel Cervin and Cornelio González.

Cornelio was on his way to the house of Doña Irinia Ayuzo to get some mescal. Lázaro González was a little ahead of him, walking casually, when the soldiers who had gathered there came down from the house of Doña Felicita Flores, where they had just killed Colonel Cervin, and hid behind the pillars of the market.

"Listen," I said to my brother Timoteo, "something is going to happen here. Something ugly is going to happen. Something is going on. Come! Really! Look how the Zapatistas are hiding here!" There were five or six of

them waiting there. "Why did Audifas Bustamante go running down the hill?
And why hasn't he returned?" I asked.

"Really," said Timoteo, and he came with me. We were halfway from his
house to where my store is now, when Bang! Bang! Bang! they shot Cornelio
in the plaza right in front of us. I witnessed how his very companions killed
Cornelio González, the one who had done so much damage to my father.
They shot him down with rifles they had taken from Colonel Cervin. Then
they went after Audifas Bustamante, but they couldn't find a trace of him. He
must have said to himself, "They're going to kill me too." He fled, and they
didn't see even a trail of dust.[13]

The Death of My Father

My father died in 1919, not in the Revolution but of an illness. He caught
a bilious fever from so many muinas, because of the injustices he had suffered,
and died. I remember in 1918, when my brother-in-law Carlos Allende and
my sister Magdalena were still living in Río Grande, my father arrived from
Oaxaca ill and suffering from rheumatism. Since my mother was an herbalist,
a curandera, Magdalena had learned how to use the remedies my mother used
to make for my father, and she cured him.[14]

When my father got better he took to the road, to go on to Tututepec.
Because of the Zapatistas, he had to go with great precaution, going from
Juquila by way of Zacatepec and then down to Río Grande. From Río Grande
he was going to go by way of La Luz up to Santa Cruz Tututepec, because the
Zapatistas didn't operate down that way, but he didn't arrive. He died of a
fever. That's how my poor father lost all his work and tools.

Leaving the Church

During the Revolution we slept in the church because it was a safe place.
While Alfonso Zárate Pérez and I were sacristans living in the church, Jerónimo Franco, from Nopala, also lived in the church with us. He fell in love
with a woman named Felipa. My obligations in the church included sweeping the church and the rectory. One day, as I was going to chime the bells for
mass, Alfonso, who had gotten up before me, went to the kitchen and saw
a niece of the priest performing an indecent act. He came to tell me. I went
there right away and saw what was going on. I wasn't going to respect that!
So, I gave the doors a push and ran to ring the bells for mass. I was chiming
the bells when Jerónimo came up.

"Don't be mean. You saw me there. I don't want Padre Soreano to know," he said, "because he'll fight with me and run me out."

"But who's talking?" I said to him. "Come to an understanding with Alfonso, because he's the one who told me that you were there. Were you doing something there?"

"You opened the door, right?" he asked.

"Well, because I thought there were some dogs inside. I heard noises, but that's all I did. I didn't see anything," I said. "So don't worry about it." He gave me fifty centavos. "No," I said, "you don't need to do this. Go on. You don't have to worry. Nothing is going to happen."

But I had lost his confidence. Jerónimo and Felipa, the servant he loved, began to act bitterly toward Alfonso and me. They began to treat us badly and give us hateful looks. She would give us some green beans that had a thick covering of grubs on them and want us to eat them. I said to her, "Hell, I'm not going to eat this!" I stayed on there a little while but then said to myself, I don't need to stay here.[15]

My poor mother had gone with my sister to my brother-in-law's ranch in Río Grande and had left me with Padre Soreano. I had been there for some time. She knew that she didn't have to worry about me; I wouldn't go out anywhere. I conducted myself very well there. I wasn't a drunk.

Anyway, after that, Alfonso and I were angry. We even swore at the padre a bit because he allowed this class of people there. But we lacked the courage to say anything about it to the padre . . . thus and thus are how things are. So that there wouldn't be any more difficulties, I decided to leave.

Working During the Revolution

During the Revolution, I began working, earning a little. I worked as a pounder in the blacksmith shop of Edmundo Franco. I worked with Edmundo, and his son Alfonso too. I worked and earned practically nothing—fifteen centavos a day. Then I worked with Alfonso Núñez for a time, working very hard. The money I earned I gave to my mother. She earned a little sewing clothes for people. I would give her my wages and she would give me what she wanted. She would give me two centavos. If there were a fiesta, she would give me five centavos. I worked as a blacksmith, a carpenter, and then after a little while, as a mason with a trowel. I worked with a man they called El Chinfras and with another called Pastor Flores. I earned fifty centavos a day working with him. As a master mason, he earned one and a half pesos a day. That was something, I thought. After a time, seeing how I bore up under so much work, Don Basilio Salazar, a good friend, asked me over.

"Why don't you come to work for me? I'll teach you beltmaking. Afterward you'll be able to earn your centavitos. Your present means of earning a living is a little degrading, and because I respect and care for you, it doesn't seem to me that that work is worthy of you."

Basilio was very kind to me. He fed me, he paid me my centavos, he taught me leather work. Since I couldn't control my hand with the steadiness needed to cut the hides, I felt ashamed. At times, I would miscut a piece and I would be ashamed to tell him. This poor man is trying to teach me, I would think, and I'm causing him losses.

"Look, my knife really slipped," I would say.

"Don't worry about it. We'll glue it. We'll fix it," he would say. At that time there weren't good cements, good glues, and he knew that.

He cared for me a lot because my aunt, Martina Aguilar, had raised him. My mother's sister married his brother, Darío Salazar. His brother, too, raised him; that is why he had him in the house. My uncle Darío taught him beltmaking, and he was a good beltmaker.

After I had learned the trade well, Basilio began to pay me my centavitos. I would hand them over to my mother. She washed my clothes, but I no longer ate there, because Don Basilio fed me. He was a very good man.

It was about this time, after I left the church, that I went to visit Padre Soreano on my way to Río Grande.

"Why haven't you come?" he asked.

"Padrino," I said, "because, well, I've been working elsewhere. I've wanted to come to see you, but . . ."

"I thought it strange," he said, "because you left here without saying goodbye to me."

"No, Padrino," I said, "it's that the way those people were treating us here was very bad."

Later I explained to him how things were. Shortly afterward, Jerónimo Franco stole this girl Felipa and took her to his house.

Life in Río Grande

After I left Basilio Salazar's house, I went to Río Grande to join my mother. In Río Grande my brother Teófilo and I worked together planting a cornfield, but since between brothers there is a certain rivalry, I said to my mother, "You pay more attention to my brother, but I love you more, I work harder than he does. I do more for you. You'll see."[16] So I challenged him. "Let's put it to the test. I'm going to plant my own cornfield, and I'll bring what I harvest here. You bring what you can harvest." I said, "I don't need to work with him. You'll see who works harder." So it went. My brother built a corn bin in a corner of the house and put the little corn he harvested in it. It was sprouting there; he didn't even bother to cover it well. I didn't just throw up a corn bin. I went to Heraclio, the father of Ricardo Velasco, and asked, "Will you build me a granary, Heraclio?" "Of course, cousin," he replied, and he built one. Well, I filled it to overflowing.

When my poor father died, a Sr. Siriaco Núñez grabbed everything my father had amassed for the support of my brothers Francisco and Berto. He treated his nephews like orphans. He didn't even give them a home, just a place to sleep. Their uncle wasn't dedicated to working, only to spending. The poor little boys suffered a great calamity.[17]

One time Berto was going to buy mescal for his uncle Siriaco Núñez, the one who took him in after my father died and spent all his money. At times, Sr. Núñez would send him without money to buy a bottle of mescal, so it wouldn't cost him anything. Berto would go do errands to earn the money to buy the mescal. He would send him to buy mescal at the shop of Sr. Lázaro Sánchez, and there Berto would play with the old man.

Well, playing there, Berto fell and cut his stomach very badly on some glass. He still has the scars on his stomach where he cut himself. It made me mad, very mad. I was sweating with anger. I said to him, "I don't like this. You'd be better off in Río Grande." It made me mad, very mad. "You're going to Río Grande! Enough is enough! No more!" I told him.

When I saw this, I said to Francisco, "Look, Francisco, you are older than your brother Berto. As you're my brother, it makes me sad to see the state you're in. I can't help you, because I'm suffering too, because I'm not asking anything from Mama, or from my sisters or brothers. But I could ask our older brother Teófilo to help you—they have the means. I don't have it in my heart to refuse to work to support myself. I want to work. It is my obligation to do so in order to teach myself to be a man, and that's what you must do too, Brother," I told him.[18]

"I'm going to return to Río Grande with my little brother," he said. I told the family to prepare him a bag of tortillas, meat, and provisions.

"You'll arrive there tomorrow," I said to him. "You're a young man. You can walk fast, right?" They went.

After they were with my brother Teófilo for a while, my brother Francisco wrote to me:

I'm very grateful to you for pulling us out of the unhappy life we were suffering. Now that we are with our older brother, everything is different. We have everything we need—above all, food; more than we need. Cheese daily, meat daily, because our brother Teófilo kills deer, javelina, or if not, he kills a pheasant or two grouse. In any case there is plenty to eat. There are plenty of tortillas. His cornfields abound in corn. At the same time, we have plenty of milk to drink, so we are well off here.

So I wrote to him: "Behave yourself, Brother! I hope that you'll cooperate in every way to help our brother with the work he has planting corn and taking care of the animals." [19]

I worked there many years, too, helping and taking care of calves. I helped my brother-in-law, Carlos Allende, milk the cows, make cheese, and I would go sell it and turn the money over to him. When they were sick, many died of worms. Jaguars killed many too. If a jaguar killed a calf, in answer my brother Teófilo would kill two jaguars. I believe he killed some twenty-five jaguars. There were many there.

After Berto and Francisco had recovered their strength, Francisco said to me, "We want to earn our own living. What do you think, Brother? I want to go to Nopala to sell some bulls. If you can help by selling us some bulls at a good price, I can sell them for a profit. The earnings will be for Berto and me. Then we'll come to plant some corn and stay with you. We just want to earn a little bit."

"All right," I said. I gave them this opportunity.[20] So after they said good-bye to Teófilo, they came to live with me. Later they decided to work on the other side of the mountain between Manialtepec and Nopala. After that they went to live on the finca of Andrés Castellanos, called San Rafael. Don Andrés liked my brother Francisco a lot. He wasn't at all bad looking. He was light complected and congenial. Don Andrés had two daughters—Virginia and Hortencia—and they had a son.

My brother Teófilo was a truly humble man. I never knew him to swear. I'm going to confess, on the record, that I was hot-tempered. If a drunk were to knock off his hat or tease him because he was an Indian, he would remain quiet. But when this would happen, I would have these violent impulses that I get when I get angry, and he would say, "Let's go."

"No, let him keep on talking," I would say.

"Are you a drunk like him?"

"No, but I don't like to see them tease and insult you," I would tell him. "It makes me mad."

"No, let's go."

"No, wait a bit," I would say, waiting to see if he would stop or not. "Well, let's go," he said. But if the drunk continued, depend on it, there'd be blows until I quieted him. Only then would I be satisfied. But Teófilo would say, "Better we go home."

"Let's go."

"Let's go, then," he would say and grab me around the shoulders.

"Well, let's go. I don't like it when they insult you, man. It hurts me when they insult you," I would tell him. "I'd feel better if they'd insult me but not you, because they take advantage of your humility."

That's the way my brother would treat me. So we would go, but every time we would go out, there would be some incident. Always. At fiestas, especially, there would be someone who would want to fight us. I would go there with the band to play the guitar. I would go to play, sing, and enliven the fiesta. We were the ones who made the fiesta in Río Grande big by going there with our band. We gave it real animation! People from Nopala, from Teotepec, from San Pedro and San Gabriel Mixtepec, from Bajos de Chila, and from Puerto Escondido came for a fling. Not many people from Manialtepec, Zacatepec, Tututepec, Acatepec, or Jocotepec came to the fiesta. Now it is a fairly big fiesta. They celebrate it on May 12, for the Virgin of Guadalupe. We would also go to Yaitepec for the fiestas of Santiago and of Santa Cruz but not to work them. We would go for a little while and then return home. In 1927 or 1928, I began to go to Nopala to work the fiesta of Santos Reyes. I'd come and then go back to the ranch and return next year.

Then I began actively to look for a way to buy some barber's clippers to work at the fiestas. At the time, I still lived with my brother-in-law Carlos Allende. He said to me, "If you want to be a barber, I'll buy you the clippers," and he bought them.

But my sister asked him, "And these clippers, why do you want them?"

"Well, I want them," he said, "so that Tino can cut hair." Tino is what they called me. "So Tino can cut Teófilo's hair, and mine, and then the baby's." The baby was Serafín. "And I'll cut his hair too. That way it won't cost us anything."

"Ah, no," she says. "Go take them back."

"You find a way to buy the clippers yourself," she told me. "No, I don't want them to teach you to be a lazy bum who wants everything given to him."

I took it very hard when my sister did that, very hard, because with that help I could have got ahead right away. I wanted to work. I took it very hard. But later it taught me to have one's own things. I said to myself, From now on I'm not going to take anything from anyone. I don't want to be suffering daily this kind of life. No, I won't take anything, not from my own mother, not from my sister, not from my brother.

In Río Grande I suffered a lot from fevers and malaria. I said to myself, I'll die if I stay here any longer. I told my brother Teófilo, "I don't want to stay here any longer." I told my brother that I was going back to Juquila. I didn't take anything from him when I left—after all I put into his ranch, all the work I did for nothing. I went back to Juquila with my arms folded, with nothing, and began to work.

After I left the ranch in Río Grande, I went to El Ciruelo to work for Don Teófilo Díaz. I earned a salary of thirty pesos a month. With the money I earned I bought two calves there, then another two in Juquila. In two years I had eight head. The herd continued to grow. I had thirty or forty head. In

1928, I bought cattle and some hillside land, and Benjamin Aguilar took care of them. My uncle Sabino Aguilar and Arnulfo Valencia sold me some other calves, which I took to Río Grande. I kept them there, and they were the ones that began to grow and to multiply. But, I didn't take cattle from anybody, not one cent from anyone. I don't like to take other people's things. I am very much against taking people's things, and I never liked that, no matter how poor I was.

How many years did I work for my brother on the ranch in Río Grande? Fifteen years. And what did I earn? Nothing. And when I returned to Juquila, I arrived with nothing. I never asked for anything. I returned to Juquila with my arms folded. I borrowed a razor, a pair of clippers, and scissors, and with these instruments I began to cut hair. What a whorish, hard life!

After I left the ranch, I took up barbering and shoemaking, just from inclination. I worked on the porch of my brother Timoteo's store. The house had belonged to my father. I would go there to work, and at times, because I was working there, my brother would heap abuse on me. Since he had gone to take the adobe, tiles, and wood from the house my father had built on the hill where the monument to the flag is and had brought them down to the plaza to build his store, he believed he was the owner and gave nothing to us. So, I said to myself, someday I'll build my own little place. But it was years before I could do so.

Chapter 2

COURTSHIP AND

MARRIAGE

When I was about eighteen or twenty years old, I started to take notice of girls, but to drink? No. I remember one time a Captain León, who was stationed in Juquila, got Alfonso Zárate and me drunk on wine. We saw the captain hiding with a sister of Silvia's in the shadows. And as you know, boys can be very scandalous, spreading gossip. He called us over and said, "Don't be cruel. Come back in a little while and we'll go and eat some sweets," and I don't know what else. He tricked Alfonso and me.

"Good enough, we'll come," I said.

"Don't go and say that you saw me with this girl."

"But, Captain, I haven't even seen you." He was a young man. He had just graduated from military college. "I didn't see you doing anything, Captain," I said.

"Don't tell me that. I saw you watching us."

"Well, yes, but one sees people all the time. It's nothing unusual, nothing important."

"All right then."

Well, a little while later we went to Doña Guadalupe's shop, and the captain invited us to drink.

"Have a glass of wine. Try it. It's very good. It's sweet."

We drank it, and ooh! I drank one, and Alfonso another. I drank another, and he drank another. We drank five or six glasses, got drunk, and after a while threw up. We went shamefaced to the house, because if the priest were to find out, he would have drawn and quartered us.

I remember the first girl I fell in love with. I was in love with a girl from the village, but I wouldn't make a definite commitment, because I was so poor that I couldn't even afford to have anyone to make tortillas for me. Besides, I had to care for the cows out there. And my mother wouldn't give me permission to marry.

"No, not until you learn to work," she said, "so that you understand the obligations that you'll have, that you'll have to work to maintain your family. If you don't know how to work, how are you going to support your family? And if you then have a child, how are you going to support him?"

She wasn't wrong. She had thought it through. She didn't really give me permission until 1932. When I went to bring the mother of my children from Juchatengo, I had her permission to find the woman I wanted.

When I was a young man I would go to Yaitepec for every fiesta. We would go to the fiesta of Santa Cruz on May 3, or to the fiesta of Santiago on July 25. We would go there all the time, and as young men we were always falling in love with any and every girl.

In Yaitepec it turned out that we had a sister we didn't know about. Her mother must have thought, No, one day they are going to grab their sister. So she went to our house to talk to my mother.

"Good day, señora."

"Good day," my mother said to her. "Come in, sit down."

"Thank you," she said and sat down. "Pardon me," she said, "don't get mad."

"Why should I get mad?"

"There's no reason for you to get mad. But, look, my daughter Chica is the daughter of Don Berto, your husband," she said.

"How's that?" That got my mother's attention. "Really?"

"Really," she said. "I was making tortillas when he arrived. He was on his way to Miahuatlán, but as it was early, I don't think he had eaten before he left. Well, who knows, since he was always going to Miahuatlán and Oaxaca. Anyway, he asked me to make him breakfast. I served him. I was making tortillas when he grabbed me and carried me to bed. That's how it was that Chica came."

"So that's what he did to you?" my mother asked.

"Well, yes," she said. "Well, it's that I have two daughters, and because Fortino, Timoteo, and others come around, that's why I've come to talk to you," she said. "I hope you'll forgive me?" the señora said very decently in Chatino. My mother answered her in Chatino with equal respect.

"I'm very grateful to you that you were so considerate as to advise me for many reasons, to recognize the family and avoid committing incest with one's own kin; and at least to be able to raise a glass and toast their health. No, I'm glad you told me," my mother said. "So don't worry that I'm going to be mad. It's in the past. My poor husband's dead."[1]

"Well, very good," she said. "If you'll excuse me, I'll be going."

"Good-bye."

The señora left. She had other children—León, Benjamín, Leonor, Ramona, Eulalia, and Lorena. Later Chica built her house where it is now. Chica had two sons, Siriaco and Valeriano, and a daughter who died of malaria when she was a young woman.

Anyway, about that time I was in love with a Dominga from Ocotlán. She went around wearing a hat of the 48th Regiment, which was stationed in Juquila. I was really attracted to this girl. I had malaria and was having chills. I was skinny, but I was naturally that way. I was attracted to her. She loved me, and I really fell deeply in love with her. She returned my love. One night I said to her, "I'd like to talk with you, but your mother is here, so I am not at liberty to express everything I desire."

"Ah," she said, "in the night I will be in a room up on the hill, in front of Nicolás Vásquez's house, next to the hotel. There we can talk."

"Fine, I'll be there," I said, "and we can talk."

But at that time the fiesta of the Virgin was going on, and someone dropped a large rock from the hotel next door onto the roof. I went out to see who did it, but I didn't see anyone. Later I learned that a silversmith named Catarino Abasolo also was vying for her attentions. He was the one who had dropped the rock. I said to myself, Jesus! What's going on?

Sra. Micaela, the girl's mother, liked me a lot. I couldn't even pass by without her pulling me aside and sitting me down to talk with her. She kept house for several soldiers. At times, she even made lunch for me there. I would say, "No, thanks. They're waiting in the house for me to eat lunch."

"No," she would say to me, "you keep me company here. I don't have other friends who hold me in the esteem that you do."

"Well, thank you very much," I would say.

Anyway, after this "friend" dropped the rock on the roof, from that time on he began spying on me. One night, he and two armed soldiers lay in wait to kill me, beneath some bushes along the path up to the house. That night I had been strolling around the plaza, and I would have gone up the path where they were waiting in the bushes if my friend hadn't warned me. Lázaro Flores came up to me. "Be careful, brother, which path you take," he said.

"Why?" I asked.

"Because there where the bugambilia tree is," he said, "just past the door to Doña Micaela's house, Catarino is there in the bushes with two soldiers. They say they're going to kill you."

"Is that so?" I said, "Now what should I do with two soldiers? I can't confront him. If he were alone, I'd laugh at him, but with these two soldiers there's nothing I can do. They are armed, and I'm not carrying anything. Well, thanks, brother."

I obeyed him and took another path. After that I took a different path; I no longer walked that way. I no longer passed by the house of Doña Micaela. They probably thought that I no longer liked them or some such thing. But the thing was that this "friend" was going around trying to ambush me, trying to kill me.

Would to God that he had been alone, but no. He went about with these two soldiers. He earned good money as a brazier and a silversmith. He had money to give to these "friends," and they did his bidding. So it was that I lost her.

The day she left town I still wanted to talk with her. She was over by the rectory and I went over to say hello.

"Doña Micaela," I said, "I hear that you're leaving, so I've come by to say good-bye to you. I hope you have a good trip."

"Good, Tincito," she said, "God be with you. We're going because they've ordered my husband elsewhere." Well, this Dominga was a gorgeously pretty girl.

Another time, my uncle Vicente arrived at my mother's house with his nieces, Hortencia and Virginia Castellanos. Sometimes their father, a first cousin of my uncle Vicente called Andrés Castellanos, would come too. Well, these girls would openly flirt with me. It was them, not me. I felt very little, because of my economic situation, because I had nothing.

Well, of the two daughters, Virginia was the one who flirted with me more. She looked for me and said things to make me talk with her. One time she sent me a letter from their ranch, inviting me to come. So that I would come she said in the letter: "My father isn't here. I'm alone. Come and we'll dance and enjoy ourselves." So I rode up to Yaitepec, and there it started to rain so hard that I had to turn back. When I returned from Yaitepec on my horse, I understood that I wasn't going to be able to go. This little horse wouldn't get me there. That's it. I didn't go. How am I to go? So it was that I lost this girl, a beautiful girl.

I said to myself, Now, I believe Mother will give me permission to marry; I think that she will make the necessary effort so I can get married. But I still wasn't resolute, because I thought it might turn out badly unless I had my own means of making a living. When I finally did, then I was ready.

We had a neighbor over there named Gabriela, a humble young woman. I liked her, but she didn't make any favorable gesture to encourage me to arrange things. So I said to myself, I'd just as soon marry a dead person for once and for all. I let it rest in peace.

There was another woman, the daughter of a judge who was in Juquila around 1921. His name was Valeriano Peralta Aguilar and he was a district judge. His daughter's name was Paula Aguilar. Well, she was a big, black woman but with very attractive legs. I declared my love for her, but, well, we didn't come to an understanding. Then too, she left town.

After that I had another girl, Felicitas Ortiz. This Felicitas was pretty. Her mother, Irinia Barrades, lived with a Sr. Abelardo Medina. Felicitas was the daughter of a Sr. Eligio Ortiz, an uncle of Rosalba Ayuzo, who is Bertita Ayuzo's mother.

We understood each other very well, but she had two stepbrothers, Ildefonso and Gildardo Medina, who lived with her. We tried to keep it secret, but somehow they found out, and they took her to the house of Sr. Valeriano Guzmán.[2] I lost another one there. After I was married, she had four or five children.

I used to go to the fiesta in Nopala every year. There at one of the fiestas I met Antonia, the woman who was to be my wife. She was coming up the hill to the plaza from the river. I was walking around the edge of the plaza to go down. As soon as I saw her I noticed she was staring at me, and I at her too. She asked me where I was from, and I told her that I was from Juquila. I asked her where she was from, and she said Juchatengo.

"And what did you bring to sell?" she asked.

"I brought some leather to sell in strips, and some whatnots, and I brought my barber's clippers because I'm a barber here. I have two jobs, working and selling. What are you doing here?"

"Well, my mother sells food," she said.

"Really? I didn't know that."

"Yes," she said, "she sells food."

"Just over there, you walk up this block. From there you walk up that block, and from there you walk past about three or four stands," she said. "It's almost under the mango tree there on the right. That's where we have our food stand."

"Will your mother extend credit?" I asked. "If she will, I'll eat there. She could charge me by the day, and at the end of the fiesta I could pay her."

"Of course, I hope you will come."

"Of course I'll come," I said. "I need to be near my stand." My stand was just up from theirs. There I had a well-made stand covered with branches for shade. On it I hung some of my things, my merchandise. The rest I had spread on a blanket. Inside, I worked with two other barbers. "All right, then, when I return I'll stop by there."

"That's fine," she said.

I passed by, and there she was.

"This is your stand?"

"Yes."

"Good," I said, "and who is your mother, then?"

"Well, my mother is this señora," she said.

"Pardon me, señora," I said, "Can you serve one by the day? How much would it be? Can you mark down the meals?" We talked. For so much, she said. "That's fine," I said. "During these days I'm going to eat here, and at the end of the fiesta I'll pay you. Don't worry, you can trust me."

Moreover, she had already told me who her father and mother were. Sr. Efren Vargas and Maximina Mauleón Pantoja. We arranged things. There I would go eat, there I would go for dinner. I had two young men who desired to learn to be barbers, and they looked after the stand when I went to eat.

So I would go to eat breakfast, lunch, and dinner there, and one of these times I said to her, "Look, I'd like to take a photograph of you with the various people who have come to the fiesta with us." But I had other intentions, well studied, and I said to her, "I spoke to Fortunata, a girl from Zacatepec." And I added, "Fulana is going to go, and some men who are from Cuixtla, and some women who are from Juquila. I'm going to have my picture taken with them. If you'd do me the favor of accompanying me, I'd be very grateful."

"If my mother will give me permission, I'll go."

"Well, good," I replied. Then I said to her mother, "Listen, Doña Nana, I wonder if you'd do me a favor." Nicely, and in this manner: "and I've thought . . . and many friends are there waiting for me to take a photograph. How would it appear to you if Antonia here accompanied us?" [3]

"Of course, gladly," she said, and off we went. But then her mother learned there was another woman there. Sra. Maximina didn't like the idea and didn't want her to go. Who knows what she knew about her. So she went to fetch Antonia, hitting her. I came up to her and said, "Well, what's the matter, Doña Nana? Why are you angry? Hadn't we agreed that we were going to have our photograph taken?"

"Well, no," she said, "because this woman is a . . ." and I don't know what else. [4]

"We didn't invite her, she just came," I said. "I couldn't just chase her away. She came on her own, no one invited her. I'm not a friend of hers, I don't even know her. I saw her there, but I don't even know who she is."

"No, she's an evil woman that . . . No!"

"I don't know the girls here well," I said. "I came to work and nothing else. Give her permission," I said. "Don't get mad."

"Of course, gladly. Go ahead and accompany the young man," she said.

"Ah, good," Antonia said.

So we went and they took our photograph. After the photograph I decently went back, but on the road I said, "Well, after so many difficulties, now that we've just met, I believe that there must be something between us. Why else would your mother get so angry? I like you very much. I feel comfortable with you, and if you want to, from here we can even go to Juquila."

"Look," she said, "I thought the same. It's not that I don't want to go but that I can't go. I came with my mother and must accompany her back. But my father is going to go to Juquila to sell corn soon, and we can arrange things there." But it was a while before they came to Juquila, some two months.

Anyway, I went, as I had promised to pay the bill I owed the señora. She was very happy, very grateful that I had come to leave the money just as we had agreed. Since there are people who leave without saying a word and never pay, these people are afraid to extend credit. I didn't do that. I've never done that anywhere.

So when her father finally brought her to Juquila I was waiting to come to an understanding with her. I was still working on the porch of Timoteo's store then. We went inside to talk so that people wouldn't overhear what we were talking about, and yes, we came to an understanding.

After some two or three other trips, I said to her straight out, "I'm not going to go to your pueblo to ask for your hand. If you want to stay, stay, because I don't want any problems with people there. They see me as an outsider. They may even do something to me, because I can't believe that you don't have any suitors there." [5]

"Yes," she said, "there are some, but since I don't want them and I haven't wanted them, I can go with whom I choose."

"Well, I can't go on this way," I said, "and that's why I'm not going."

"All right," she said, "we're going to leave shortly, about three in the morning." She was going with a mozo who had some five mules. So I said to a friend, León Muñoz, whose brothers have become killers, "Go get your gun and come with me. I'm taking my pistol, because I am going to steal Antonia."

"Let's go," he said.

God, it was ten at night. It was so dark that one could no longer see the mules at the house where they were staying. Were they missing? We moved closer to the edge of the river. I said to him, "We'll wait here. When we see them coming, we'll tell her to get down and let their hand go on by himself with the mules."

Their hand, Alejo, passed by, but they weren't with him. Nothing happened. When I returned I said to Enriqueta, the owner of the house where they were staying, "Don't you have any mescal? Give me a bottle," I said, since León really wanted to drink.

"Of course," she said, "here."

This Enriqueta lived with a cousin of mine named Bartolo Cuevas Aguilar. She gave me the mescal and I passed it to León, who chugged down half of it in one drink. I took a drink too, and then gave the rest to him, and he finished it off. We went home.

Then I went to work, but I couldn't restrain myself, and I asked Enriqueta what time they had left.

"It would have been twelve at night when they left," she said. But I came at ten or eleven o'clock.

Enriqueta came to speak to me. "Look, don't get into trouble, brother," she said.

"Why?" I asked.

"Well, I know that you want to steal Antonia now," she said, "but Efren entrusted her to me. I'm your friend, and you know that we care for you a great deal. But Sr. Efren has seen that you come here at night with your friends, that you sing and play the guitar. He's come to know that you're interested in Antonia. If you steal her from my house," she said, "before this friend leaves, he's going to believe that I am in league with you. Better for the sake of peace that you leave it alone. At least wait to see what you can do, because Antonia also told me that no matter what, she is going with you!"

That's what happened. Their hand probably took this gossip about how things were to her father, as well as on what path we were waiting. So he no longer came to sell corn.

Then she wrote me a letter saying that I should come to get her. Then I said to myself, Should I go or shouldn't I? I didn't like the idea. I was ready to give it up when Don Luis Comas, a telegraph lineman, said to me, "Listen, compadre Tino, what's going on? Let's go to Juchatengo." He knew that Antonia was my sweetheart. "I'm going with the line gang, and we can pass you off as a pole climber."

"Well, let's go then," I said, and off we went.

In a place they call the Alhaja, below the Plan de Minas, I meet Sr. Efren, who had a large salt bed there. I had made a large bowl of orange juice to drink. I passed it to Sr. Efren. "And what are you doing around here?" he asked.

"Well, you know what? These friends are paying me a salary not to work. Since I wanted to earn some money," I said, "and as I play the guitar, sing, and they like it, that's why I've come."

"For Christ's sake, it isn't worth it, wandering all over the countryside with this gang, entertaining them. You were better off with the job you had."

"Yes," I said, "but they duped me, and so here I am. I'll see. Maybe I'll only go as far as Juchatengo or Sola de Vega with them and then return."

"Well, that's good, friend," he said.

"My mules have gone on ahead."

"Thank you for the refreshment," he said.

"Well, be seeing you."

"Have a good trip," he said.

I thought to myself, If this poor man only knew where I'm going. I felt ashamed. One always feels bad when one knows how hard a person works to live honorably and then it turns out that one dishonors his people, his house.[6]

Anyway, I went on and arrived in Juchatengo, and I spent a night there in hiding. No one knew where I was. I hid because one of Antonia's suitors had made an agreement with one of her kinsmen, Virgilio, to keep other men away from her. I saw them riding there one day because I spent two days shut up, not going out anywhere either by day or night. And I said to Saúl Díaz, "Ask your wife to go see how things are over there without saying anything. Just find out what is happening. Tell her to be careful not to say anything. If she sees Antonia over there, tell her that I want to talk to her."

Saúl's wife went, and right away she found Antonia and told her, "Go over to my house. Fortino is waiting for you."

"Is that so?" she said, and she came running. She entered the house and asked, "How've you been?"

"Well, fine," I said.

"Did you receive the letter I sent you?"

"Yes, I received it," I said.

"Well, if you want, I'll stay once and for all," she said, "and I won't go back to my house."

"No," I said, "not yet. Go, and about ten at night, you come." But the reason was that about ten in the morning I had seen Virgilio and this other "friend" go by and turn up the path to Yolotepec. Ah, no, I said to myself, these "friends" are going to make that a bad route. This is going to be a little difficult, but I don't care. So I began to think, For these to get the upper hand, they'd have to study me a lot. No, they're not going to get the upper hand. So I said to Saúl, "Go find Pedro. Antonia will be here in a little while, and she is going to stay here." He went to fetch Pedro, and when he returned I said, "Come in."

"What's going on, brother? How've you been?"

"Fine," I said. "You're a man, and we have treated each other as friends. When you come to Juquila I put you up as a friend."

"That's true, brother. I won't find another friend like you. You're macho, as we say. When I've needed you, you've helped me wholeheartedly, and I'll do the same for you."

"Well, you see, it's this way," and I told him about the matter.

"Really," he said, "she's my niece, but that doesn't matter. If she's willing, you can count on me."

"I want you to guide me to Amialtepec," I said. "From there I know my way to Ixpantepec, and from Ixpantepec I'll go down to Juquila, and that will be that."

"But right now I don't remember this path," he said. "It would be better if I took you up the path to San Juan Lachao. Of course, up there Emiliano Vargas, Antonia's uncle, has a house. You can stay there."

Pedro took us up there that night, and there were heaps of mosquitoes, nothing but mosquitoes biting me. What a barbarity! All I had left was twenty centavos. I had spent all the money I had in Yolotepec, so we had no choice but to spend the night there.

We were on the edge of Juchatengo, on the upper side, toward San Juan Lachao Viejo. There were mosquitoes, and in quantity. We arrived there on the peak, and I started to sob to my friend and threw myself down. I had been drunk for three days, and now without anything to eat, I lay there stretched out where I fell. I was exhausted.

I was just thinking about the problem as we arrived, and I heard the rooster crow two or three times. "Now's the time," I said to him. "I can't stand these animals crowing anymore. Let's go." There was nothing else to do but to brush the mosquitoes out of one's eyes and ears.

"Let's go," he said, and away we went up this very high peak that is over to one side of Juchatengo. We climbed the first ridge, and from there to another, and another, and another. Up and up we went. I carried two rocks in my pants pockets and a jackknife. Those were the only arms I had. I didn't carry a pistol. "Damn it!" I said. "This is it!" But I had a real strength in my hand to throw rocks. We reached the summit over there, and I had a great thirst. I dropped to drink water from a pool that ran by the side of the path. We were exhausted.

After we had rested a while, I grabbed her. I had to carry her. Off we went along a little arroyo that was near the village. A Valeriano from Sola de Vega came along with a few bulls and cows and said, "Where are you going, brother?"

"Well, I'm heading toward Nopala," I said. "Actually, I'm going to Temaxcaltepec, because my niece Juana Aguilar is there. She said she wanted to see me, so I'm going there."

"And this girl?" he asked.

"Oh, she's coming along with me. I'm just accompanying her."

"Ah, could it be that you've stolen her, brother?" this friend said to me.

There were two others with him. "Be careful," I told them. "If you go through there, be careful what you say."

"Don't worry, brother," he said to me. "Do you need anything?"

"No," I told him. I didn't ask him for anything but just kept going.

We got to San Juan Lachao Viejo. Over there, with the twenty centavos I had left, I got a bowl of *atole* and two big tortillas. We split the tortillas and atole. We had to spend the night there because it was raining hard. The people in the town were very nice—poor, but nice. They dried my clothes, and I changed again. They also dried the sarape I was wearing and then gave us a mat to sleep on.

We didn't sleep that night. I kept thinking that her family might find us there. I worried that someone might have told them which path we took, that some of her suitor's friends might be waiting for us on the other side by Yolotepec, but they didn't find us.

It was still raining when we left Lachao. I thought we could get to Temaxcaltepec right away, but the river was flooded and I didn't know how to get across it, so we took another route. We followed a path that took us from almost the foot of the mountain up to a rancho called El Plantanar on top of this peak. There I ran across Florencio Núñez, may he rest in peace. He asked me where I had gone. I told him that I had gone to Juchatengo. Then this other man, Julio, Florencio's stepfather, showed up.

"Good afternoon," he said to me.

"Good afternoon, friend," I replied. He asked me where I was coming from.

"I'm coming from Juchatengo," I said.

"And this girl?" he asked.

"Well, she's from Juchatengo," I told him.

"She's the daughter of Sr. Efren Vargas, right?" he asked, "or have you stolen her?"

"I should steal her? No!" I told him. "I'm just going to see my niece in Temaxcaltepec." This Julio was from Temaxcaltepec.

"So your niece is there. She's a fair-complected girl, right?"

"Yes," I said, "that's my niece."

"Yesterday when I left my village I saw this girl. She's a teacher."

"Yes, that's her."

Then they gave us some yellow venison mole to eat. How delicious it was! I've never again had such a delicious dish—tasteful, not plain, but food with a sauce, salt, and venison flavor such as you've never seen. Then Florencio made a fire in the hearth. I put on a blanket and hung up my pants. The steam came out like a factory smokestack. In two turns my clothes were dry: shirt, undershirt, and then my sarape. Then I said to the poor drenched woman, "Now cover yourself with the blanket and I'll dry your clothes."

"Don't bother, I'll do it."

You should have seen all the troubles we went through that day. The following day I didn't know what to do. I didn't have any money.

When we were getting close to Temaxcaltepec I said, "Christ, we don't have anything to worry about. My niece lives there." It took such an effort to get to Temaxcaltepec! There was a poor fellow there, crossing the arroyo just above the place generally used—a high place where the river widens. He was on a horse.

"Don't be mean," I said. "Do me the favor of taking me across the river. I'll pay you, but we'll talk about that in a minute."

He took my wife across first, and then I crossed.

"Look," I said, "I don't have any money, but how much do I owe you?"

"No, señor," he said, "nothing. You're known around here."

"Oh, thank you very much."[7]

I didn't have a cent on me. Then we had to cross another arroyo, a fierce little stream. Well, I tried, but I couldn't. Then I said to myself, What am I going to do? I refuse to get stuck here.

I found a rather sturdy pole and stuck it firmly into the bottom against the current. On the other side there was a cuajenicuil tree with a branch sticking out over the middle of the river. I said to myself, If I can get to there, I will have made it. So then I stuck that pole in there and grabbed onto it and secured myself well.

"All right," I said to her, "give me your hand." She did, and I told her, "Don't be afraid. If the river pulls your feet out from under you, I'll pull you out, no matter what it takes."

"All right," she said, and she grabbed my arm with two hands. There was no way she was going to let go of me! She hung on, and we finally got across. We crossed another small stream after that, but it didn't have a lot of water in it, and the current wasn't strong.

We got to Juana's house, and she said to me, "Dominga is here." Dominga was an aunt of ours that we respected very much, like a mother. She was my mother's sister.

"Oh," I said, "I don't want her to know what I'm doing out and about."

"Oh." She finally figured out more or less what was going on. "Only God knows what you're up to, Uncle."

"Well, we'll be going now," Juana said.

"Well, let's go see her then," I said to her. We said hello to Aunt Dominga.

"Tell me, son, how have you been?"

"Fine, Aunt." We greeted her very affectionately. She was a very good person. She died without ever marrying, and she was quite old.

"Look," I said to my aunt, "I'm going to leave Antonia here." You see, she had already told me that my mother was in Teotepec. "I'm going to go see my mother," I told her. "I'll come back tomorrow, and then we'll leave."[8]

I arrived in Teotepec. Right away my cousin Benjamin said to me, "God, it's good that you came."

"Well, I dropped by for a little visit because I found out that my mother is here," I told him. "I'll be leaving today or tomorrow. Then I'll be going to Juquila."

"All right," he said.

As I was saying, I arrived and went to say hello to my mother, my aunts, my uncle, my cousins, and all my aunt's children.

My aunt said, "It's so good you came. You can cut our hair, cousin. Look how long it is!"

"Of course," I said.

"I have my barber's shears you sold me right here," she said.

"Then let's do it!" I said. I cut Benjamin's, Santos's, Bartolo's, and my uncle's hair. He was still alive then, may he rest in peace. I got them all fixed up. Then some other fellows arrived and they wanted their hair cut too. I earned about five pesos. At that time it was cheap. A shave and a haircut cost twenty centavos, so I earned myself five pesos.

Then my uncle said to me, "What's the matter? You look like something's troubling you."

"Why should anything be bothering me, Uncle? I'm not a murderer or a thief!"

"No, son," he said. "There are many reasons for being troubled. Sometimes you're troubled because you hurt yourself. Sometimes because somebody hit you. Sometimes because you've fought someone and have to run. Sometimes because you've stolen something and have to flee, whether the robbery was a success or not. And if you steal a girl, it's the same way."

"Now you've hit the nail on the head," I said. "That's the truth of the matter. Why should I try to fool you? With all the problems caused by yesterday's rain, I brought a girl with me from Juchatengo, and that's the trajectory I'm on. You aren't letting me lie about what's happened."

"Oh, it's all right, son," he said. "You're a hard worker, and it doesn't bother me. So, if it becomes necessary, your uncle's with you."

"Thank you, Uncle," I told him.

Then my mother said, "What are you up to, Son?"

"Well, look Mother," I said to her, "this is what happened and this is what I plan to do . . ."

My mother had already given me permission to look for a wife, the one that I wanted, and that's what I did.

"All right," she said, "there's nothing more to be said." [9]

Then I went back to Temaxcaltepec, and on September 29, 1932, I left for Juquila. Yes, I think that's the way it was, because Licha was born in '33. We went to my aunt Modesta's house when we got to Juquila.

She said to me, "What are you doing, son?"

"Well, look, Aunt, this is what I'm doing, and I came to ask for you to let us stay here until I go back home," I said. "I don't want a lot of fuss and people gossiping."

"All right," she said. "Come in, young lady. Come in here, daughter. Stay here until my nephew comes back." Then I went to say hello to my sister at home.

"And where have you been?" she asked. "You don't even say where you're going."

"Oh, I just went on a short trip," I told her.

A little while later my aunt arrived, and I told her, "I went to work in the plaza." When I got back I had saved up some money. I was all paid up and working, and that night I went to get her.

My sister said, "What are you doing? Mother worries a lot about what you're doing."

"She doesn't have to worry," I said. "Time is slipping by. I'm already more than thirty years old, and I found a little wife for myself." [10]

After a short time we made peace with Antonia's family. It wasn't too hard, because it almost wasn't a kidnapping. Others take women by force, but I wouldn't kidnap a woman like that. No, ours was a voluntary union. In my case, I can assure you that some of her people were in favor of it. My father-in-law's older brother, Emiliano Vargas, the eldest of all the brothers (because there was Don Emiliano, Don Manuel, my father-in-law Efren, and Irinia Vargas, another sister) came to visit me after we had been together a little while because they were in favor of it.

No, there weren't any problems except from her mother, who was a little put out. She even sent her eldest daughter, Sidronia, to chide Antonia. She tried to make her go do who knows what. Well, Antonia told her sister off, saying freely what she wanted to. I was at work, and I didn't know. Well, if she had said something to me . . .[11]

Changes After the Revolution

AN INTRODUCTION TO

CHAPTERS 3 THROUGH 6

Although by 1917 the bloodiest phase of the Revolution had ended in most of the country, its violence went beyond the battlefield. The Revolution had displaced millions of people, haciendas and plantations had been destroyed, and the power of the central government had been seriously weakened, leaving the countryside in the hands of regional caudillos, petty despots. Between 1920 and 1934 a series of presidents attempted to reassert the central government's authority over the semi-independent regional leaders by again resorting to the ruthless tactics of the Porfiriato. Political assassination was rife; Emiliano Zapata, for example, was assassinated in 1919. In the district of Juquila, however, Zapatistas continued their fight for "land and liberty" well into the mid-1920s. They were only destroyed when their constant demands caused the very Indian communities they depended on for survival to turn on them.

By 1926 the efforts of President Plutarco Elías Calles to bring regional caudillos under control had largely succeeded, and he turned his attention to the Church, the only power in Mexico that still remained independent of his system. In his campaign against the Church, Calles deported foreign clergy and closed Catholic schools. In retaliation—hoping to pressure the government into backing off—the bishops ordered priests to close their churches and abstain from administering the sacraments. Almost immediately mass hysteria swept the country-side. Catholic laymen calling themselves Cristeros drove federal troops from rural areas where Catholic priests were still administering the sacraments and went on a rampage of murder, shouting, "Long live Christ the King!" The government responded in kind. Between 1927 and 1929 the Cristero rebellion turned into an excuse to loot churches and persecute conservative elites. Even though the Cristero rebellion was not particularly violent in Juquila, it helped finance more-enduring local factional struggles.

The struggle for power ended with the establishment of the national party, which incorporated almost all the competing sectors. Under various names (the current one being the Partido Revolucionario Institucional, or PRI), this party has ruled Mexico ever since. While the PRI achieved peace on a national level, factional struggles within the region brought continued violence.

The election of Lázaro Cárdenas to a six-year term in 1934 saw an intense and dramatic revival of revolutionary goals. The long-promised land reform began in earnest, and it created a complex series of conflicts in the district of Juquila which pitted Indians and peasants against the mestizo elites. During these conflicts the caciques competed for political power by championing local causes, and in doing so they divided villages and created a state of near civil war.

Fortino, whose family was impoverished by the Revolution, recognizes that the factional struggles in his region were a continuation of the conflict over communal lands between the holders of private property and the Chatino villages. He explicitly links the endemic violence to the introduction of coffee as a cash crop on communal lands. Detailing these factional struggles, Fortino argues that coffee created the same structural contradictions in every pueblo in the district.

Chapter 3

THE BEGINNINGS OF

FACTIONALISM

At the end of the Revolution, two or three groups of Zapatistas were operating in the countryside. The last one was that of José Próspero, whom they killed in Teotepec in 1927 or 1928. The Zapatistas were moving swiftly this way and that, and every couple of weeks they would come to Teotepec to demand food and money.

A municipal secretary and teacher, Artemio Beltrán, organized the people and raised the flag to end it. (Long before this, General Juan Rodríguez had died in Nopala of an illness.) Artemio Beltrán said to them, "They come here every month, every couple of weeks, to demand money, to take chickens and food. We've lost patience here." They formed a plan. "Look," Artemio said, "next time these people come, we'll have a plan. Everyone should have a musket or whatever arms you have prepared. When these people arrive, we'll feed them. We'll tell them to put their arms over there. While they are eating we'll have the town criers go and tell everyone they are here. At the first sound of the church bell, come with cudgel or whatever you can."

So that's what they did. When the Zapatistas were eating, the villagers came—bullets and machetes—and wiped them out. There were some ten of them. That was the end of this band of guerrillas, which had operated around Teotepec, Nopala, El Camalote, Cinco Negritos, La Esmeralda, Zacatepec, Jocotepec, Acatepec, Santa Cruz, and down the other side to Tataltepec, Tepenixtlahuaca, and Cinco Cerros.

The Revolution of the Cristeros

No sooner than they had finished off José Próspero's group than another revolution erupted—that of the Cristeros.[1] They came in search of money, because the churches had the obligation to give, since they were soldiers of Christ. Father Rosalino Soreano was still the priest in Juquila when they came. God, how they robbed the church!

They established a citizen's committee to care for the property of the church. They tried to appoint me to the committee in 1928. This was the year after the Revolution of the Cristeros of Don Plutarco Elías Calles had begun. They appointed me as a representative, along with I don't know how many others, to go and guard the church.[2] But I didn't want to, and I told them no. "No," they said, "you've been named, and you have to complete your obligations."

When we arrived at the church to see the padre, the people crowded in to hear the town's presidente, a follower of Calles. Then Padre Soreano said, "All of you here can serve on this committee except my godson, Fortino. I don't want him to serve."

"But, Padre, we've already named him. Why do you say no?"

"This is an honorable young man, and they will corrupt him," he said. "I don't want him to serve. You can do and say what you want, but I won't allow him to come here with you."

"All right," they said, "we'll excuse him." So it was that I didn't serve even though I had been named a representative on the church committee.

Christ! I said, when I saw how the Cristeros robbed the church.[3] The presidente municipal, Valeriano Pozas, was having an affair with Micaela, the grandmother of Anselmo Valentín. He went to a convention of presidentes municipales in Queretaro in 1928 and came back with a load of hats. When she saw this, she went to him. "I'm told all you do in the church is rob it," she said. "Why haven't you given me anything?"

"Go, grab what you can in your two hands."

She grabbed a handful of these large silver pesos with her two hands, a few pesos.

"Well, have you grabbed them?"

"Yes," she said. "I'll be going now."

Later they said these two had taken two twenty-liter cans full of pesos but that this money wouldn't let them sleep. Pozas died. The money killed him. They say that Micaela wanted to return the money or that she sent it back, but I don't believe it. I never saw it returned, and I was in the church for a long time and saw many things.

I saw how Alfonso Zárate Pérez, who married my comadre Tina, carried off boxes of old gold pesos. His brother, Audifas Villanueva, liked to drink. So every so often—every two or three days—he would open the box and take a handful of gold. Audifas wasted good money, gold. He didn't know what to do with it.[4]

After they had spent all this money, the citizens' committee of Lázaro Sánchez took over. Since Alfonso had helped Padre Soreano dig holes in the walls of the church to hide the church's money, when Sr. Sánchez took over he grabbed him and said, "Come, show me every place where there is money here. You know that I'll give you what you want." Sr. Sánchez carried all the money off to his house. He gave Alfonso practically nothing, just a few pesos. Since no one made trouble, Alfonso had the audacity—when nothing else remained—to take even the Virgin's crown. He even stole the Virgin's dress with all its ornaments. He broke up the crown and began selling it piece by piece in the pueblo. It was a very deeply felt injury for the people of Juquila. Everyone cried bitterly at the lack of respect that they had for the Virgin.

At least I confronted Alfonso. "I'm going to teach you a lesson," I told him, "so you'll know to respect the place that has supported you for so many years. You didn't know to respect the church. You abused the trust that was placed in you. Don't you remember that Padre Soreano was our godfather? He taught us honor. He taught us respect. Why did you abuse his trust?"[5]

"No, it's that they tricked me, that . . ." and I don't know what else.

Finally he confessed how they had taken the Virgin's crown, put it in a basket, and had Mariana Palacios sell it. When I learned this, it made me very angry. I was going to beat his brains out. I was the boxing champion of Juquila, and I said to him, "I'm going to hit you. I'm going to teach you a lesson so you'll know that you're good for nothing. You're going to make a confession." Alfonso confessed, and he, his brother Audifas Villanueva, his companion Amado Muñoz, and several others went to jail.

The Beginning of Violence After the Revolution

When I was growing up, the only killing that I knew about, in Juquila, was that of Blas Ramírez, the father of Eva Ramírez. She's the wife of Sr. Sánchez. The father of Amado Muñoz, Edmundo Muñoz, killed him. Apart from the Revolution there were very few killings.[6] During the Revolution they killed a Vicente, a *pistolero*. They killed the father of Diego and Urbano Núñez after the Revolution. I don't remember any others, but it was a rare occurrence then. It was afterward that people began to go around buying pistols and celebrating this work, saying, "I'm very macho, and if anyone gives me difficulties, I'll kill them."

When the people of the pueblo began to plant coffee, about 1930 or 1935 in Juquila, that's when things began to become very violent. People started accusing one another of witchcraft and started killing witches. There was a man from Juquila named Sierra who they accused of being a witch. He was the father of some Sierras who have some coffee now. They're rich. He was always a hard worker, but the people of Camalote came after him. I don't know who he had done some harm to, but one day he was taking a bath and this fellow went and killed him. Jesus! By now they've killed a lot of witches, a lot of them.

The killing became very intense. Yes, when everyone began planting coffee, that was when it began to catch fire. When the price of coffee went up, everyone wanted to plant coffee and harvest it the next year. There was too much ambition and greed.

People began to grab land and fence it in so no one else could enter, which meant that others who wanted to plant a small plot couldn't. That was the difficulty. They began to have difficulties in the hot lands down around Camalote, Cinco Negritos, Miramar, Barranca Honda, and La Esmeralda (which are communal lands of Juquila), and even in the pueblo in the Barrio Grande and on the Loma del Toro, where the house of Teófila Mendoza is.

The house of Olga Salazar was where the first casualties began to occur, when she began to sell mescal there. That's where it began. Soon after, it was becoming a custom that over that way, on that path, there would be a continual succession of fatalities. Many men have been killed there, but in vengeance over these things, over land. In the heat of mescal, these shameless men reach the point of killing one another. That's why there have been so many men killed there.

Factionalism in Chatino Communities

All those towns where coffee has been introduced have the same characteristics. They are divided and fight among themselves. First it was San Juan Lachao Viejo, then it was Nopala. In Lachao, it was the Barrio Abajo that rebelled, very intensely, and moved off to form a new town. Lachao Nuevo is now stronger than Lachao Viejo. Lachao Viejo is calmer and more peaceful than Lachao Nuevo. It was all the outsiders from towns in the district of Miahuatlán (from San Jerónimo Coatlán, Almolongas, Santo Domingo Coatlán, and Santa Ana de Cuixtla) who stirred up trouble. It was money that talked, even setting brother against brother. These friends have a lot of land, and the poor Indians don't have anywhere to work. Their land has been taken over by these outsiders.[7]

Teotepec was divided because the townspeople didn't agree to the amount of land that Sr. Florencio Valencia took for himself. So they started fighting for a while, but these poor, ignorant people weren't strong enough. León and Ramón Escamilla were educated outsiders who lived there. They helped the people recover part of that land. There was a time when Ramón Escamilla started planting his coffee crops around there. Everybody was immediately against them. Even the priest, Nicolás Serrano, participated in the protest. He offered his support to the people so that they could regain their right to have what was theirs. Nevertheless, Ramón Escamilla bought off government officials and even the Church hierarchy. The office of the bishop denounced the priest; that's how big the gossip got. These powerful people gave a lot of money to the office of the bishop so that they could get Padre Nicolás Serrano out of the way. This was just a spark that grew and ended in the killing of the Escamillas.[8]

Later, some courageous people from Teotepec tried to take over. There was a young man named Francisco (nicknamed Chico) working on the finca of Sr. Valencia. He loyally defended Don Florencio's interests, so when he realized that sacks of coffee were disappearing from the finca, he began to investigate. Chico found out that Sr. Florencio's brother, Gilberto, was the one taking the coffee and trying to blame it on their opposition. He confronted him and told him, "Look, we are going to put a stop to this. What do you think they're going to say when they find out that you're taking the coffee away? They are going to say you're a troublemaker!" He was attacked and killed by Don Florencio's brother, Gilberto.

His name was Francisco Rodríguez Aguilar, and he was a son of León Eustorgio Rodríguez. The night they brought his body to Juquila I went to see him. I was sad because I had loved him as I would love any member of my family. They say that those Aguilars were related to my grandfather León Aguilar. They had killed him because he was trying to bring Gilberto to justice.

Suddenly things started to get confused in Teotepec. After they killed Chico, the federales and a sergeant got into it, hitting and kicking, and Gilberto became an important person. A brave man from Teotepec hit the sergeant, but he was killed immediately after. The federales attacked the town, imprisoned people for several years, and took them to Juquila. Some had to go, and some didn't. That's how the town was divided.[9] It had been a free municipio, but now it is divided into two agencias, all because of Don Florencio. Since he had the money, he gave the orders. Everybody would obey him. This is what he wanted to accomplish in Juquila. We have all this conflict because of him.

It was Don Florencio Valencia who began this division. When he died, Sr. Sánchez took power. Sr. Sánchez's father was from Teotepec. His name was Nicolás Valencia. He was from Teotepec but I think Don Nicolás spent some time in Juquila, but I'm not sure, because he would take Sánchez to the finca to see his brother, Padre Valencia, a priest. Padre Valencia had two women: María Acevedo and Mariana Colón. There were many priests like him in town, but in Juquila it was Sr. Sánchez who made all these changes in terms of land. He wanted to steal land without giving any reason for it. People here were easily turned off by him.[10]

Anyway, that was Teotepec's history. It was divided into two parts. Nowadays it still explodes. There were a lot of deaths in Teotepec the other day, but they were losses for the Cerro del Aire side. The perpetrators went back to Teotepec, but the police caught them. Now they're in Juquila. The people from the other side, from Cerro del Aire, have more peace. I think there were two or three criminals, and the people of Teotepec got together (they didn't tell me why) and caught them and took them to jail in Juquila. They were fighting with the people from Cerro del Aire, but the latter are considered weaker. Teotepec used to be the main municipio before, so it's considered a stronger town. That's why they could imprison the others. I saw them when they brought them to Juquila. It was too bad; justice never existed for them. One can't do very much about it. I couldn't spend my time raising hell because of that. It would have been too much work.

Political Divisions in Juquila

In Juquila from about 1935 onward Sr. Sánchez began to fight politically with my padrino Saúl León Villanueva, and they began to divide the people. It was business. The manipulation of people defined Sánchez's and Saúl's politics.

Lázaro Pantoja Sánchez of Tlaxiaco had come to Juquila during the Revolution, and since he had become accustomed to doing wicked deeds during the Revolution, he continued to do them afterward. Despite his being an outsider who wasn't very well accepted by all the people of the pueblo, he opened a store to compete with that of Saúl Villanueva, who was from Teposcolula in the Mixteca Alta.

Don Saúl had been there since before the War of the Pants in 1896. He fled with my father when the Chatino, led by the Indians of San Juan Quiahije, attacked Juquila in 1896. He must have come to Juquila in 1890, because in 1896, when they fled, he went with my father and Don Eusebio Guzmán and some others to Tututepec. Since my father knew the country, knew everything well, he led the way. They fled because the Chatino were going to kill every mestizo. But they weren't able to do anything to my father or my godfather Saúl or Don Eusebio Guzmán, or the others who went with them.

Anyway, Saúl León Villanueva came to Juquila in this epoch and built up a business. Later he became secretary to the judge of the district court, because he was very knowledgeable in law, in everything. He was always the first person they would call to arrange any business in the court, because he was very competent in everything.[11]

So he had his store when this Sr. Sánchez arrived and opened a tiny shop. Things were favorable and Sánchez started to do business. Then he opened a store in competition with Don Saúl León Villanueva. Since Sánchez had his supporters, he began to divide the people. Saúl Villanueva had a lot of followers, Sánchez only a few. They started to divide the pueblo and form groups, which were sometimes armed. They used to kill each other's followers, and the resentments from this are still rooted in the community.

The difficulties increased daily as the suporters of Sr. Sánchez increased, so much so that he won the election in 1935 and was made presidente municipal. It was in 1935. I remember it well, because it was on Independence Day —when Santos Aguilar, Alfonso Núñez, and I went to dance El Jarabe—that Sr. Sánchez went about on the night of September 15, waiting for the hour to give the cry of Hidalgo to animate everyone, yelling, "Viva la independencia!"

Well, Joel Morales, Agusto Morales, and Nicolás Morales were around, but before the cry of independence Sr. Sánchez had already organized a defense of armed men there. Don Saúl's supporters couldn't go around armed because they didn't have anyone to give them political protection, but they carried concealed weapons. Sr. Sánchez's guards carried theirs openly. There, in front of my shop and along the porch in front of the shop of Maximiano Salinas, they stood looking toward the town hall.

Suddenly they encircled the Morales boys. I thought, It's in the realm of possibility that they are going to kill them any second here. But just then the others made their move. Two came up behind those who were encircling the Morales boys, and another two stood in front of them. So then Sánchez's men couldn't move out from the middle, because of the two behind them. If they made any move, they would have had to die too. They let them go. They filed out of the plaza and down the street past my shop. Then these friends took the path for their house. They said, "Better we go before something happens," and they went to their house.

They were already a little high—half drunk—and they wanted to continue drinking, but when they arrived at the house there wasn't any mescal to be had. They lived in a house above the house of Olga Salazar, in the house on the crest of the hill. This was the house of Joel Morales. Delfino Olivera was going around drinking with them. This poor man wasn't a troublemaker and was going around with them because he was a neighbor of Joel's father-in-law. "Let's go get some mescal," they said.

Meanwhile, Sánchez's men had followed them over there. Two brothers, Abdón and Gregorio Pérez, were there waiting to see what they were going to do. These poor souls went to Olga's to bring some mescal, and they were waiting there. They fell on them with daggers. They killed Delfino, but Joel was still able to do something before he died. He managed to stab Gregorio in the leg and just about severed the great artery, which, if severed, would have killed him too. These two, Delfino Olivera and Joel Morales Guzmán, died that night of September 15 on the orders of Sr. Sánchez.

At the time, I was the justice of the peace. To prevent the investigation into the Sánchez affair from being executed as it should be, they accused the district court judge of being an accomplice in this affair. It was done invidiously. There was nothing to it. It wasn't true. After the judge left, since I was justice of the peace I was summoned by the prosecutor to assume the post of assistant judge. I was to present myself to the court immediately to receive the office. I went and was sworn in. Then I turned to my kinsman Santos Aguilar and said to him, "Look, they've already done their investigations, but we are going to proceed duly. It pains me to have seen what these men have done. Personally, I don't like it. If it's possible, I'll use a heavy hand to punish these evil men."

"It's certain," he said to me, "that they've done . . ." such and such, "and that's how this friend in jail was wounded."

Despite the fact that both Abdón and Gregorio went to prison, Sr. Sánchez continued as presidente, but after that the party of old Sánchez languished. It no longer had these two leaders to head it. Sr. Sánchez went about in fear. A son of Captain Joaquín even tried to kill him. He always went to Sánchez's store to drink. He became drunk. I don't know what Sánchez did to him, but he stabbed Sánchez in the back. The knife struck the spine. If it hadn't, he would have killed him. As it was, he was a long time healing. Sánchez's business went down and down until it was practically ruined. But despite the fact that Sr. Sánchez was behind these murders, he continued as presidente. The thing was that he had many relatives in the government. A cousin of his was a senator. The senator put his foot down hard. So it was that nothing happened to him.

After that calamity in 1935, as I've said, Sánchez's business fell off. He went into debt and they seized his store. After some time had passed, he was elected presidente of the church committee. There he was able to do what he wanted. With the money he stole from the church he paid off his debts and put his business back on its feet. But after that, in political matters his power was gone.

Nevertheless, Lázaro Sánchez—backed by the Muñoz family—continued to divide the pueblo. Because the people were divided by Sánchez, wherever they would meet they wouldn't get along very well. And, because of mescal, or whatever, they would begin to fight and kill each other. Things went on chaining themselves together until this old man Sánchez died. After that his followers didn't have anyone to protect them. My padrino Saúl Villanueva died soon after.

Then Florencio Valencia grabbed Sánchez's old banner, and my brother Timoteo and his son took up the battle against him. Florencio Valencia also had the Muñoz family's backing, and they began to divide the pueblo.[12] The time came in which the bitterness came to an end. Things were appeased. Don Florencio withdrew from politics because he was old and was no longer able to take part effectively. He wanted to be a cacique, but my brother Timoteo was able to force him out of power. After that he didn't get involved, because he couldn't. Don Florencio didn't let his sons get involved, because he knew they would be killed right off. This was over then.

Sr. Sánchez gave me a lot of trouble in 1933 when I built my shop. I built a tiny place where my store is now, but it cost me a lot of work, a lot of suffering, a lot of anguish, and many disputes—conflicts even with the presidente municipal. I lit into the presidente, verbally abusing him even though he threw me in jail. I had evil, evil thoughts. I thought, Why is he ridiculing me? Why won't he give me a lot like he has given everyone else? He gave Sr. Lázaro Sánchez a large lot in the middle of the plaza, even though he isn't from Juquila, because he has money, but since I am poor, he doesn't want to give me one.[13]

But as luck would have it, my brother Teófilo was serving as *síndico*. I didn't take advantage of him. Instead I made a petition to the presidente municipal, because I didn't want people to say that my brother had given me the parcel. My brother was a very meek man who would never say to the presidente, Help my brother, or some such thing, but he advised me to talk with the *regidores* on the town council.

So I went to see Uncle Ricardo at his house and won his affection.[14] "Look, Uncle Ricardo," I said, because he was the first regidor, "I'm thinking . . ." thus and thus.

"Look, young man," he said in Chatino, as he was a Chatino Indian, "you are a servant of the pueblo. Yes, I've seen you. You do your duties here. You help. You're from the pueblo here. You've suffered with the pueblo, and you performed your duties during the Revolution with us here in the town hall too, yet this presidente doesn't want to help you now."[15]

"Tomorrow," he said, "when I toll the bells at twelve o'clock, come to the town hall and speak with Cuberto González, Isaac Ríos, Mateo Ríos, and me. There are four of us, and the presidente is only one. I can sack him if I want."

"Alright," I said, and so it went. I simply waited there, and when I heard the bells go dong! dong! dong! I went in. He had already spoken to the council's regidores. When I arrived the regidores were there. I spoke to the first regidor.

"Good afternoon," I said. I greeted the presidente too, but he was sitting in the shadows and I couldn't discern him clearly. "How fortunate it is that you're all here," I said to them. "Señor First Regidor," I said, "I've presented three petitions to the presidente for a small lot on which to build a barbershop, because there are none in Juquila. I want to work honorably. Why not give me a small lot and aid me in this way. Of course, those who occupy places that everyone uses, those who have lots on the plaza or a piece they've grabbed over there, are paying monthly. I can't afford that."

"Ah, yes," Uncle Ricardo said. "Señor Presidente, why have you denied this young man a small lot where he may work honorably? He's from here. He's of this pueblo. He didn't come here with the Revolution like Sánchez. You gave him a large parcel over there without advising me, and now you deny this one because he's a son of the pueblo, right? And to that one, who is not a son of the pueblo, you've given a large lot in the middle of the plaza."

"No, it's that . . ." who knows what. "And after this, we'll give it to him."

"And why after this?" I asked him, "Why does it require so much thought? It's not an inheritance from your fathers. It's an inheritance from the pueblo of that which the government ceded to us centuries ago. What reason have you to refuse? None! That's why, Señores Regidores, I've come to speak with you now, to ask you to take my needs into account. I don't want your help to do some evil deed. I simply want your help so I can begin to work as I should. It's past time. I'm thirty-two years old."

"Of course," Uncle Ricardo said, "Let's see. Mateo, grab that yardstick. You, Isaac, grab the rod. Remain seated," he said to the presidente, "you're very busy. Don't stand up. You don't need to go."

We went to make the measurements. "Here you put your posts. Here, in this square, you can build your little shop."

But Sr. Sánchez was a jealous man. "No, there he'll block the view of my store, it's that . . ." and so on.

I told him, "Don't speak. You're not even from here. They're doing you a big favor by giving you a place, and now you even want to give orders. Now, I understand it's because you've given money to those here and there, to Sr. Lauro Ramírez, who is the presidente."

"No," he said, "it's that . . ." and who knows what.

"You," the regidor told him, "you be quiet, or are you a native of this town?"

"No," he replied.

"Then what right have you to speak here? We are the ones who give orders here. We are the authorities. You are nothing, so shut your mouth." [16]

Do you know how much I had in my pockets in those days when my first child, Licha, was born? I had $1.25, and with it I bought two posts to start building my shop. A while after I had spent that money, Pablo González, a finquero from the finca Las Delicias, came and asked me to cut his hair. He gave me a peso. At that time I charged twenty centavos, but he gave me a peso because he saw that I needed it. After a while my godfather asked me to cut his hair, then someone else did, and so on. Then with these centavos I bought the other two posts I needed for the four corners. I still needed two long center poles for the roof. I worked some more and bought them for a peso—oak beams that will never rot, cheap. I had some roof tiles, but I didn't have enough to cover the entire roof, so nearly half of one side remained uncovered.

A compadre of mine, Felipe Varela, came by. "Compadre," he said, "why haven't you finished the roof of your shop? Look at it!"

"Compadre," I said to him, "I'm going to be frank: I don't have any tiles, or the money to buy them." Tiles were worth forty or fifty pesos a hundred then.

"No, compadre," he said, "I've got a big pile of them at home that are going to waste. The children go there, jump on them, and break them. Better you use them here. Let's go. You count the ones you can use, take them, and when you can, pay me."

"Thank you, compadre," I said to him. "Let's go right now."

I went and got some young men to carry them and put them on the roof. Now the shop was shaping up. It still didn't have any walls, just posts and a roof. So then I framed it round with laths and slats, and stuffed this framework with mud, pieces of tile, pieces of adobe, pieces of whatever I could find. Now all there was left to do was to hang the doors. One of the doors Don Silvino gave me. It was made of knotty pine and was more than a hundred years old. The other door Luis Comas made for me for $2.50. He also made me some shelves, which went from the floor to the ceiling and covered the entire wall, and three stools for four pesos. Four pesos was cheap. And where did those four pesos come from? I had to work and work. I did a little carpentry. I would pound nails for a day and earn a peso. I would work half a day and then cut hair. People began to ask for me, and I would go down to the shop to cut hair.[17]

Even after I built my shop, Sr. Sánchez continued to bother me, because he wanted me out of there. One day, he came into my shop and I confronted him. "You've ordered killings. You've killed. You committed all kinds of evil deeds, and then some, when you went around here as a soldier during the Revolution. But this time you've made a mistake. I don't have any reason to fight with you, but if you continue to bother me," I said, taking a revolver out of the cash box, "I am going to liquidate everything you've got left. So don't mess around with me or I'll empty all five shots in you." After that he was afraid of me. He never personally bothered me again, but he would do so indirectly.

Soon after I had built my shop, I established my field at the edge of town. My brother gave me a little barbed wire, and I planted my corn there, but this Sánchez lit into me with relish. I had a lot of trouble with him. I was a young man then and could stand up like a man. It was those from the Barrio Grande who did the most damage to my fence. I awoke one morning to find all the barbed wire around the field cut. Almost everyone in the barrio was involved, out of envy. Not that I had enough land for five or ten people but that they were simply told by Sánchez to go damage it. I planted corn, squash, beans, and everything there. I was a hard worker in the field, too, not just in the plaza. I would leave the plaza early and go to the field. I would return for lunch and then to the plaza to work cutting hair, fixing shelves, selling the few little things that I carried in the shop. Out of bitterness, I went to Río Grande. I said to myself, What am I to do? Well, I'll sell a cow, and with this money I'll return and repair my fence. When I returned from Río Grande, my compadres Felipe Varela and Benjamin Ríos came to help mend and repair the fence. It was like new. Since Felipe worked at the telegraph office, he had tacks to drive fasteners into the posts and leave it well secured. My compadre helped me a great deal; the poor man, that's why I admire him highly. He treated me like a brother.[18]

I have had compadres who thought a lot of me, like Felipe, and others who were compadres and nothing more. Compadrazgo isn't like it was before. Compadres aren't sincere the way they used to be. They don't fulfill their obligations like they did before. They have only their self-interest at heart. It isn't a free favor anymore. People are too busy to do you a favor—to get firewood, to work a while in the cornfield. Because sometimes people can't say no, they even take the liberty of deceiving you, saying that they are going to fulfill their obligations.

Well, my compadre Felipe wrote a complaint about the affair that went all the way to Mexico City. In Mexico City there's an office of complaints, an annex to the presidency of the republic. He wrote them a complaint, and they transmitted the order that they should give me justice. Seeing this, the señor who sustained these "friends," this Sánchez, clearly said to them, "Look, this friend has complained all the way to the president. We are going to get in trouble. We had better leave him in peace."[19]

I finally got a title for my field from the presidente municipal in 1940. I had been petitioning him for it. I told him, "It's this way. I've invested time and money on this field, but I don't have any authorization." So he gave me a title saying, "I authorize Sr. Fortino Santiago, native and citizen of this district, that he may, when he can, enlarge his field for planting. By order of the presidente," on such and such a date.

Sánchez pulled a really dirty trick in the town hall while he was presidente. He put the municipal archive in the jail and let the prisoners use it for toilet paper. The archive, of course, contained all the documents on land that had been litigated. There was the documentation of the lands of Rancho Viejo. Sr. Sánchez and his wife had made plans to grab the lands at Rancho Viejo. That is why they put the archive there, so the prisoners would destroy it, using it as toilet paper. Now they claim that the land is private property. They want to grab this land, but their papers are false, because the communal lands of Juquila adjoin those of Panixtlahuaca, San Juan Quiahije, Jocotepec, Zacatepec, Yaitepec, Ixpantepec, Teotepec, and Cuixtla.

When they told me how the prisoners were using the archive, it burned me up. I protested their placement of the archive in the jail, but no one would confront Sánchez and make him return the archive to the town hall. That's how it went. They destroyed it.[20]

Now the "owners" say they have titles, but the pueblo won't let them get away with it. When they tried to fence the property in 1973, the pueblo took their machetes to the barbed wire. If they had found Sánchez's son-in-law Don Esteban, they would have killed him.

Don Esteban is a stubborn fool about these things, but he hasn't filed suit, because he knows the pueblo would rise up right away. He would lose. The communal lands office would tell the judge, "Here are the titles if you care to examine them. It is clear that these lands are communal property, not theirs. The titles they have are false." Well, Don Esteban hasn't filed suit, probably because it's worth more to him to work the lands as a member of the community.

Don Esteban knows that the people in the mountains have turned very criminal, that they would kill him. After all, they can't expect justice. There isn't any justice. Justice is bought, and laws are bent to suit those who can pay.

Now there is no justice. What witnesses are there to see? Do you believe that in the mountains—where they go around killing people—there is going to be anyone watching? The people know that even if they do have encounters with criminals, if they were to go to court and make charges against them, they had better not return, because they would be killed. "Why did you go and say that? So you won't do it again..." bang! They would shoot them. That's why justice is worth nothing. One can't expect to live, if one wants to make them respect the law, by going to the authorities. Take Yaitepec. They practically killed Concepción Nicolás in the town hall. They no longer respect the law. There is no authority now.

It's clear that Don Esteban is abusing the law. Nothing is right about this. They forge documents and have the effrontery to say "It's mine" when it's not true. It's too much. I'm a son of the pueblo, born and raised here, but

I've never said this. They gave me a field, a piece of land for planting corn. At the time it was some distance from town, but because the town has grown so much, now it is on the edge of town. Houses border my field. But I received my land legally, not by abuse of the law.[21]

The Nopala War

In 1937 a very violent conflict broke out in Nopala. They began to fight among themselves. It began with Angel Aguirre. Actually, it started with his father, Diego Aguirre, who fought with practically everyone. Then, when it reached the point that Diego was killed, his son Angel took up the campaign. He formed a band, and they did a lot of damage in Nopala. Later they chased him out of town, and he went to San Gabriel Mixtepec. He then began to attack people in Nopala at night, and so on. In Nopala, Gustavo Venegas drove Angel's gang out of town, and formed another band. They were the ones who ruled, and those who didn't like it had to leave.

I knew Gustavo Venegas's father. He was a little old man who I'm fairly certain was from Sola de Vega. He was short and fat, with a protruding stomach. He rarely wore a shirt. At times, when I would come for the fiesta I would see him from the road, cutting up the pigs he had butchered, because he was a cook. Gustavo Venegas was a foreman on the finca Las Delicias.[22]

When Gustavo's men would get drunk, they would kill those they didn't like—that's how it went. I don't know exactly how, but another band formed, and they began to fight among themselves. There was another massacre in Nopala. Then this new party took up the challenge and went after Angel's band in San Gabriel Mixtepec. A son of Manuel Bustamante hit Angel's band and killed many of them. He told them that next time he would finish them off. Then Angel's band prepared. They learned what day Bustamante and his men were coming. They found out from where and by what path they were going to come. So, once they entered San Gabriel, they surrounded them. They finished them off, and they killed the son of Manuel Bustamante. They even set fire to them. After this the conflict between San Gabriel and Nopala ended, and Gustavo Venegas remained in charge in Nopala.[23]

In 1940, during one of my many trips to Nopala for the fiesta, Nicolás Pérez —a countryman of mine from Juquila and a son of a Zapatista, Lauro Pérez— was riding a merry-go-round with a pistol in his hand. I was talking with an uncle of mine from Miahuatlán, Arnulfo.

"I came to the fiesta to enjoy myself," he said. "Let's walk around, Tino."

"Let's go, Uncle," I said, confident that I had no difficulties with anyone. Well, each time Nicolás would go around he would aim his pistol at me. The second time, I said to my uncle, "This one's going to shoot at us on the third time round. Let's go. It doesn't take long to go around."

Fast, then, we went running around back of the town hall. That's how we escaped Nicolás Pérez shooting us. After that I didn't go to Nopala for three years. "I'm not going anymore," I said to my mother.[24]

"Why, Son?" she asked.

"Because I'm not. Things are very ugly there. They don't respect people. They'll shoot at anybody, kill anyone. That's why I'm not going," I told her. "Even though the fiesta helped me earn some money for my children, I'm not going."

"Well that's good, Son," she said. "Why should you expose yourself to danger even for work? We'll get along here."

So instead of going to Nopala, I would go to Río Grande or Oaxaca to buy what few things I could. So it went for three years before I risked going to Nopala again.

In Nopala there was an Ignacio Aguirre, a butcher, a good friend of mine. He was short, had a mole on his cheek, and was widely known. Shortly after this happened to me, Ignacio started to organize the people, holding secret meetings at night with the town leaders and telling them, "Let's take up arms, the whole town, but not as one party or another. We're not going to exempt anyone. We'll let them all have it, kill them. Those who manage to escape, let them go. But let them not return, because if they do, they'll die."

"Well, then, it's agreed," they said.

On the day that was theirs to get drunk and boldly threaten and kill people, on that day they surrounded Tavo Venegas and his men. They fell on them. Some they killed there, some died running. Some managed to flee, some escaped, but the rest they killed. After this there was peace in the village.

So it was three years before I returned to Nopala. Before leaving Juquila, I told my family, "I'm going to sell this donkey in order to buy some merchandise to put in the shop." I sold it and went to Nopala. That night I ran into Ignacio Aguirre. I couldn't get away.

"What's new, brother?" he asked me. "How have you been?"

"Well, fine."

"Why haven't you come, brother? I've been waiting to see you at the fiesta. I've asked for you. Some tell me that you've gone to Río Grande. Others say you've gone to Oaxaca, others say that you're not there."

"I didn't come, brother," I said to him, "because this Nicolás Pérez was about to kill me the last time I came. This is what he did . . ."

"Ay, man!" he said, "They were doing well then, but you should have seen how it went for them later. I've finished them off, brother. And those who fled, fled. You can go about in peace now."

Well, he wouldn't let go of me, and he wouldn't let go of me. I was carrying seventy-five pesos in my money belt from the sale of the donkey. There was a band of forty or fifty musicians accompanying him—and to buy beer for them all!

In a very short time I finished off the donkey. Yes, I had thought that that money was going to serve me to make some change, so I wouldn't have to go around asking favors here and there, to let me buy the few assorted things I carried in the barbershop—the earrings that I sold. Well, they drank up my donkey. What a barbarity! All of this because I met Ignacio, the chief, the principal commander of Nopala. I, well, couldn't deny him.

"Boys," he says, "you know this gentleman?"

"Of course, chief."

"Don Fortino comes here every year to our village, to work the fair, to work and sell. He's a good man. We care a lot for him. Ah, good," he says, "you'll take care of him for me wherever he goes. You'll watch out for him. If anybody wants to do something to him, you know what to do, hey? That's how it will be. So, brother, don't worry about a thing. Let's dance and enjoy ourselves."

Well, I finished off the money from the donkey there. Since then it has been attention to business. But I finished off the donkey there—and seventy-five pesos was a lot then.

Chapter 4

JUSTICE, SOLDIERS, AND

THE POLICE

When national military service began during World War II, the comandante, a sublieutenant called Saúl Sánchez Sáenz, who was the instructor of recruits in Juquila, made me the sergeant of a platoon. The thing was that in 1914, when I was in school, they had taught us military drill. They said, "Attention, about face, forward march, double time." So when they named me sergeant to instruct the rest of the troops, I already knew about military discipline. The platoon wasn't very large; it consisted of ten or twelve men. But there were so many recruits in the pueblo that we couldn't all fit in the plaza nor in the streets. We stretched out to the cemetery, all the way out to the field of El Pila. Since the comandante couldn't supervise everyone, even though we were packed tightly in the streets, he named me top sergeant, instructor of recruits.

Federal and State Troops

Our duty during the war was simply to guard the district and the plaza. When we were soldiers we would go out on patrol through the countryside. Now the soldiers just sit in town. Even when someone is going about making trouble they won't grab him. They will only do something if the public prose-

cutor or the presidente municipal asks them, but on their own they won't
get involved, nor will the state troops there. Only if they see there won't be
any real resistance will they go and do a number and a half on them. They
hit and beat people, take their money, take away their machetes. Worse yet,
if they catch some poor bastard with a pistol out there! But if it's a real criminal, they go after him with fear. They go slowly, giving him plenty of time to
escape. He can come to shoot up the plaza and neither the state police nor
the soldiers will show their faces.

One time I told off one of these "owls," one of these state policemen, who
had said to me, "We are going to lay down the law now."

"Look," I said, "I'll give you five hundred pesos the day you pass through
the plaza with one of these real killers. I'll give you the money as a gift, on
my word of honor." And I would have given him the money if he had had
the guts to grab one of these real bad characters.

One time, a bunch of drunks started raising a ruckus over there, and these
armed state police went to arrest them. The drunks took their guns away
from them and beat them up. I said, "What are you that you let a bunch of
drunks beat you up?" I've told them to their faces, "You bring in one of these
real killers that are out there by the cemetery, or by the edge of town, and
I'll give you five hundred pesos. I'll give you five hundred pesos the day you
bring in one of these real outlaws.

Once there was a comandante of the federales there when some prisoners
escaped from the jail. The comandante told the public prosecutor that if he
wanted their help, they would give it to him. These prisoners were making
a real mockery of them. A kid from the barrio of San Nicolás who escaped
from jail with some fifteen or twenty others came to town carrying a pistol
and started shooting at them and mocking the authorities. One day they
spotted him out there on the edge of town, near my field, and they told the
comandante that this "friend" was out there.

"Let's get him," the comandante said, "once and for all, because daily he
comes here to cause trouble."

"Let's go," said a light-complected sublieutenant. And they went and got
their machine guns and some soldiers. They sent some of the soldiers around
one way, some around the other, and they came up the middle. They fell
on this kid where he was, and he fled along the path that goes by my field.
There he turned around and shouted some obscenities at the sublieutenant,
who shouted at him to stop. The soldiers were sweeping along one side and
along the other. "No," he shouts, and the kid pulls a .38 special and starts
shooting, bang! bang! He just missed the sublieutenant, who then swung his
machine gun up and let loose a volley, and that was it. He left him doubled
up there.

Justice

There is little justice, especially if one doesn't have money or connections. Felipe Varela was a kinsman and a good compadre of mine. He took on the government twice, and twice he won. He was very intelligent. He was a telegraph worker and line inspector. He once asked the president of the republic, "For what reason did you allow the suspension of the National Telegraph Service? We are the ones who earn the money, and you are the ones who eat it up. We have the right to a better salary, not what you pay us. If you don't pay us what we want, we won't renew the service."

They put him in jail and threatened him. "I don't care if you kill me," he told the president, "if it is written in history that a barefoot Indian from Juquila died demanding his rights. Even if you kill me, it doesn't matter. I'm a man. And don't think that it's because I come from a wicked race. Even if you kill me—right now if you want—it will be written in history that they killed me for demanding rights."

Felipe Varela Villavicencio was very educated. He was the uncle of my brother Timoteo, but he was from a very bitter family. He had an uncle, his mother's brother, whose name was Enrique Torres Rojas. Enrique arrived in Juquila during the Porfiriato as a replacement soldier. At the time, they got soldiers from the prison in Mexico City. Enrique had been sent to prison for some misbehavior or other, and they made him be a soldier. He came back to Juquila as a soldier. I remember it very well. He was always talking about the soldiers.

"Lazy. You lazy men do nothing but eat the food given you. You people don't know what the duties of a soldier are like. Talk to Enrique Torres and he will tell you what you must do to earn your money," he would say. "You, with your knapsacks, you walk along dragging your feet in those old sandals. You don't even deserve them. Those of us who worked were Porfiristas. We were the ones who fought, who went to the north to fight—who knows with whom, but we did." He was always insulting the soldiers, insulting their mothers, and saying very strong things to them.

Once he went to their quarters with a machete and said to the guard, "You are worthless as a soldier."

"What did you say?" said the guard.

"What you heard," and chop, chop, he cut him with the machete. He chopped him. Fortunately the guard didn't die. But the guard would be completely within his rights to kill someone who shows such disrespect when he is on duty. He had gone there and chopped him with a machete. He was lucky they didn't kill him. They put him in jail. When he got out, he knew how to make very good brooms for sweeping houses, how to make straw hats and fans, and things like that. He was a barber, too. He had a good-sized place of business, which he later bought, and a small house over there where the late Carmen lived. He had some bamboo that he sold. That's how he made his living. And then, since he was very honest, they asked him to be an *alcalde*.

"Sure, an alcalde, watching prisoners, and then they'll put me in jail, too. No, thank you," he said.

"We'll defend you if there is any trouble."

"In that case, I accept. But don't back out on me, because Enrique Torres is a man, and whoever promises me something will keep his promise, or I'll make him keep it." That's what he told the authorities, that he would be tough, and he was. Then he was out of office for a little while, and after two or three years they asked for him again.

"Of course," he said, and took office again. Then they didn't pay him his salary, and he worked at his barber's trade in the alcalde's office. That's how he made a living for himself and his wife, Graciela Mendoza. That's how he stayed alive. They didn't pay him and they didn't pay him, though he demanded his salary.

"Well, what do you people think I'm going to eat?" he would protest. But they said no, not until the fiesta, because they didn't have any funds, and so on.

"Why did you ask me to be an alcalde if you couldn't pay me? I'm not going to eat grass while serving you here."

He would get drunk and yell at them and call them ugly names. One day they locked him up, because of all the things he said, and afterwards they let him out.

"All right, you had a good laugh at my expense, didn't you?" he said. "But you don't know Enrique Torres."

One day at about twelve he took off for his house, but before going he told the prisoners, "Here are the keys. You can leave. If you don't want to go, don't go."

He took his machete and tortillas and went to Oaxaca, where my relative Felipe Varela lived. He told him, "Look, nephew, that's how our countrymen treated me in Juquila. It's true, and there's nothing I can do about it. They put one over on me."

"Why?" Felipe asked him.

"They didn't pay me," he said. "I worked so hard and was good to them. They put me in jail, but they let me out the next day. So I said to the prisoners, 'Here you go, boys! Here are the keys! If you don't want to go, don't go, but here are the keys!' And a few of them left, and some didn't, because they didn't want to."

Later he came back to Juquila. He went to the government in Oaxaca and got an injunction against them. They wanted him to serve as an alcalde but wouldn't pay him, and they wouldn't accept the keys, because they wanted him to go on serving. But he didn't let them get away with it. He threw the keys to the prisoners and left. When he came back, he had an injunction that prevented the authorities from jailing him. He was very smart. His nephew, my relative Felipe Varela, got him the injunction.

Chapter 5

AFFAIRS

I fell in love with Esperanza Pérez. She was certainly very pretty, and I told her I loved her. She was living with her mother in a house opposite their shop. Well, her mother didn't like me, because she knew positively that I lived with my woman. But I would pass the nights carousing. One night I fell asleep on the bench. I was awakened by a stick poking me. I had a net bag full of beer, another with soft drinks, another with bottles of mescal, and my guitar.

"Get up," she said, "you shameless lout! What is this, your house? What business do you have here? Don't you have any shame? You are the same shameless lout that your father was!"

I thought she must have known him. Why else would she say this to me? Yes, I said to myself, she knew how my father was; there's a reason she's saying this to me.

"That's how your father was, shameless!"

"Goodness me, did you know him?" I asked. "Well, because why else would you get mad? In the fiesta of the Virgin, the pilgrims come and do so many things. They come to defecate, to sleep here, to drink until they vomit, and one stands it. And I, your countryman, you treat so badly. You hit me with a stick. Goodness! Instead of saying to me, 'Look, Tino, drink a little coffee, since you've slept here.' "

"Well, so you won't have come here for nothing, drink a cup of coffee. Esperanza, come and see your 'daddy' here. Bring him the coffee he's asking for." She's really giving it to her inside, I said to myself.

Nevertheless, this girl loved me. Later, we agreed that I would take her to Miahuatlán. I would leave my family in the house with my mother, and I would leave my shop, my little store that I have there, for them. And I would go with Esperanza to Miahuatlán. What a bitch! I don't know where she was going to take me, but it hurt me, you know?[1] It's all right. After a while, the señora saw I was very determined.

Well, one morning I said, "Look, I'm going to open a beer, so you can drink with me. Don't get angry. I've only come to visit. Is that any way to receive friends?"

"No, dog. You didn't come to visit me," she said. "Your 'mama' is inside. Go on in and see her."

"No," I said, "I'm not so forward."

"I'm giving you permission," she said.

"No," I said to her, "in a little while you'll be beating me here outside; inside there you'd kill me." I also said, in a very polite manner, "I'd better not. Here is fine." I got up to give her the beer.

"No," she said, "I don't want it. Don't open it."

"All right, here it is unopened. You may drink it when you like."

"All right, that's fine then."

"Friends, then," I said, and she took the beer.

"Well, I'll be going with my little cantina on my shoulder now," I said. "Pardon me that I came here to sleep a while. We'll see when I come to sleep here again."

"Whenever you like, you shameless lout. The bench is at least big enough for the big ass you have," she said.

"Well, good enough," I said.

After that she talked with me like a great friend. She would greet me nicely, right. When no one was in my house or in hers she would come running to talk with me. I thought things were fine, but a little later—who knows what she was thinking. The señora took Esperanza to a pueblo they call Chilillo, where they lived for a time. From there they went to Oaxaca, where she had a sister and handed her daughter over to her, because she no longer wanted to be responsible for her behavior. She couldn't do it any longer, it wore her out.[2]

God, there's no doubt that when something's not for one after all, something will happen to prevent it. This sister who had her there, like a daughter, made arrangements with a shoemaker for her to marry him. Then her mother told me, "I've received word that Esperanza is going to be married. Now I'm going to see just how much of a man you are."

"Well, what do you want me to do about it?" I asked.

"Let's go," she said. "I'm going to bring her back. I just want you to help me with the expenses, because I can't afford it."

I too was poor. "Wait two weeks," I said. "I'll go to Río Grande. I'll leave tomorrow." I had my gray horse. I rode all day. When I got to Río Grande, I fed my horse and curried him well. But unfortunately I got sick there. I was bedridden for a week. I couldn't sell a cow or arrange anything, and I owed people about forty pesos that I borrowed to meet expenses. I went to a local moneylender.

"Loan me fifty pesos," I said.

"Yes," he said to me, "here you are." I then paid off my debts and rode back to Juquila to go back to work.

When I arrived, Esperanza's mother asked me, "What happened? Did you get the money?"

"You can't imagine what happened to me," I said. "I did . . ." this and that, "and then I was sick for a week. I couldn't catch a cow, and I decided I'd better come back before they buried me there."

"I can see that you're very pale," she said.

"Yes," I said, "I was very sick. Ay, if only you could bring her here. Anyway, I should be better in a few days, and I'll go back to Río Grande, and then I'll go fetch her." Well, I couldn't arrange things in time, and she married the shoemaker.

Sometime afterward, I had a girlfriend called Natalia Vasilides Aguilar. She was my little fiancée from the night to the morning, when she got up. Then her mother, Sra. Euladia, and her husband left town with her, and I was left whistling on the hill again.

About fifteen years later, Urbano Núñez showed me a photograph that the Otter (that's what they called Raimundo Ortiz, because he was always drinking) gave him. When I saw it I said to Urbano, "That's so and so."

"That's her," he said.

"Jesús!" I said, "Where was this picture taken?"

"Well, here she is on a trip that she took with her uncle to Veracruz. That's her in the hammock."

"Christ!" I said, "Very good. Well, it makes me remember something stored away in here."

"Whoa, man," he said.

"Yes," I said, "You'll see. The day we meet again, she's mine."

The years went by, and I couldn't look for her. I was living with the mother of my children when I met her in Oaxaca. We had gone with my aunt Justa to cure my cousin.

"Careful what you say," I said to my aunt. "Don't say I have a wife, don't burn me, because there is Talita over there."

"Really?" she said.

"Yes," I said, "but don't say anything that would make me lose face." I had my plan in mind, no?

As soon as she saw me, she gave me a hug. "Now I've trapped you," she said to me.

"Yes, we're trapped."

"Doña Leandra," she says, "Aunt, I'd like to introduce you to a country-man. It's been many years. I haven't seen him since I moved here. He used to be my fiancé there."

"Is that so?" said her aunt.

"Yes," she said, "but as we separated there, this was left dead." But she wasn't satisfied with this and made signs to me behind her aunt's back.

"I'm going inside, Aunt," she said. Behind her aunt's back she signaled me to go out the door, turn the corner, and come in the other way.

"Well, if you'll excuse me," I said and left.

Yes, right off she hugged me and kissed me without further ado, because this was an old account. She began to caress me right away.

"I've thought of you so often," she said, "but I had no way to see you."

"I couldn't leave," I said. "Well, to tell the truth, the situation there wouldn't let me, that's why. But I saw a photograph you gave to your cousin Mundo, the Otter, it brought back many memories. And I said to Urbano, 'This has come to revive many things that have been left hanging.' "

"Really," she said.

"Yes," I said.

"Well, that's good," she said. "If you don't have a woman, I'll marry you right away."

"No, no, I don't have one," I told her.

Juana, my niece, well, she was half crazy too. She went and told her that I had a woman. Justa said to me, "Juana has told Talia that you have a woman."

"You tell Talia that she's crazy, just like her brother Erasmo." So that is what she told her.

"Did you believe what Juana told you?" Justa asked Talia.

"What was that?" she asked.

"That Fortino has a woman."

"It very well could be true. But it's all the same. That is why we've reunited, to cure him."[3] Talia replied.

So things worked out well. We went around together. Later she had a son by me and after that no longer wanted to see me.

After Talia separated from me, others came. I was in love with a poor woman called Isaura Cuevas, the daughter of Sr. Andrés Cuevas. I fell in love with her, but another was quicker. Alfonso Zárate took her away from me. He took her away from me because he won her over. I didn't go over to her house a lot. I'm careful. I only go to a place if it's very safe. I don't go to take chances.[4]

Chapter 6

BRUJOS AND CURING

One time, Sr. Emiliano Vargas, the elder brother of Sr. Efren Vargas, who was my father-in-law, may he rest in peace, lost a stud burro and I didn't know it. After two months he came to Juquila to tell me, and he said to me, "Look, Tino, I'm going to ask you to do something."

"Well, go ahead and ask me," I replied.

"Well, you see, I've lost a stud burro, an excellent donkey," he told me. "Every time he mated with a mare they would give me five hundred pesos. I'll give you one thousand pesos if you tell me who has him. It is this color and carries the brand E. V."

"All right," I said to him, certain that I could do it. I kept my eye out everywhere, but I didn't leave the store very often, because I was waiting on the customers there. It's not easy for me to get out like before, when I used to plant my cornfield. At that time I got around a lot on horseback, but with the work in the store I got out less. I used to find a lot of people's animals.

"I'm telling you again," he said later. "I'll give you a thousand pesos if you find the donkey for me." I already knew what the brand was, and the shape of the letters that formed it, and that the burro was a pretty black one. Well, I had never seen it, but he told me that it was very pretty, and since he was my wife's uncle, I believed him. "All right," I told him, "I'm going to try." But since I couldn't go out, I just asked people about it, and nobody told me anything. Then I spoke to a friend I had whose name was Porfirio Olivera.

"Porfirio," I said, "since you know about witchcraft, I want you to do me the favor of finding out where a black burro is that was lost. The letters of the brand on it are like this."

"How long has it been lost, brother?" he asked me, because we were very close. Sometimes I would get him drunk. Sometimes I would give him a free shave. I liked to chat with him because he was a good-natured fellow, and he sort of stuttered. "I'm going to try, brother. Don't worry," he said. "If I find that burro, it won't get away. I'll catch it."

"Well, I want you to do it today," I said.

"No," he said, "tomorrow, because tomorrow is Friday, a day on which it can be done. I'm going to take the saint," by which he meant eat sacred mushrooms.[1] "I'll see what comes of it," he said. "Give me a quart of mescal and seven small, five-centavo candles, and let's see what I see tomorrow or the day after tomorrow. I might not come until Sunday, brother, because I stay up all night, and the next day I'm always in very bad shape."

"Don't worry," I told him. "I'm going to give you five hundred pesos." But I had already thought out my plan. I said to myself, If Don Emiliano gives me a thousand pesos, I'll give this fellow five hundred pesos, and I'll have five hundred pesos left for myself.

"Don't give me anything, old chum," he said, "because you're my good friend."

"Fine, brother," I said, "but I'll give you five hundred pesos. Of course, I won't advance you anything. If you want, I will pay you. If you don't, I won't. But I'm telling you this clearly, so that you won't be bickering with me about it afterward."

"No, brother," he said, "you're my friend. I'm not going to charge you. But if you want to pay me, that's your business."

He left, and the next day, Friday, he ate the sacred mushrooms. Sunday, there I was, watching and waiting, and he didn't show up and he didn't show up. Finally he came.

"I saw the countryside," he said. "I saw corrals. I saw burros. I saw horses. I saw cattle. I saw everything." And finally he said, "I found a corral, far away, and the burro was tied in the corner of the corral with three thick ropes. It was tied to a thick stake. And a man came, but he didn't show me his face, brother, so I couldn't see who he was."

He told me that on a Sunday, and I said to him, "And now what are you going to do? Are you just going to leave it at that?"

"Oh, no, I'm going to try again," he said. "Now, give me seven more candles, a handful of incense, and some mescal to drink while I'm waiting in the darkness to see where the animal is."

"All right," I said to him. "Here's your quart of mescal, the seven candles, and the handful of incense." He left, and came back on Tuesday.

"This time I saw him, brother," he said. "I got a very good look at the burro, and it has your uncle's brand. And I saw that fellow, but he's a stranger. I don't know him."

"Whose face is it?"

"I didn't recognize it, but I saw it very well," he told me.

"Where is that place?" I asked him.

"Well, it is to one side of Sola de Vega, farther up," he said.

"Is that right?" I said to him. "And, what were you waiting for? Why didn't you take the burro away from him?"

"Oh no, brother," he said. "I was unarmed and that fellow was watching me. And, look, he had a gun. But now I know what to do. I have three *nahuales*, big spirit dogs, and I'm going to send them after the burro from far away. And that fellow isn't even going to see me, since it is the spirit that is out working. My dogs will frighten him away."

The next time I saw him, the next Friday, Porfirio told me, "I sent the dogs after him. Right then the burro hee-hawed, and the pack went running, three big dogs running after the burro, and the burro spooked. It was standing there, and when the dogs attacked, it reared up three times. It balked, pulled the stake loose. It jumped the corral fence and went running away down the rocky road. The rope kept getting stuck on things, but the burro kept running. Finally the dogs let him alone. Near there he found a herd of mares. He had already worn out his rope; just a little piece of it was dragging along. And the burro mounted one of the mares there, and he kept himself busy with the mares. He was heading home when he found the mares, but then he didn't continue on."

The story that he was giving me was unfolding well. The burro came down from Santa María to be able to go in the direction of Juchatengo. "And since there were colts there with the mares, that damned animal got one and bit and kicked it to death," he said. "The owner of the mare was there. 'This animal can't come to kill my colts!' he said. 'I won't put up with that. I don't care if he is a stud burro!' He shot and killed the burro. That's the way it is, brother. There's no more hope, because they killed the burro on a ranch below Sola, on this side, going down toward Juchatengo. They killed the burro there, and there's no hope left, so tell your uncle that he's gone. So I didn't earn anything on what you and I did, and you didn't earn anything. Both of us lost out, because if they were going to give us something, now they're not going to give us anything. But that's life."

"Well, all right," I said to him, "drink another half-quart."

"Give me a shave, give me a shave!" he said. "I don't have any money on me. I'll pay you later."

I used a razor on his head—a razor! I left his head bald!

"Now I look handsome, brother. I'm going now."

"All right, see you later."

He came back about a week later.

"Since you didn't shave my beard the other day, shave it this time."

When he arrived he had been drinking and was a little drunk. Then I started to have some fun with him.

"Give me a drink. Don't be a bad friend," he said.

"Of course," I said to him, "I'm going to give you a little drink," and I gave him a big glass.

Curing

With that, his head started to nod, and what was I going to do? His head was falling down, but I shaved him like that. I had to hold his head like a child to be able to shave him. Since he didn't wear a mustache, I finished shaving him and covered his head with a towel to put alcohol on his face. And, since he was already half asleep, I began to go through his pockets. I took out a little bag that he had in his shirt pocket. It had rocks in it, shells, dog teeth (or who knows what animal they were from). It had big maguey thorns. It had cocoons that are found on guava trees, each with a worm inside. He carried them around, worms and all. He had chunks of red dirt, pieces of sugarcane, pieces of bamboo. He carried all of that in there. He carried small thorns, straight-pins, and needles in there. I took out a little bit of each thing after I had put alcohol on his face and all, and then I put his things back in his pocket again. I had taken a little of each thing, and I left him sitting there. I went to do my shoe-repair work and to take care of orders until another client arrived to have me cut his hair or shave him, because I charged very reasonably. As I looked over all the things that I had taken out of the bag in his pocket, I said to myself, So that is what they do to people.

He sucks on a person's leg, arm, hand, back, or stomach. While he is sucking he already has his things at hand, already dried out. Then when he is curing someone, he says, "Bring me a bowl of water." Then he puts those things in his hand and washes out his mouth very well so the person will see that there's nothing in it, right? He rinses out his mouth and starts sucking. Then he says, "Go and bring a corn husk with a little bit of ash in it." The corn husk is like a little canoe, and he begins to spit in it until his sucking opens the person's pores and he draws blood. "Go out there," he says, "and come back in a few minutes, because something big is about to come out." Then he puts those things in his mouth. I have seen them. They've done it here in my own shop. They put whatever they have in their mouth: a piece of glass, a piece of a rock, corn silk, locks of hair or whatever, a thorn or a worm in a cocoon. "Look! Look what came out of you! That's why you were in so much pain, because of what came out, but now your pain has gone away."

And the people believe in those things. Even though there's no hole in the skin, you know, where the animal came out, they believe it. It's the power of suggestion. Then he washes his mouth out with the bowl of water, and after he washes his mouth out he begins to speak in Chatino, so that the evil spirit will come out, so that the man's suffering will end. He speaks in Chatino and invokes God. He begins to blow out the evil air that he had inside him. Once he has blown it out well, he puts his shirt on him and passes his hand over him. "The sickness is gone. You are cured," he tells him. "You're fine now."

Then he goes over to a table and drinks his chocolate and eats some pastry. Then they wrap up some toasted tortillas or whatever in a napkin for him and give him the money he's earned, and he leaves. That person's pain goes away. It goes away because of suggestion. The power of suggestion cures the people.

Porfirio was a good friend of mine, but I had to use tact to ask him about his craft. I would say to Porfirio, "I want to learn to do that. I'm really interested in witchcraft." But I said this only because I was digging away to see what else I could get out of him.

"Oh, that can be done, brother. Look, brother," he would say, "I'll come over on Sunday."

"I hope you're not just saying that."

"No, man, of course not. I mean it, brother. I'll come over," he said.

When Sunday arrived, I was taking care of people in the store. "Hey, old buddy," he said.

"Oh, yes," I answered.

"Yes, today I'm going to teach you that work so that you'll learn it in three days. You'll be ready."

"No," I told him, "I won't be able to today. Look at all the people I have to attend to, brother." He didn't say that again. Well, I had to attend to business.

"Look," I said to him, "wait, and I'll give you half a glass of mescal. Have a drink instead, and we'll talk when I have a chance, because I can't right now. Look how busy I am."

"No, you can't," he said, "there are a lot of customers."

So it was just dropped there. That was it. I didn't have any more trouble with him, because I calmed him down with a drink. And, in so many words I got it across to him that I didn't have time for him. Well, I had told him that I wanted to learn, but I was just joking. It wasn't true that I wanted to learn to do that. What did I want with going around sucking on people?

After that he would say to me, "Whenever you want, just let me know, and I'll teach that business to you."

"Fine," I said. "Don't worry. I'll let you know."

One time, Porfirio flew into Juquila in a light plane, so I said to him, "Well Porfirio, where did you go?"

"I went to San Gabriel Mixtepec, brother."

"Why did you go?"

"I went to cure a person who was very sick."

"What did he have?" I asked.

"A very high fever."

"And what happened? Did you cure him or did you kill him?"

"No," he said, "he got well. I earned myself a thousand pesos."

"Is that right? That's good," I said to him. "And what do you plan to do now?"

"I'm going home to leave off my things, and then I'll come back and have a drink over there at your shop."

"All right, I'll be waiting for you there," I said. And that's how it was. A little while later he was over there drinking his mescal.

When brujos take the "saint," they go into a state of mental concentration to wait for the answer to what they've been asked. That's when they say that everything is revealed to them. Then they see very well who it is that did something to the person. Then they say, "It was so and so, and in such and such a place he buried the image that's doing you harm." Then they go to the place and dig down, and there it is. They find it. I haven't seen that myself. I haven't gone to dig it up. It hasn't happened to me. It hasn't happened to us.[2]

The brujo has to know very well how to plan affairs. Depending upon how he sizes up the situation, he says to the people when he arrives, "I see that this person is very sick. I'm not responsible for what happens to him. I'll do the best that I can. He's very sick. If God wills it, I will cure him, but if God doesn't allow it, I won't be able to."

Elizido Rojas was another brujo who was a good friend of mine. He liked to spend a lot of time around me, and he often used to come to visit. He would come to get drunk at my shop. Since we sold a little liquor there, he would show up to drink and to have me give him a shave and a haircut too.

He would say to me, "Give me a good shave, because I'm going to leave on a trip today."

"Where to?" I would ask him.

"Well, I'm going to Tataltepec to treat a sick person, but I'll be back in four or five days."

"And what does he have?"

"Well, he has a fever," he would say.

"And can you cure that?"

"Well, let's see here. I have my bunch of herbs that I'm going to use for the treatment."

He would go off and come back in four or five days, and since I like to joke around so much I would ask him, "Did you kill him, or is he still alive?"

"No, brother. God forbid!" he said. "If he dies, I don't get paid! Nothing! But it went well. I earned a thousand pesos, and I cured him quickly. The fever left him."

One day, Elizido Rojas came into my store and said to me, "Give me a little quart of mescal on credit, Fortino." He spoke very loudly, and he was quite short, not too tall. He was already drunk. He had his eyes shut and didn't even open them. "I'll pay you. Elizido's not trying to trick you."

"I'm not going to give you any, because you're already drunk. I'd like to have a drink, too," I told him, "but I don't have anyone to buy it for me. We could both drink if one of us had the money."

Ponchito, an Indian from Ixpantepec, came in and saw Elizido sitting on the little bench in the shop, and he went up to him. Ponchito greeted Elizido in Chatino. Then I spoke to them in Chatino. Ponchito said to me, "Give him a drink." So I gave one to him.

"Here it is, father," he said to Elizido in Chatino. He carried the drink to him very reverentially, as though it were a big deal. Ponchito told him in Chatino about his knee and all, where it hurt him, and Elizido said in Chatino, "At this very moment your pain is gone."

He grabbed a piece of paper, and then he closed one eye even tighter. You see, he was going to do some work. "Even you are going to drink now," he said to me. "Yes, even you are going to drink now. With your permission."

"No," I said, "with God's permission."

He started sucking on Ponchito's knee where it was hurting him, so hard that it bled! Then he crawled outside on his hands and knees. They had spread a lot of red earth around out there, and he found an evenly shaped little ball of clay. I was holding the piece of paper for him where he was spitting. Then he came back and grabbed Ponchito's knee again and started sucking on it some more.

He seemed to be struggling, as if to extract whatever was inside there. He shook his head gravely to signal that what was in there wouldn't come out. When he finished doing his maneuvers, he finally did spit it out.

"What is this thing we have here?" he said in Chatino. "I'm drunk. I can't see very well. What was it, Fortino?"

"Ahhh, it's a piece of red earth. Look, Ponchito," I said. "Look at what came out of you, a piece of red earth."

"Ahhh, so that's what was doing me harm," Ponchito said.

"Now you are well," said Elizido. "Give that to me. I'm going to dispose of it," he said, "because you can't throw that away just any old place."

He put it away nice and safe somewhere, out there where the red earth was. That is where he got the piece of earth; it wasn't far at all, and that's where he threw it away again.

Well, he had just finished taking the pain from that "friend" away when his brother-in-law said, "I have a pain right here. I can't go on like this, the pain's so bad." His arm was hurting him, and Elizido cured him right away. Ponchito gave him about thirty-five centavos, and the other "friend" told him that he didn't have but eighteen centavos. Well, it would be worse not to have anything, he must have thought.

"That's fine," he said, and he cured him too and put the money in his pockets. He wrapped up all of that saliva he had spit out in a thick piece of paper there and put it away. And then he went and spent his centavos.

"Now I'll buy a drink!" he said. But back then a little quart of mescal only cost fifteen centavos!

Fortino the Herbalist

What I do know something about, what I learned from my mother, is herbal remedies. For example, one time I cured a son of Angelina. He had a fever. He had been treated by this army nurse José. He had been treated by this Dr. Marcelino. They weren't able to cure his fever. "He doesn't eat. It's been two months," Angelina said. "It appears that he's going to die."

"Ah, well," I said to her, "go to my field. There I have some *espinosilla* bushes growing wild along the fence above where the avocado trees are. Bring a handful of leaves, and I'll give you some pills too." She went to pick some and brought back a bunch. I told her, "Boil half tonight and half tomorrow morning, early." I gave him six *bromoquino* pills. He took them and was cured after so many injections, doctors, and everything. It's positively true; ask Angelina. To another, who had a pain in his neck, I gave espinosilla and garlic. You should have seen it. It's great how it took away the pain in his neck. I've cured many people from Yaitepec of malaria. They get better right away. I don't charge them, I don't exploit them for this.

There is a medicine, however, that I have charged for, because it's very good. It is a little expensive, and I have to bring it from Mexico City even though I don't go to Mexico City just to bring it. I bring other things besides, but I always bring this *Hitorro real*, which is a purple vine, as well. It's good for blows. Now, if a bull or a cow is urinating blood, defecating blood, they know where to find me, and they come to get the remedy. I charge twenty-five pesos a dose, but it's going to go up. A cow is worth 4,000 pesos. It's not fair that they pay me so cheaply for such a good medicine that I discovered.

These simple remedies are pure herbs. Well, as one tries and experiments with this remedy and that one, as time passes one links all these things together and discovers which ones are good and which are not. I only wish I had learned all that my mother knew.[3] My mother was a *curandera*. She cured people of many illnesses. For example, she knew how to cure bilious discharges with herbs and olive oil. She used an herb that they call the *irritación*. It's an herb found in damp soil, as is water cress, and has a little yellow flower. She would put it in boiling water with *ruda* and myrtle. After it had boiled, she would add three green limes. She would give this to them to drink with olive oil, and they would get better. If people suffered from *empacho* or indigestion she would give them this preparation with a purgatory of lard, and they would pass all that bad stuff that was making them ill and get better. I've never made that preparation, but I saw my mother do it. She would give it to people who were ready to die, emaciated from so much suffering, and they would recover.

For fevers, sometimes she would give people espinosilla and put strawberry leaves around the bed and under their *petate*, and it would take away their fever. But if it were an intestinal fever, she would give them a purgatory of castor oil to drink with orange juice. Even when she was sick she used to go to people's aid, day and night. My brother said to her, "Mama, it's not such a good idea for you to be going out at night and before daybreak. You are old, and something could happen to you. We wouldn't want something like that to happen to you."

Afterward, my mother came and asked me what I thought. She said, "What do you think, Son, about what your brother said to me?"

"What did he say to you, Mama?" I asked.

"He said that I shouldn't go out to cure people, that I shouldn't go out at night, because I'm old and I could fall, or something could happen to me. And he wouldn't want something to happen to me."

"Well, in part I think it was good that he said it to you, Mama," I said. "Because you're a person of experience and know what you are doing, I can't stop you from doing it. You are my mother, and you know what you are doing. But up to a certain point, I think that what my brother said was good."

Then she told me what she thought. "But look," she said, "I'm thinking about you. If I were to die, there would be no one to do you favors. As we are isolated, living in this small town where there are no doctors, where there is nothing, if I didn't go, someone might die. It would hurt me to my soul not to go to see them."

"Well, Mama," I said, "I'm very sorry that I can't give you advice. But it appears to me that what my brother said was good. I can't tell you to do this, or I'll take away your liberty. I simply can't. You are the owner of your will. You know what you are doing."

She took our advice half seriously, half not. Anyway, on one trip to cure someone, a dog bit her and she fell and broke this bone in her iliac. No one could cure her. Four years she spent in suffering. My brother was killed in 1945, this accident took place in 1946, and she finally died in 1950.

I remembered my brother's warning to her, but I couldn't reproach her by saying, "My brother warned you that something like this would happen." I didn't say anything. She lasted four years, suffering like that.

At the time, I had young children in school. My wife would get sick, or one of the children would. I was often half sick and would have to go to work to support them all. On a mountain near Juquila, I had some cows that I had bought. I sold them. I said to myself, We need the money to live; I can't let my mother die.

But there was no road then. There was nothing. I thought, I'll take her to Oaxaca on a stretcher. But I only had enough money to take her, not to cure her or bring her back. What was I to do? I resigned myself to suffer. To say it more clearly: I had to resign myself to the fact that I couldn't provide my mother with the kind of superior medical attention she needed. Instead, at least four bonesetters came to see if they could set her bone. I sent for a bonesetter in San Pedro Mixtepec. He came and set it. I paid him his centavos, and he was very grateful, but he came in vain. She died.

Amalia came, and she cared for my mother. My daughter, Licha, also cared for her. She was sleeping with her when she died. The whole family was there. I can't tell you how deeply I felt her death, how sad it made me feel.

The Renewed Capitalist Economy

AN INTRODUCTION TO

CHAPTERS 7 THROUGH 10

When Lázaro Cárdenas stepped aside in 1940, leaving the presidency to Manuel Ávila Camacho, his revolutionary methods and socialist policies were quickly abandoned. Under Camacho, a devout Catholic, Mexico's land-reform program came to an abrupt halt. The outbreak of World War II provided an excellent excuse for halting any further land reform. Breaking up large estates, it was argued, would affect production at a time when secure food supplies were essential to the war effort. Moreover, the war gave the Mexican economy a terrific boost. The United States was eager to buy raw materials from Mexico, and the absence of imported consumer goods stimulated Mexican manufacturing. Mexico's growing prosperity and the Camacho administration's positive attitude toward foreign capital encouraged British, American, and European investors to deposit small fortunes in Mexican banks.

Fortino's emergence in this period as a small-businessman and landowner was a consequence not only of his stopping drinking and reinvesting money in his store but was also of the changing national climate, which now favored capital accumulation. Under President Miguel Valdes Alemán, who was president from 1946 to 1952, the government moved ever more sharply to the right. Alemán "firmly believed that wealth must be formed before it can be distributed, or as his critics put it, growth first, justice later" (Riding 1986, 81). Development became the guiding principle of his regime. Strong industrial and commercial elites with extensive government connections emerged. Government spending focused heavily on industry, trade, and private commercial agriculture. To encourage the cultivation of new export crops, government policies protected the lands of private commercial farmers from expropriation, and land reform became an economic stepchild.

During this period the district of Juquila, too, was undergoing a boom. Because coffee prices were at an all-time high, Chatino villagers, using loans from coffee buyers, began to plant coffee on communal lands on a large scale. The increasing coffee production greatly expanded the flow of cash through the market in Juquila, which opened commercial opportunities for Fortino and other merchants.

Chapter 7

I STOP DRINKING AND

GET AHEAD

The main reason I stopped drinking was that I couldn't get ahead in my work, because drinking took up too much time. I've been a friend of all kinds of work. I've done a little carpentry, a little shoemaking, a little blacksmithing, a little masonry, a lot of barbering and shopkeeping—selling general merchandise. But drinking prevented me from getting ahead. I had young children in school. Little by little I started to think this wasn't for me. I had some cows on the mountain, and as I said, I had to sell them when my mother fell ill. I had some others in Río Grande. After my brother was killed, there was no one to take care of them, so I decided to sell them. I finished them off. I was left with nothing, except the field I have at the edge of town.

I remember that when my mother died in 1950, I was still drinking. After my mother died, my aunt Modesta kept after me. "Go to work," she said, "delouse your children, wash them, bathe them, see to it they iron their clothes. Do what you like, but see to it they're fed. That's your obligation."

But about three years after my mother's death, in 1953 or 1954, my aunt Modesta died. I said to myself, There is no one left to care for or keep after me now. My aunt Martina was the only one left, but she lived in Teotepec. This humble woman loved us very much and would always come to visit, but she was very old and tired. I said to myself, I'm not going to wait for her to come and scold me; the time for this is past. From now on, I'm going to stop drinking.

The first time I swore off drinking I didn't drink for ten months. I wasn't one to get drunk every day, but every fiesta for sure we would all get drunk, celebrating merrily the day of the fiesta. I had left off for ten months, but during the fiesta I grabbed the cup, while playing, and started up again. I then said to myself, No, this is just a waste. After that I stopped for a year. Then I started to grab the cup again. My friends wouldn't let me alone. My brother would say, "You're a good drinker. As delicious as it is, nothing's going to happen to you or to me. Let's go drink."[1]

I then stopped for four years, started up, and stopped another four years. One time, they were waiting when I came back from Río Grande to celebrate my saint's day. I came into it blind. I had arrived in Juquila about noon and left my horse in the corral. I just gave it some hay and water and left it saddled there. But as my daughter Licha knew of it, she said, "Don't worry about it, I'll do it. Many people are in the shop asking for you."

"Well, I'm going, Daughter," I said. Although I had just finished a six-hour ride, what tiredness, nothing! When I got there everyone was waiting. My cousin Benjamin said, "You old goat, we've been waiting for you to give you a hug. We came, well, because it's your saint's day. I suppose you didn't know?"

"What's the date today?"

"Nineteenth of May."

"Right," I said, and I gave my cousin Benjamin, the biggest drinker, a bottle of mescal. The poor man had no limits.

"Drink up," I said.

"No, Cousin, you first."

"You know I don't drink."

"No, it's just that now that you've come in time and that we have the desire . . ."

"Well, I'll have one," I said. I drank one, and they drank another and started serving one another.

A little later, Timoteo went to get his violin, and I my guitar, and we began playing and singing and enjoying ourselves. Since I was the one paying, soon the place was filled with people who had just come to drink. There was nothing to be done. Finally, late at night, my eldest daughter, Felicitas, came to fetch me.

"Papa, let's go," she said. "You haven't even rested or eaten."

"I'll eat here," I said to her.

"No, let's go," she said. Slam! Slam! The doors closed, and she threw everyone out. "My father has finished drinking with you!" she said. "Please leave."[2]

The counter was filled with bottles. When we started we were just a few, but those who came were many, although few were invited. Well, I got up and left. The next day they came about noon.

"Look, we brought . . ." this and that, "we brought . . ." I don't know what. "Well, have another bottle and stop bothering me," I replied, but they went on and on.

What a barbarity! The next day, there was another fiesta there in my shop, and so on successively. Everyone knew that I was very generous, that I would give them drinks. My brother would come and we would drink, singing and singing, and in a short time friends would come in. No one would buy anything. I was the only one buying. Then I said to myself, After four years of withstanding them, I'm going about with a bunch of drunks again. No, I didn't continue for very long. Here this guitar is going to hang and that is all. It has hung there so long that I've forgotten the positions already. I play a few chords and I've lost the thread and can't remember the rest. Now when they say "Let's go hear a band" I tell them, "No, not if it means drinking. I'll tell you clearly, if they are going to bother me there, better we not go. If we go, I won't drink." Anyway, the guitar has hung in the house ever since. When they come to ask me to play, I say I don't have it any longer. If I didn't, they would continue to bother me.[3]

Once in a while these drunks would come to bother me, but I had a recipe to fix that. I used to make big pots of strong tepache in the house, and I would have it in the shop to sell. When one of these very talkative little drunks would come and bother me, to shut him up I would take out a large bowl of tepache, not too full, into which I would pour a bottle of beer and then a big cup of alcohol. The tepache, then, would boil, bubble, and froth as it fought with the alcohol in the bowl. And I would say, "Did you come to talk or to drink?"

"Give me a drink and I'll pay you later, brother. Brother, I don't have any money."

"No, man, I'll give it to you free. Here's a bowl of tepache for you, but drink it down at a gulp. I don't want you just to sip it, because flies will get in it."

"All right, I'll drink it."

"Good, go on then. You know my tepache's good tepache."

Well, just as soon as he had finished drinking it, he would take two or three steps and fall. There in the doorway he would sit or lie. The tepache would shut him up.[4]

Getting Ahead

After I stopped drinking, I began to get ahead. I started to build up my shop. The fur trade was what really got me started. I would buy furs: ocelot, otter, marten skins, deer skins, rattlesnake and boa skins. I would send them to Navojoa, Sonora, to Ciudad Obregón, and to Alamos, Sonora. The buyers there paid me very little, but like one who likes to hunt deer, I continued in this business. I had a lot of faith that someday this business would help me, so I began to search and investigate where they could give me a better price. One day on a trip to Panixtlahuaca, I walked into the shop of my compadre Pepe Flores and saw a calendar: LÁZARO MÉNDEZ, BUYER OF FINE FURS. I wrote the address on the palm of my hand and headed home. Lázaro Méndez paid me top dollar, and he has been my buyer in Mexico City ever since.

During the fiesta of the Virgin, I would invite as many as four shoemakers and six or eight barbers to share the shop. We would crowd in there, everyone working furiously. They would give me half of what they earned.

Finally I was making a few centavos. I would buy my merchandise with cash, and the suppliers began to offer me credit. At first, I didn't want it, but they kept begging me. Friends who came to sell in Juquila during the fiesta were begging: "No, man, don't worry. No one is going to charge you interest if you're a month or two in paying. Nothing will happen. It's what you should do."

Well, I started to act like a man. I took 2,000, 3,000, 4,000, 5,000, 10,000, up to 40,000 pesos in merchandise on credit and put it in the store. I don't like to say things that are untrue. I don't like to lie. While I began with four, five, six, or 10,000 pesos on credit, what is in the store now is my own. It is no longer other people's. It is no longer on credit. No longer.[5]

So, little by little I've advanced. As the business grew, I began to buy some coffee properties. I bought a *cafetal* near El Platanar from my compadre Benjamin Ríos around 1955 or 1960. I don't remember exactly what year I bought it from him. Then, about eight years ago, a half-nephew of mine named Ricardo Velasco (a grandson of my mother's cousin, Micaela) sold me another cafetal. His father, Heraclio Velasco, takes care of it for me.[6]

I used to see Ricardo Velasco. He would walk past me, so one day I said to him, "Do you know that I'm a relative of yours?"

"Yes, I know," he said to me, "but I'm ashamed to say hello because you are of a higher class."

"What do you mean? No, no, here we are all equal. What's more, I know that you are the son of my cousin Heraclio."

"Well, it makes me ashamed, because my grandfather told me that I was the son of a valley man, that I wasn't the son of your cousin Heraclio. That's why I've kept to one side. I don't have a blood link to your family."

"No," I said to him, "you're the son of my cousin Heraclio. When you need something, let me know."

Well, when it came time that he thought his son should serve as a mayordomo in the church and sponsor a saint's fiesta, he came to me. "Look, I'm thinking of selling a cafetal," he said. The first cafetal he offered me I didn't buy. He sold it to Alfonso Zárate. I didn't want to buy it because I didn't have anyone to look after it. Later he said that he was going to sell another piece with two thousand trees.

"I'm not going to sell it to Alfonso. He's a very bad man. But I'll sell it to you for two thousand pesos."

"But I don't have anyone to look after it for me," I replied.

"Well, if you like, I'll look after it for you," he said.

"All right," I said, "I'll buy it to help you. Because your son is very young, if he becomes a mayordomo, you can save him from doing a year's service as a topil for the town council.

"Well, that's what I thought to do if you'll buy the cafetal from me."

"That's fine," I said. "Here's the money, and now the cafetal is mine. What do we need with papers?" I said to him.

"No," he said.

Then I said to Nico, "Go and inspect this cafetal and tell me how it is."

When he returned he said, "It's nice, Papa."

"Ah, good."

"It's ready to be harvested," he said. "It's a mature cafetal. Its first fruits were last year. This year it should be a fair harvest."

Nico went to work it, and then I let him have it. He picked it, and then they began to process it there, but it was too much work. So I said, "No, no, leave it. Do it however you can there. Just spread the beans out to dry."

Since there were only two thousand trees—and young ones at that—it wouldn't yield more than six or seven sacks. Well, I got three sacks. I get six thousand pesos annually from this small cafetal. Then I had another two thousand trees planted, but he did it the way they felt like doing it. He sent a hand to do it and everything, but they did a poor job. They tell me the cafetal is in sad shape.

"Look," I said to Nico, "I asked you to do it for a reason, so that it would be done right, but they didn't do a good job. That's why it is in such sad shape."

"Ah, but they're fixing it."

"Well, good, then we'll leave things the way they are."

There were four thousand trees there, and another 1,700 trees that we had in El Plantanar. But the trees there were drying up, and already the yields were dwindling. Then there was a fire and I don't know what else. I want to replant that field but since I can't go do jobs in the fields, I let Heraclio Velasco take care of this cafetal. He sold me three sacks of coffee, the same three that he had already sold me in advance. I said to him, "I'm not going to pay what they pay at harvest time. I'll give you so much now, and that's it. If it goes well, then I'll profit, but if it goes badly, I've lost."[7]

"Well, I'll let you have them for one thousand pesos a sack."

"Fine," I said, "here's three thousand pesos."

Then a man from Panixtlahuaca came and offered to sell me sacks of good dried coffee at 800 pesos. I said, "I'll buy them."

"Good, I have four sacks."

I gave him 3,200 pesos, but they are worth 2,000 apiece, or 8,000 pesos. God helps one.

Chapter 8

CONFLICT WITH KINSMEN

I brought Agustino back from Río Grande when my brother Teófilo died in 1945. I told my mother (may she rest in peace) and my brother in front of all of them, "Look at your boy here. It seems like we're not even family that he has no mother or father.[1] Do you think that it's right that my nephew Serafin doesn't take responsibility for his children? I don't think it's right. Serafin is not even responsible for himself, so Agustino is staying here. Right here, where his mother laid her head. Don't you remember where you grew up? Who made you into a man? Who supported you? Who clothed you? Who took care of you when you were sick? Who made sure you finished your elementary-school education so you could have your certificate? To whom do you owe all of that?"

Then Serafin said to me, "I'm going to take Agustino with me."

"Why?" I asked. "You can't support him. You've never been able to support him."

"Well, I can't keep him in school," he replied.

"Well, I can," I said. "That's why I brought him from Río Grande, because I saw what his situation there was."

Because I saw there was no father or mother for him, I said to him when he arrived, "Since you're my nephew, now that mother has died you can live with us, and you'll continue to go to school. Here you'll be fed and clothed and everything."

Agustino and his sister Amalia were there when my mother died. They were with Licha. Then Magdalena, my sister, took care of Amalia's grandmother. I'm grateful to her for that, because she did more for her than what little money Serafín might have given them would have done, because I used to give her some money every day, a few centavos. I'm not saying that I gave her a great deal. But I would give her three or four pesos every day, as much as I could afford and still support my own household too.

I also did the same thing for my mother when Amalia's poor mother died. Serafín was in Río Grande taking care of the airstrip. I sent him the news that night, but he didn't arrive until about ten in the morning the next day. That's the truth.

"God," I said to him, "were you so far away when your mother was on her deathbed? I sent word to you so you'd come to see her and say good-bye to her, because her life was coming to an end."

"But I have to take care of the place over there."

"Oh, that's fine," I said to him. "Something else is more important than your mother. I'll leave anything, but never my mother." I was by her side until her last moment with my children and Amalia.

Serafín told Amalia, his daughter, about a sewing machine my father bought for my mother so she could make clothes for us. Serafín told Amalia that in a very magnificent way, as though he wanted to butter her up, and he gave her the sewing machine. I said to him, "What happened to the sewing machine?"

"I gave it to Amalia," he said.

"Well, I don't think that it was wrong for you to give it to her," I said, "but I'm going to tell you something. Your father didn't sweat to get that sewing machine, and neither did your mother. My father bought that sewing machine to support us. In turn, your mother took it to support you, but that machine should belong to all of us, so we all would know where it is and each of us could use it a little bit. Not the way you handled it. But in spite of everything, I'm not angry about it, because I am grateful to your daughter Amalia for working and taking care of your mother and my mother as best she could."

After my mother died in 1950, I treated Agustino like a son. He was still living with us when my sister Magdalena died. Later, when Agustino and his wife came to Juquila for the fiesta, my wife told them that she had loaned the house to some people from the valley of Oaxaca. She had had it cleaned and had rented it out.

Agustino's wife started saying, "Why are those people in my father-in-law's house?"

My wife told her, "Well, we rented it because it was unoccupied. I had it swept to earn a few cents, and I rented it out."

"Well, you get those people out of there, because my father-in-law had that house there for us to live in." She doesn't even know about that house.

"But why do you say that?" my wife asked her. "You've always stayed here in the house with us. Even though that house is unoccupied, you always stay here. You already know the situation of that house and that you can't stay there, so you can stay here with us."

"No, no," she said, "tomorrow you're going to get those people out of there, because the house belongs to my father-in-law. It is for us to live in."

They went to the house and told the Oaxaca valley people, "Give us the money, because this house is ours." And Agustino was saying the same thing, and they gave them the money.

It's too bad that I wasn't there at the time, because I would have said, "Did your father-in-law build it? You don't even know who built the house. You don't have any right to live in it or to talk." But it was too late. I wasn't there. Well, that's how it was.

Just before the next fiesta we had a telephone conversation. Serafín called, using another name so that I wouldn't refuse to receive the call. When I got to the telephone I said, "Who am I speaking with?" (because they said the call was from a Benito so and so).

Then the voice said, "I'm Serafín."

"Oh. Well, what do you want?"

"Look, I want you to take your things out of the house before the fiesta, because I'm going to need to use it. Agustino and his wife are going to go there," he said.

I told him, "I can't vacate it just like that. I can't just throw away the things I have stored there. They're worth some money."

"That stuff is just about nothing but trash now," he replied.

"Well, we poor people call trash money," I told him. With that I tried to make him understand that for us poor people trash is money. To him money is like trash. "Since I've always been poor, I think it's a shame to throw my things away, and I won't vacate it," I said. "On the contrary! But if you would like, we could make some other kind of arrangement."

"No," he said, "no arrangements. I'm leaving for the fiesta today, and we'll work this thing out in whatever way is necessary."

"Whatever you want," I told him. "If you say so, I was a boarder with my mother. Or if you want, I was just raised by her. If you say so, I'm whatever you want. But I am not my mother's grandson. When you get here, they will tell you who they think is right. The authorities will set things straight." I had the receipts that prove I've been paying for the house since way back when.

"I am the son of Carmen de Dolores Aguilar," I told him, "and you well know it. Isn't that right?" That's what I said to him. Then I told him, "You can come whenever you want. You already know that I am not a grandson, or boarder, or just a child raised by Carmen de Dolores Aguilar. I am Fortino Santiago Aguilar, and they are going to put each of us in his rightful place here. If you have the right to my mother's property, then you will be the owner. But you have the least right, because at the time my mother needed you the most, you weren't there. How long have you been living in Río Grande? What did you contribute to the house? How many receipts do you have?" Well, he doesn't have any. That's the way things are.

When Serafín got to Juquila he came and said to me, "Did you vacate the house?"

"I didn't vacate it," I told him, "because I don't have anyplace to put my things." I told him, in a very magnificent manner, "You're crazy. What right do you have?"

I had to go out of town, and while I was gone his daughter-in-law went to yell at my wife, "Why are you renting out my father-in-law's house?" And she went and asked for the money from the people who were living in the house. "Give the money to me, because we are the owners," she said. My wife is the one who suffers.

I have never taken other people's goods that way. I got a house from my wife's father, Don Efren, and I gave it to my wife. I still have the document, the power of attorney. When they began to divide Don Efren's estate—land, mules, cattle—whose consent did they ask for? I have the authorization signed by Don Efren and signed by Guillermo Zavaleta and Timoteo Santiago as witnesses, that I am Don Efren's executor to take care of any matter having to do with his goods. He said that was what he wanted. That's why he gave me the document. I still have it.

I never took any of Don Efren's goods. When he wanted to give me cows, dogs, pigs, or turkeys, did I say, "Bring them over"? On the contrary, I told him, "You take care of them. When I need to, I'll tell you to sell a bull or a cow, and then you give me the money."

I have the document there, the authorized power of attorney registered by Sr. Efren Vargas, which told me that I could do anything with his goods whenever I wanted. But I'm not going to do that. Let them tear it to pieces. Let them waste it all until it's gone. What do I care? What can I say if I didn't take anything when he was alive, even though he was a man of his word? I didn't take anything. Now I could do it with more satisfaction, because I have a document that authorizes me to control those goods. They've already finished off all of the cattle; they've sold all the land. The only thing left is the house, but why should I say, "I'm going to claim this, and I'm going to fight"? Why don't I do it? Because it doesn't concern me.

When my brother Teófilo, with whom I used to work in Río Grande, was killed, I should have gone to fight to get the cattle that he left, to get some for myself. That would have been fine. I worked for those cattle. But no, I left them to my nephew Serafín for him to do whatever he wanted, as he usually does. Afterward, he sold all the cattle. He even sold the house.

Later I said to him, "Look, man, what you're doing is no good. You sold the house. You sold all my late brother's cattle that he got from his mother, and they didn't give me anything. Do you remember how many head of cattle and mares were to be mine? And where are the mares that they left to me? I never took a plate or a cup, not even a single grain of salt. I don't live off other people's sweat. I've always worked for a living."

There was a reason that I didn't take any of their things. I already had a lot of experience because of things I had seen. I would go on some of these trips without even having money. Sometimes I had to go into debt in order to take my furs to Mexico City to sell them, because that was the business that helped me earn a few centavos. But at least no one can say that I got what I have from other people. I don't like that.

For example, Serafín finished off his mother's and my brother Teófilo's cattle, even the house, and now he wants to take my mother's house on the basis of being a grandson. Just because he says so. No matter what, he must have an agreement with me.

A person should be ashamed to say "This is mine" if he doesn't have any proof that it is his. But Serafín, without any receipt of payment at all, was saying, "I paid during such and such a time," but he didn't pay one centavo.

His brother Rutilo's mouth is even more treacherous than Serafín's. About eight years ago, Claudia, the daughter of Rutilo, accused my wife of being a witch. You see, Rutilo said that he was going to hit my wife. It's been a while since this happened. It was over some money that my wife had loaned him. When she asked him to pay it back, he got real mad. I told her not to keep on lending him money. I told her, "You're going to have trouble one of these days."

The property on which Rutilo's house sits doesn't actually belong to him. Not one of them is going to be able to do anything when they come before the authorities. He'll have to ask my permission the day that he wants to sell. My mother gave it to him. I know that she gave that to him, and it's a fact. My mother told me, "My son, I'm going to give a small piece of land to Rutilo so he can build his little house."

"That's fine, Mother," I answered. "Whatever you want. Just remember who Rutilo is, so you'll know what you're getting into. But I won't tell you not to give him the land. Give it to him," I told her, and that's how it was. She gave it to him, and that's why someday when he wants to sell it, he won't be able to, because it's part of my mother's property. He won't be able to because he doesn't have my mother's signature proving that she sold it to him. What's he going to say when he wants to sell? It's part of my mother's property.

He built the house with his work, that's true. He leveled off the little piece of land, but the land doesn't belong to him. It's part of my grandfather León Aguilar's inheritance, which now belongs to my mother.[2]

Chapter 9

MY YOUNG SON'S DEATH AND MY WIFE'S INGRATITUDE

I was just starting to get ahead, to build up my shop, when my youngest son fell sick. He had rheumatic fever as a child, and his heart was affected. He was sick, but I had to go to Oaxaca to take care of some business. So I told my wife to send him to Oaxaca in eight days and I would take him to see the doctor. But she didn't send him, and fifteen days passed.

I was in Oaxaca eight days waiting for him. I told her to send him with my daughter, Licha. But she didn't send him, because it has always been her habit to disobey me. I had planned to go to Mexico City to sell some furs and buy what merchandise I could. I was about to go, but I returned to Juquila because I couldn't stand it. I felt desperate. I felt that something awful was happening in Juquila, and I told Adriana, "Daughter, if it weren't for this business that I've had to take care of, that I've finally taken care of, I'd have gone to Juquila already. But now I want to go back. I don't know what I feel."

I was just saying this when Irinia Pérez exclaimed, "Look what a pretty butterfly has alighted on your hat!"

Who was to know, right? I took off my hat, and there was a butterfly, black and white, like the Virgin of Soledad in Oaxaca—identical, just the way they represent the Virgin. I put my hat back on, but I had an awful feeling.

"Let's get our tickets," I said.

God had told me that something grave was going on there, but I couldn't get tickets for that night. We left for Juquila the next day. I had wanted to go that night to be able to sleep well. I did everything I could. Look what happened. This Otilio came, and he gave my boy an injection. An hour after this "doctor" gave him an injection, he died. What a barbarity! The poor man gave him an injection that wasn't the right one, because my son said to my sister, "Aunt, everything is getting dark."

"Ah, son, it's just because you're afraid," she said to him.

"No, Aunt, I'm not afraid, but everything is getting dark. I can't see well," he said, and died.

I'm not responsible for what happened to our youngest son, and it hurt me too. I had already realized that I couldn't get along with my wife; I just had to get out of her life.[1] I would like it to be like it was when I met her—very kind and obedient. She was, most of all, good at preparing my food. But once she got comfortable she didn't do these chores anymore. I would come home from a trip, at night with wet clothes, and she wouldn't even give me a cup of coffee. She would always say to my requests, "I'm asleep already. I don't want to get out of bed." What else could I say?

Twenty years ago we went to Huaspaltepec. Her father wanted to take his grandson, Héctor's son, and he joined us. So, we went to the fiesta. We took two mules I had just bought in Río Grande. I chose the bigger one because I thought it was in better shape. I was wrong. The small one was better, and I gave it to her. I saw that mule getting ahead. Once we arrived in Tepenixtlahuaca, I took the animals and went to look for some hay. It was already night, so I didn't find any.

I asked Marcelino Ríos if he had some hay, and he said, "I have some, but there's nobody around to help me bring it in." I told him I could help him cut it and carry it to the house. He accepted the proposal. If we were to reach Huaspaltepec the next day, we were going to have to get up early and go a long way. The animals were very tired already, and we had to get some hay. So I got a bale of hay and carried it on my shoulder. We then fed the mules. Right after that I said, "I have to get some corn now. I hope when I come back I can have some coffee and tortillas."

When I got back with a bag of corn, I asked her if I could have some coffee. She said, "I'm tired." I told her all the things I had done for us to be able to continue our trip early in the morning. And she was tired!

"You could've sent the boy to bring some water," I added, but she didn't do it. I finally said that this was going to affect our relationship. That is exactly how it was. I didn't want to go anywhere with her anymore.

She made me fall out of love because of her lack of care. Fifteen years ago she used to tell me she was going to Juchatengo or other places. Now that I travel she doesn't do that anymore. Nobody can be happy in this kind of situation. For example, my daughter always tells me where she is going and what she will be doing so I know where she is, but my wife doesn't tell me anything.

Now we are separated but still live in the same house. If I wanted to have a relationship with another woman, everybody would be against me, even her. But she really doesn't have a say in the matter. A man has the right or the necessity to have a relationship. I'm already old anyway. I wouldn't get involved with another woman now. Besides, people would talk about it, and my children would lose all the things I wanted for them.[2]

I can have women, not because I'm cute or young, but because they need some money. Some of them ask for up to fifty pesos. So I tell them, "If it's not inconvenient for you, we can have a relationship, and I can help you out when you need it. You don't have to pay me back." In a matter of a few minutes everything is arranged. Some women seem ready anytime. I guess they really want to be in my house, because I have so many things to sell. I say that if God gives me a long life, I will have a longer life of quarrels.[3]

Anyway, that was the main reason why I broke up with her. I fell out of love and got out of her life. It is not my fault. God saw it. She hurt me because she didn't obey me. We can't live together anymore. She won't even wash my clothes. I used to give the laundry to Señora Ursula, because my wife wouldn't even bother to give it to her. She, however, always sent for soap to wash her and the others' clothes. In the meantime, my clothes would pile up in a room that she used to lock up. My heart couldn't stand it.[4]

I wouldn't wish this kind of life on anybody. That is why I always tell my daughter not to do the same things her mother did. "Try to behave well," I tell her. "The life your mother leads is not good." I tell Licha and Adriana the same thing. But Licha acts dumb. Her husband does whatever he pleases, but that is her problem, right?

I don't want to talk about these things, it hurts me. Nevertheless, it is a reality. When I had a woman in Mexico City, my wife used to send her nasty letters. One time I read one, and it was full of nasty things. This woman, however, told me, "Don't you ever hit her or leave her. I care about her and love her. I love your kids even more because they're yours. If you ever want to come here, as we said you would, we can get married."

We always had a serious relationship. "You can bring your wife, your kids, your mother, your brother, and everything you have. Here, you will be able to earn a lot of money because you are hard working. I know you very well. With whatever I make we can set up a beauty parlor. I know how to make creams, lotions. I just have to buy the right type of scents, and you can stay and work here. We can have a good life."

I didn't have the courage to do it, because of my kids. Besides, I had some cows in Río Grande and in the mountains. There weren't very many, but they constituted what I had saved up, my security. Cattle were cheap then, but as I said earlier, I had to sell the cows from the mountains because my mother was sick. I had to sell them to support my family. I especially wanted to give my mother everything I could, so she could live well.

If my wife would change her ways, I would go so far as to forgive her and make up with her. If she doesn't, I won't go back to her. I don't want to suffer anymore. That is what I told her one time. But when I went to Mexico to sell some furs, I came back and found out that she had moved into another room without my permission. I only saw the beds of Licha, Adriana, and Nico, and my own. I didn't say a word about it. If I had needed to, I would go to Mexico City and Oaxaca every month, because it is important for me. What bothered me was that she separated our rooms without telling me why. I'm not dumb, so I started thinking about things. I did not say anything for a while, but later I decided to say what I thought.

"I can see that you want to leave me. Why don't you go to your own house? Nobody will bother you there."

She didn't answer me, because it wasn't to her advantage to do so.

"You're here because it's convenient for you. That's why you don't leave."

She didn't stay because of me or our kids but because she is comfortable here. I built an oven for her so she could bake bread. She never gives me half of the money from it. Because of my diabetes I don't even eat bread. Only once in a while I eat a piece.

Chapter 10

NICO'S COURTSHIP

AND MARRIAGE

I planned to marry my son to a girl named Catalina Ríos Villavicencio, the daughter of Viviana Villavicencio and Basilio Ríos, but there was some interference, because Nico got involved with another girl. Not to tell lies, he had two children with this schoolteacher Ausencia Flores. But at the time there was a running relationship between this girl Catalina and Nico. And I said to him, "Look, Son, your playing around with two women is no good. Catalina has already given you her word that she'll marry you. It doesn't seem right to me that you should be going around with the *maestra* Ausencia Flores. Anyone would feel hurt. Señora Viviana is easily annoyed and will play nasty tricks on you. You'll see, that's the way it's going to be." We spoke this in secret.

Well, a few days later he said, "What you said would happen, happened, Papa."

The señora took her daughter to Oaxaca, to Río Grande, to Tampico in order to erase my son Nico from her daughter's thoughts, I suppose, until she found a better marriage for her. One day my son said to me, "I'm going to Río Grande."

I said to him, "Look, I don't think that you have any business there."

"I just want to go to amuse myself there, Papa," he said.

"Well, I understand, more or less," I said. I knew that this girl Catalina was there with her mother. "Go on," I said, "but don't go around among crazy thugs. Don't go around doing this or that. Try to fix things decently, if by chance that's why you're going."[1]

He went, and he was there about six or eight days and then returned. I asked him, "How did it go?"

"Well, things are a little opaque. The señora is a bit unhappy, but she said that they are going to come in order to analyze things."

But nothing came of it. I said, "Remember what I told you. You'll see."

When they came back to Juquila, the señora had the jewelry returned that Nico had given to Catalina, saying that her daughter had become engaged to Diego Rojas. There were some dances in Juquila, and my son went to them. This Diego Rojas came, and Catalina didn't let go of him. She danced with him and everything. I saw them. Later I said to my son, "Did you see? Weren't the results what I said they would be? That's why when I tell you something, listen to me. Don't be so stubborn. I was very well disposed to your marrying her, but you did what you wanted. Look at the results. Even her new fiancé came, came to torment you."

"Don't worry about it, Papa," he said. "I'm not an old man, I'm young. If I were an old man, then it would make me sad, but now it doesn't matter at all to me. I'll find another."

Courtship

He began to have dances at the house. These dances were attended by the Ayuzo sisters, Berta and Rosalba Ayuzo, and the other young ladies of what little society there is in the pueblo of Juquila, as always. There would be a dance—every six days a dance, every three days a dance.

One day they said it was my saint's day and that they had come to congratulate me. They brought me flowers, a little gift, and a wheel of fireworks. Then it was Adriana's saint's day, they said, but it wasn't true. They just wanted an excuse to dance with Nico.

I said to Nico, after more than half a year of dances every eight days, "It doesn't bother me to spend the money, but I'd like you to tell me ahead of time if you are going to marry some girl. I'd like to know."

"No, Papa," Nico said, "there's nothing. Why should I say there's something when there isn't?"

He was preparing a plan, according to what I understood. Time passed and the dances continued. A year passed, more than a year, and again I asked him, "What's happening? I'd like to know if you have a relationship with one of these young ladies. I'd like to know ahead of time if you're going to get married so I can work with you, because we can't continue to waste so much time. Not that we don't have enough to meet our necessities, but as you know, and as we all know, when one begins to spend the little one has, the next thing one knows, one has nothing."

So it was then that he told me, "Well, it looks as if there is something developing."

"With which one of these two young ladies, or is it with one of the others?"

"Well, with Bertita," he said, "but it's, well, a thing that doesn't have any formality."

Marriage Negotiations

In the meantime, the dances continued as ever. If there wasn't one in the house, they would offer a dance in the school hall, or for the saint's day of a friend, or at public meetings, and there we would be. Finally the time came, and my son said, "Now, Papa, Bertita has told me that she'll marry me."

"Yes," I said to him, "well, do it. I'd be very happy to have it at once so you'll calm down and work."

"Then you'll give me your permission?"

"Why shouldn't I? I was ready for you to marry last time. It wasn't my fault that you didn't get her. Well, as Bertita and Catalina are second cousins, I don't know how her family is going to react. Well, it doesn't matter, it wasn't your fault, nor Bertita's, that she changed fiancés because you abused your engagement and went with Maestra Ausencia."

"Well, I'll arrange it," he said.

One day at about dusk, Bertita arrived at the house with Nico and said, "Good afternoon, Don Fortino."

"Good afternoon, Bertita," I said. "What a surprise! I feel honored by your presence."

"Well, don't thank me for the visit," she says. "I've come to an agreement with Nico."

"What would that be?" I asked.

"Well, you may have noticed that we have acted as though we were engaged officially," she said. "We have decided to be married."

"Well, good, I am very pleased to hear it," I said, "and above all from you, because I want things to come out in an honest, correct, and decent form. But I want you beforehand to take note of all of our flaws, from the father to the mother to the children I have, and principally those of my son, Nico."

"About this I've absolutely nothing to say," she said to me. "I already know everything. I've already decided to marry him."

"Good! On that account things are settled, but I want you to take note of another thing. You should understand the economic situation in which we

live very well. We are not hacendados. We're not millionaires. We're not rich.
We don't have large properties, only the small shop that I have. It is where
we all work to make a living. This is not a fine house. It is not well made, and
if you marry Nico, well, you'll have to bear living in it.

"No," she says, "I know all this. I've seen it. I've absolutely nothing to
discuss. I've already taken note of all this."

"Well, then, I'm very happy, very delighted. With great pleasure I shall
make the sacrifices to see that you celebrate this matrimony. You need only
tell me how you desire things to be, and in what form, so I can arrange them
in accordance with your wishes."

"Well, look," she said, "I'm going to Oaxaca tomorrow or the day after to
see my father."

"That's fine."

She went to see her father. When she returned she told me, "I've spoken
with my father. Well, he's a bit opposed. He would have preferred for me not
to marry Nico but to continue my studies."

"That matter is between your father and you. I can't interfere," I said, "because there's nothing I can say to your father."

"No," she said, "you don't have to discuss it with my father. I've already
told him to give me honorably in marriage to your son so that I may begin to
work. I told him that I'll continue my studies sometime in the future if I can.
I've fixed it with him. He has given me his permission. I told him that I'll
be very happy, but I wanted to show him the honor due to a father. 'I don't
want to do as I like. I don't want to show any lack of respect for you,' I said to
him. 'That's why I beg you to allow me to get married, to deliver me to the
church where I am going to be married to my husband.' He said, 'It is alright.'
So he'd like you to come to the finca El Ciruelo tomorrow to talk with him."

There weren't any obstacles to prevent my going, so I said I would be
happy to go speak with Sr. Genaro Ayuzo. Then I considered with whom
I could go. I asked my brother Timoteo, because he is Nico's godfather of
confirmation, to go with me to El Ciruelo to ask Don Genaro Ayuzo for
Bertita's hand for Nico.

"I'll pay our expenses," I said, "but I'd like you to come with me since you
are Nico's godfather, to see what we can arrange. I'm sure that he's going to
create some pretext to prevent it."

We went to El Ciruelo the next day and sat down to discuss the affair with
Don Genaro Ayuzo. As expected, he put up a few obstacles. He asked us
about the economic situation in which we live. As I have been a barber and
shoemaker, and always a small merchant, I had at the time a fair-sized store
with about 60,000 to 80,000 pesos of merchandise. But he knew this. He has
known me for a long time. I was his barber for many years. Well, we got along
well, and there was nothing in our relations to object to. So after discussing

the matter with him it was concluded that he would accept the marriage. He asked when we wanted the marriage to take place. We had decided that we wanted to have it on August 14, 1968. So that is what we arranged with Don Genaro. He made an appointment for us to come see him in Oaxaca in five days to make the rest of the arrangements.

On my return to Juquila, I told Bertita that I had made an appointment with her father to visit him in five days. She then sent him a telegram saying that it wasn't necessary for me to go, that she was going to leave for Oaxaca to buy her wedding dress and everything. Nico had already given her money to do her shopping. Meanwhile, I would stay at home, preparing things with the family.

She selected as a padrino Genaro Ayuzo, Don Genaro Ayuzo's son, who later died in a plane crash. He was the godfather of the marriage. But with so much going on I didn't notice the others, except that among those dressing Bertita and making preparations was a godmother of the thirteen marriage coins, a godmother of the bouquet, a godmother of the garters, a godmother of the rings, a godmother of the prayer, a godmother of the rosary, and a godmother of the wedding knot.

The Wedding

On the evening before the vespers of the marriage, a small band of violin and guitar players came to the house. The next morning there was still the small orchestra of eight or ten musicians when we went to bring the bride to our house. All along the road we came, playing and singing songs appropriate to the occasion that we were celebrating—joyous songs, songs of love, regional songs that are customary in the pueblo of Juquila. The orchestra played its pieces along the road and arrived at our house. The violin, guitar, and accordion would stop and the orchestra would start. We danced, and we drank a delicious milk chocolate with some egg bread that my wife, Antonia Carmen Vargas, made. The fiesta went on almost all night. It was nearly dawn when we went to leave the bride at her house.

That morning at about 7 A.M. I went with my son to the church. Don Genaro Ayuzo, Bertita's father, accompanied her in the procession that brought her along the whole road through his barrio to the church. We joined him outside the church, then together we entered the church. The priest received us and took the couple to the first row of seats before the altar. There they knelt, and we began to celebrate the mass. When they exchanged the rings, fireworks were set off. In the middle of the mass, more rockets were set off. While the priest was marrying them, exploding wheels were burnt. At the end of the mass, exploding wheels and large and small rockets were set off.

Then we invited the priest to come have a lunch of enchiladas with us at the house, and he came with us. Meanwhile, Don Genaro Ayuzo—who, to tell the truth, still wasn't very happy about the marriage—didn't wait to eat even the enchiladas or anything but grabbed his plane and returned to Oaxaca. But his son, Don Genaro, stayed and went on the second flight with his wife. That is how we celebrated the marriage of my son Nicolás Santiago Vargas and Bertita Ayuzo de Santiago.

So it was we celebrated their marriage. We held it over five days, five fiestas, holding a dance at each fiesta and burning all kinds of fireworks, making a grand ruckus to celebrate our great pleasure. Many people came to visit us. Many people participated in our joyous fiestas.

Land Reform and Factionalism

AN INTRODUCTION TO

CHAPTERS 11 AND 12

The land reform promised by Article 27 of the Constitution of 1917 did not become a meaningful national program until the presidency of Lázaro Cárdenas, from 1934 to 1940. Even when land reform did come, little came of it in Juquila, partly because large plantation owners have been able to buy off the authorities at the local, state, and national levels and partly because various administrations have run hot and cold on land reform. For example, in 1947 President Valdés Alemán led a "counterreform" in agriculture. Amending Article 27 of the Constitution, which provided the basis for land reform, he introduced the amparo agrario, an injunction to prevent expropriation. To further guarantee the rights of private landowners, he expanded the definition of small landholdings. Since even large estates could be divided among individual family members in order to keep them within the defined limits, they could be protected from expropriation. Even though since the end of the Alemán administration over 30 million hectares of land have been redistributed as ejidos, little of this land is arable, and not a single hectare has been returned to Indian communities in the district of Juquila. Not only have Indian communities been unable to recover communal lands lost to plantations during the Porfiriato, but mestizos have actually carved out new coffee plantations from communal lands.

During the early 1950s, as the coffee trade became ever more lucrative, conflicts between competing coffee buyers heated up. Assassinations and blood feuds were rife. It is worth noting, too, that although these factions had political faces, Fortino talks about their mafialike politics and assassinations in terms of families, not parties. Though political parties exist, they are less important than family politics, because it is family politics that determines access to political power and resources in the community.

⸝Fortino argues that coffee is also at the root of the vicious feuds that have divided Indian communities.⸜ When coffee began to be planted on communal lands, it created a market for suitable land, which rapidly transformed communal land into a de facto form of private property that could be bought and sold within the community. This created a new form of land tenure that pitted claims to land based on usufruct rights and traditional inheritance against claims based on a capitalist contract. The upshot of this was that when land was sold, those who stood to inherit concluded that the purchaser had stolen the land from them. Because many of Fortino's close kinsmen and compadres were directly involved in the blood feuds and factional struggles that flowed from this process, the following chapters provide a detailed and intimate view of the conflict.

Chapter 11

POLITICAL FACTIONALISM

IN JUQUILA

Following the death of my godfather Saúl Villanueva, who used to fight with Lázaro Sánchez, my brother Timoteo entered the picture. I wasn't afraid of my brother getting involved, but I just didn't trust anyone. Anyway, when my godfather died, Timoteo was the one who confronted Sr. Sánchez and the Muñoz family. That is why they started to hate him.

The Muñoz family went after my brother Timoteo and his son Diego. First they shot Diego in the foot. Timoteo used to hide all the time. At night or in the middle of the day he would get out of town before people could find out. When people would find out, the house was already empty. Instead of going to Zacatepec—where he said he was going—he would go to Nopala. From there he would take a small airplane and go to Zacatepec or Río Grande. Sometimes he would go through Panixtlahuaca. He was constantly hiding when he had to do his business traveling. When they shot Timoteo, the fight was at its peak. They shot at him from the corner of the market. Timoteo wasn't doing anything but passing by the market. He was lucky. They tried to shoot him in the head, but they didn't aim well enough. They shot him near the liver, but he didn't die.

An Indian from San Juan Quiahije shot Timoteo in his store. This Indian had been sent by the Muñoz family. They even gave him the pistol he used. They say that they even trained him how to shoot. They had him practicing every day in their house. The bullet went under my brother's heart. This happened in 1958, after they tried to kill Diego. When they shot Timoteo, his son Diego got very angry. He told his father, "Do not get involved anymore. It is my turn."

So Diego got involved, and they've already tried to kill him twice. The first time they shot at a shadow, and he was able to escape. The second time they shot him from up front, but the bullet only grazed his leg. He was lucky. Timoteo and Diego continued to try to pull out, but they always managed to find new enemies. They are very good at that, even now.

About this time I was elected presidente, but Florencio Valencia paid the PRI to have my election annulled. I still have the papers. What happened was that my brother Timoteo had just served a term as presidente, and he came to me and said, "Look, there's no one who we can put up for presidente. I've come to an understanding with the regidores and with all the barrio presidentes that it would be better to have you."

"All right," I said, "I accept because I see how things are, but it really isn't convenient. I've a lot of work to do, and it's not in my interest. I don't really like politics, but we'll see. For the good of the pueblo I will ask God to let me serve the town honorably."

I was going to show them how I would serve, how I saw it in those first years, when I began to understand what authority was. Came the elections and I was elected. But then, because Timoteo was my brother and this "friend" Florencio Valencia was fighting him, he paid off the PRI and I wasn't allowed to become presidente. Constantino González took office instead. Everyone in the Barrio de Jesús was mad. They came to me and asked me for arms in order to go kill the presidente. They said to me, "You were elected. We voted for you. Why should we let another go sit there?"

"No," I said to them, "I'm a poor man. I don't have money. I don't have any arms. But even if I had them, I wouldn't do it, because it would just be a waste of oneself."

So we waited until we could protest. Esteban Emiliano, along with others from Barrio Grande, invaded the town hall. I had given the sergeant, who was in charge of taking care of the town hall, an order not to let anybody in. I had asked for all this security. The sergeant heard them come into the building but couldn't stop them. There was Ernestina's son, Gregorio Rojas, that killer. The Muñoz family was also there. Everybody was afraid of them because they were killers and the rest were not.

One time, I passed a Muñoz on the path up to the house, and I said, "I'll order these bushes cut around here. If I don't, one of these days an assassin will hide in them." He heard my remark, but they didn't try to do anything to me. They knew I wasn't going to take advantage of them. And when it came down to it, I was more effective than the others. They saw that I wasn't vicious, so they didn't bother me. That is why I was never armed. There wasn't any need for them to kill me. I was by myself, and my son was still very young. I said to myself, If they do something to me, they'll also try to kill my son.

Anyway, I didn't take office, because I wasn't able to give them the documents on time. After that, Don Florencio began to buy the authorities whenever he could, and when he no longer could, the priest, Padre Modesto, began to do the same thing.

One time a public prosecutor who was bought by Florencio Valencia came here. We were all at a party, and whenever a person would get near him, he would reach for his pistol. I was fed up with this, and I decided to approach this clown without giving him time to grab his pistol. He tried to grab his pistol, but I took him by his shirt and grabbed it from him.

"Look," I said, "let's go outside to straighten out this matter, because you've gone too far. You're using your pistol to scare all these good people. Why are you doing it? Are you a real man or not? You should know that I'm more of a man than you, because I don't have to carry a pistol to be brave."

I remember that Comandante Reyes arrived. He was a top sergeant, and he yelled at me when he saw I was cocking the pistol.

"Tino, you're my friend. I've always loved you. Please give me that pistol."

I explained, "First you, as an authority, have to look at the disturbance that this man is causing. He pulls his pistol out whenever he pleases. That's not good. That's what he tried to do to me, but now I have his gun. I'm not going to give it back to him. Now, take him away. I'll wait for you here."

The comandante called the public prosecutor aside and invited him to the dance saloon. "What do you think about this whole matter?" he asked me.

"I think we're at the mercy of those in power," I said. "I don't carry a pistol, but this man does, and he even challenges the authorities. It shouldn't be this way. I took his pistol away to teach him to respect people and the law."

"Be a good friend. You can continue dancing if you like," he added. I told him that I wanted to go home and that I would give him the pistol there. So I did. "I only wanted to show that guy that a pistol doesn't give courage," I said.

I have taken five pistols away from people who were ready to wipe me out that way. I was strong then.

I used to think to myself, I'm not going to get out of this one. But everybody was afraid of me. I had many fights and difficulties where people ran away. Nevertheless, one has to be careful and not expose oneself to danger. For example, I haven't gotten drunk since 1953 or '54. When my aunt

Modesta died, that was the last time that I got drunk. Alcohol is a factor in getting people in trouble. That is why I only played with alcohol for twenty or twenty-five years. After that, I didn't drink anymore.

I've been in very many tight spots, but I've never wanted to kill. It is true, there were times when I couldn't stand it anymore, but I commended myself to God, and I was at peace with them. God's the one who has protected me. I've never carried a gun.

At first, I didn't say anything when they tried to kill Timoteo. I told myself, This isn't going to be of any benefit to me; although I have a son, he's still very young, and they could easily kill him if I get involved in this kind of quarrel. Moreover, I realized that as soon as Timoteo and his son got to be politicians they would use their positions for whatever material benefits they could get out of them. They didn't even get water for the town. It wasn't because of their selfishness, but I don't think politics should be used for business. I told my son all this, every day, because they wouldn't stop trying to involve him. My son thought they really liked him.

"They are my family," he used to say. I told him that they only wanted to get him involved because they needed to blame somebody for whatever they did. I kept on trying to convince him not to see them. "Doña Juliana is sort of a twisted character," I warned him.

What bothers me is that they are getting my son involved in the whole thing. Diego is a bad influence on Nico. Nico trusts Diego too much. The Muñoz family, who started the fight, are vicious. They are the ones who shot Timoteo. Their kids have continued the fight. There is no doubt about it. The Muñoz family shot Timoteo. I am sure he was shot on Amado Muñoz's orders. He was the key person. He was mean, offensive, and a killer. Money gave him the right to be that way. At that time he was keeping an eye on Diego's money.

Diego used to take Nico to different parties. Tomás Muñoz was Diego's compadre. Diego used to provoke him, and when Tomás reacted, Diego would pull my son into the whole thing. I always had to intervene, especially the day that my son started beating up a young man. I wasn't there at the time, but when I found out about it, I went and took him home. I had to force him to come home. He was twenty-four or twenty-five years old when they tried to kill Timoteo and Diego. I always told him that Diego was bad news. Only when he was disillusioned did he believe me. That is why I used to tell my son that throughout life one should be careful and not to get under the mandate of any specific people. It is strong ties that would drive him to participate in political matters, which could only end in his death. He heard me all right, but he got involved again and again.[1]

I think he is disenchanted with the whole thing now. He has finally recognized the truth in what I've told him. He said, "I am sorry, Father, you've always advised me well. When you used to make your business trips to Oaxaca and Mexico City, I always disregarded such advice. The first thing I would do is disobey you. So many terrible things have happened to me. I got out of going to jail only because some people helped me. You would have found me in jail. They set me up. They even gave me a pistol to shoot this kid who was saying wicked things about my aunt. I did shoot him, but I didn't hurt him."

I asked what he would have done if he had killed him—who could he have blamed? He said that he was sorry. I told him to take the whole matter as a lesson. "The next time you should know what to do," I said. "I never taught you to be vicious. I've always told you to do good things in life."

I think he understood. When this happened he had already become entangled with that enemy. Since I never defined my posture as against these people, the Muñoz family knew what to expect from me. That is why I've been able to live in peace in this town. I've always been on the fringe of things, so I was never disappointed by anybody.[2]

When Padre Modesto entered the political arena, things went from bad to worse. Of course, he financed his political ambitions by stealing from the church. For example, a man from Puebla donated money for a church clock, but the priest didn't buy it. Instead, he bought his mistress, Sabina, a two-story house with electricity. He has built three houses now, the two that they built where the late Cuca lived and another one that he built down by the riverbank next to Jorge's house. They also had some coffee land near it, which they had bought from González. That is when they started claiming that they got their money from it. What money could they have made from that? They didn't even take care of those coffee trees.

The old mosaic from the altar in the church was set into the brick wall of the house in that coffee finca. Everybody knows it. On one occasion they took some good beds there, to go and enjoy target shooting with fine rifles and pistols, and enjoy all the money they had taken. Later on, an Indian from Yaitepec stole the mattresses. This Indian is a real criminal. He is a son of Teresa Carmen. The year before last he served as a policeman. This year he didn't serve, because he was afraid, because they had killed his brother. Since he is a killer too, he didn't serve, out of mistrust. He was afraid they might catch him off guard. So he didn't go but fled Yaitepec instead. It was this guy who stole the mattresses, a bed, and pillows and took them to Yaitepec. He took them to a house in the country. A friend of mine told me about them. "What fine beds this guy has," he said. "He got them from where Arnulfo Palacios lives." It is nice, I suppose, that someone's making good use of them.

Anyway, when Padre Modesto Valerina entered the fight against Timoteo Santiago with his father-in-law, Arnulfo Palacios Gutiérrez, they pulled the Muñoz family and everyone else they could over to their side and started the killing anew. They went on killing and killing until the day came that the state police grabbed Ezequiel, a son of Amado Muñoz, and killed him. Comandante Rufino killed him. Then a grandson of Amado Muñoz took up arms. He was named Darío Muñoz and was the son of Leonor Muñoz. He was a very dangerous character.

One time Darío Muñoz went to visit Luisa Calvo because he was her daughter Rosa's lover. There were rumors that his nephew Bartolo was Rosa's lover too. One day they met in Rosa's house and began to argue. Bartolo pulled out a pistol, and his uncle shot and killed him.[3]

After that, Darío's uncle, Tomás Muñoz, also got into it, and his involvement in politics turned ugly too. Then Amado Muñoz's other son, Diego, was killed. They killed Bartolo, Ezequiel, and Diego, and the others continued their revolution against the Ramos and Santiago families, killing them.

The Muñoz family had become enemies of the Ramos family, the sons of Ausencia Mendoza, because they had stolen her cattle. They had gone well armed and openly to steal her cattle. This upset the Ramos family. They went to spy on them, and a few times they tried to kill them, but they weren't able to do anything.

After this, Tomás Muñoz too began to declare himself a strong enemy of the Ramos family. Because the Muñoz were fighting with the Chenchos (that is what they call the Ramos family, because their mother's name is Ausencia and they call her Chencha) a lieutenant who was engaged to the daughter of Silvia Santiago supported these sons of Aunt Chencha.

This lieutenant was always pursuing the Muñoz family because they were going around doing their wicked deeds in the countryside. So one day, who knows what they did, but the lieutenant went to pursue them. Out toward Chorro Conejo they ambushed the lieutenant and killed him. This caused great turmoil in Juquila. That night I felt pity. I said to myself, This poor man, there wasn't any reason for him to die, and he died.

The thing went on, and in the middle of things some of the Muñoz supporters got involved. One time they were bringing some cattle of Sra. Chencha. Among them was a cow that they had brought from Tututepec. They hid the cattle in a pasture near town and came into town. But instead of going back to bring the cow in themselves, they sent one of their hands to fetch it, one of the Ramírez kids.

This poor kid went down there with a rifle to untie the cow and bring it into town. And there waiting, armed, were the owners of the other cows, guarding them, waiting to kill anyone who came to take them. This kid went there. They saw him untie the cow, thought, "Ah, all right," and with the cow and everything, they killed him.

Well, we surmised that it was the rivals of the Ramos family that killed him, but one can't point them out, because who saw them? It happened in a place where people don't go walking, out of fear. So the feud continued. After having killed this kid, they began to go after Tomás Muñoz, and so he left town.

Later the Chenchos learned that Tomás was on a ranch near his wife's village in Piñas Negras, and the sons of Aunt Chencha and some others went after him. They surrounded the house and opened fire from in front while the rest lay in wait. When he came out the back door, they shouted at him not to move, because there he had to die. He set off running, and they shot and killed him as he ran. This Tomás Muñoz died there. And after that the killing continued, first here, then there, and it didn't stop. What a barbarity! It was a thing that had become disgusting.

Then they learned that the señor and this Sra. Chencha had hired a pistolero, one of those from Tututepec, and they had him there on their finca. So one day Amado Muñoz, the father of Tomás, was walking with a tray of meat when this man stepped out just in front of him and killed him in the entrance to the market. Ramona, the wife of Leonor Muñoz, went running after the killer. She ran after him all the way to the arroyo that runs behind the town hall, where Berta has this cantina, when he turned around and said, "Look, you'd better not follow me, because if you do you'll die where you are."

I actually saw this. I was in Berta's cantina when I saw a man coming with a pistol in his hand and behind him ran Ramona, and he turned and fired at her and she ran into the cantina.

That is the way it was. It was the Chenchos who killed him. After that, things calmed down, and Leonor said to him, "This isn't going well. Look how many have died already." For some reason, they didn't catch them.

I had a lot of experience already when they went after my son, Nico. I urged him to be careful when he went to Panixtlahuaca or anywhere to bring coffee. What happened was that they had shot Tomás Muñoz at night. They killed him, but they said that Nico had done it. We were afraid, but we knew he hadn't done it. God only knows which one of his killer friends murdered him. They never did anything to my brother, because they knew who did it, but people like to gossip.

Nico had punched Tomás in the nose while they were taking a walk somewhere. He didn't have anything to do with the whole situation, but they involved him. Yes, that is the reason why now people talk about Nico. I had already told him that he shouldn't mingle with his cousin Diego. He realized how they were, but even so he would still hang around with them. They knew what would happen if a shooting took place, but none of them said anything. I asked Nico to remember this incident. "They didn't even go to see what had happened at the time of the shooting. Only my uncle Timoteo went," said Nico. I said it was good that he realized it, so that he could learn to protect himself rather than let others use him.[4] I myself taught my sons and daughters how to defend themselves on all fronts. If things go wrong for them, it is their own fault. I already taught them everything I know.

Shortly after Tomás Muñoz was killed, Nico and Berta were ambushed on their way back from Panixtlahuaca on this side of Rancho Viejo. Nico was driving along and came to a tree that had fallen half across the road. A truck had just gone by ahead of them and moved it aside a little. If they hadn't, Nico would have had to stop. Only because there was a little space left was he able to pass. As it was, they opened fire as he went around it. He sped up and pulled his gun and started shooting, driving and shooting, but he couldn't aim. He could only shoot wherever he heard the bullets coming from. He didn't see who was shooting at them. Who is going to stop to see? He couldn't see who the killers were, but they hit his car. He sped on, running until he hit a place where the road was bad, near the Río Concha. He left the car there, and he and Berta walked to Juquila and arrived at night. Right away they asked the police for help. The next day they sent a truck back to pick up the car. Then he left for Oaxaca, since there was no reason to stay.

I don't understand why people do things like this. They have stolen so much from the church. They are clever people, yet they still envy those who work, and they don't let them work. But it is God who arranges things. I can't be the judge.

They ambushed Nico out of envy, because he doesn't have anything and doesn't owe anything to anybody. I'm an old man already. I don't want them to kill either my son or me. If I were dead, my children would ruin things, because they don't know how to manage the business.[5]

My son is still young, and I told him, "Let's see how we can arrange things, God willing, without compromising ourselves, because if we don't, we won't last long before they kill us, because these neighbors have a lot of money." On the other hand, Nico has a lot of relatives on his mother's side, people of determination.

Nico has an uncle in Río Grande, Demetrio, and he told him, "You just tell me who did it and nothing else, and then stay out of it. Who was it?" He is an honest, simple man, a hardworking man right now. But when his father was killed, Demetrio and his brothers Basilio and Erasmo became killers. They tried to shoot Nico out of envy. I think it was the priest's woman, Sabina, and her brother who put out the contract. So I told myself, Neither my son nor I will touch them. In Juchatengo, Nico has many relatives who are already experts. One worked a short time for Nico and Berta in order to figure out who had tried to kill them.

My daughter Adriana was taking care of the store the day Nico left with his wife for Panixtlahuaca, and Sabina's people were running around. It was around April 4, 1973, when Adriana heard one of the maids saying, "The barbecue will be here soon, right?" And the woman who was with her told her to shut up, but Adriana heard her. She was standing outside in the corridor, thinking that it was already ten at night and Bertita and Nico hadn't come back yet.

Quite honestly, we thought there wasn't anyone left who wanted to hurt him. He was scared before, but not any longer, because Nico now is the one who rules the coffee business. His father-in-law has been the coffee king. He was the main coffee buyer and the promoter of the coffee business in Juquila. He insisted that everybody plant coffee, explaining that it would bring money. Actually, Don Genaro Ayuzo is responsible for the relative wealth of each family who owns coffee.

My son had told me that he was going to Oaxaca to try to fix things. He went to see the archbishop. "I don't want to wait here in Oaxaca forever, because I have a business to take care of," he told the archbishop. Then he added, "I'm spending money I don't have. I'm a father and I have to work," and he left. The archbishop must have intervened. He must have said he was going to hold Padre Modesto responsible, because he sent word that it was safe for my son to return. Padre Modesto didn't have anything to say, because my son told the archbishop the truth. I was also trying to do something. And my faith in God helped me through this, even though I knew they were treating my son and daughter-in-law very badly. But God, watching over us, did not let anybody kill them.

I thank God and especially Señor del Rayo, a very beautiful saint. I lit some candles and asked him with all my heart to save my son and all my family from those evil people. I know that God realized the kind of people they were. We certainly didn't deserve any kind of punishment. I left it to his will. I prayed, saying, "I am in your hands. We commend to you our souls. You know whether they did wrong, because you know what you are doing. We do not want commitments. We want to respect you because you have given us life and made us good people, not criminals."

Chapter 12

LAND CONFLICTS

In Cárdenas's time, when agrarian reform came to Juquila, everyone jumped in to reclaim their land rights.[1] Formerly the municipal síndico was the only authority on communal lands; now there is a president of the communal lands committee. During the Díaz regime the plantation owners wanted to grab the communal lands of Juquila, but they weren't able to. In Juquila there are no plantation owners, nor have there been, nor will there be. The people never would consent to any, except the ones at El Plantanar. They were the only ones they allowed to have a small area to work, good land for coffee. But in other municipios the plantation owners were more successful, since the authorities always have had the custom of selling themselves. So when there was agrarian reform, those who had taken the lands of Teotepec and Yaitepec did not surrender them. Instead, they went to Oaxaca, and even to Mexico City, and made agreements, and nothing was done to take away their lands.

Just like the poor people of Yaitepec, years have gone by and nothing has been settled, nothing. I told them, "Go to see the president of the republic. Tell him. Speak to him clearly about how things are, and he will take care of it right away." But no. What happens is they offer authorities in Yaitepec their small bribes, behind the people's backs, and things are quiet, and so it goes.

For example, there is a very old conflict that Ixtapan has with Santiago Minas. It is a long-standing conflict over what little good land Ixtapan has. As Santiago Minas had money, they beat Ixtapan out of it in court. But that was the only way they could do it. They had tried previously to wipe out Ixtapan. In 1971 they had gone to attack Ixtapan, and the trip came out lefthanded;

those of Ixtapan really let them have it. They killed some thirty Santiago Minas men. Since then, every so often they have tried the same foolishness: to try to wipe out the pueblo. They haven't been able to. After that, those from Ixtapan began to rob those of Santiago Minas, and those of Santiago Minas robbed the Ixtapaneros. Finally they made sort of a truce. They came to an agreement among themselves that as long as Ixtapan didn't molest Santiago Minas, they wouldn't come to harass them. So little by little they came to an understanding that this was the remedy, simply among themselves. On various occasions the government had been called in, but it was never able to fix things.[2]

Many of the fights over land are really over coffee. In the 1930s the Chatino began to plant a little coffee, but very little, just for their own use, because coffee was only worth twelve centavos a pound. They didn't start to plant coffee in quantity until the price began to go up, because it wasn't worth very much and it required a lot of work.

About 1950 coffee reached a price that was fair, even profitable. The one who gave the business of planting coffee real impetus was Don Genaro Ayuzo. The Chatino planted coffee not only on Don Genaro's advice but also on that of finqueros from La Soledad and La Aurora. Everyone had worked there. They brought back with them the enthusiasm for the work. There they began to have more faith in the coffee trade. In Juquila it was Don Genaro, I can testify, who pushed the development of the coffee trade. It was he who inspired the people to plant coffee, who persuaded them it was profitable. He not only pushed it, he bought it from them. He went on giving better prices until they reached where they are presently. He still continues to buy, and the people continue planting.

The pueblos that have the most land of their own for coffee in the district of Juquila are San Gabriel Mixtepec, Acatepec, Jocotepec, Temaxcaltepec, San Juan Lachao Nuevo, and San Juan Lachao Viejo. Yolotepec has some on a fringe of land on the border with Yaitepec. Some pueblos, like Ixtapan, are too hot for coffee. Yaitepec works in Las Placitas, and they have a lot of coffee too. Juquila does too. Beginning from the edge of town, coffee grows along the path to Tututepec, along the mountains, and all through the valley to Rancho Viejo. Rancho Viejo is in Juquila on the boundary with Panixtlahuaca. There is coffee along the whole ridge above the Río Mano that borders San Juan Quiahije. And up that way they have some lands in a semitemperate zone, and all through there they've planted coffee. They planted coffee along the path that goes to Tututepec—in Yerba Buena, Santa Cruz, Tataltepec, Tepenixtlahuaca. All these villages have coffee now.[3]

All the towns where coffee has been introduced are bitterly divided, because there is very little free land left on which to plant coffee. Now they are just blocking things, because some greedy individuals grab a good-sized perimeter of land in which one could plant 100,000 trees, and they go plant a hundred trees here and a hundred there, all around the edge of this property, so that no one else will enter, and then they plant a few trees in the center. This simply blocks the economic development of the pueblo, but the authorities haven't filed papers to reduce these people to what they can work, because they can't, because then there are conflicts. If they do something, it is not just a little conflict; it turns into a big one—killing, grabbing land, and everything.

For example, about the time that they started to grow coffee in Yaitepec, a vicious fight started. It began as a feud between the family of Samuel Saldivar and the Cruz family, who were sons of a man from Ixtapan, León Cruz. He had a son, Sabino. He was the oldest, and he lived in Yaitepec. He had another son, named Santos, but it was the one in Yaitepec who had children. Anyway, they started to fight with the sons of Samuel Saldivar, and they began to kill one another.

Samuel Saldivar had a son-in-law. He was a short kid, not too tall, but a real killer. He was the grandson of a Federico Contreras from Yaitepec, but he was the son-in-law of Samuel. Anyway, during a drunk he was on he got into a fight, I don't know how, with a music teacher from Teotepec who was living there. They were already fighting with the Cruz family, and this teacher liked to fight, but unfortunately this kid was carrying a machete and cut off his hand. This added fuel to the feud, and it burned even stronger than before. This incident helped the other side gain support, since they had cut off the hand of a man who was of service to the pueblo. He was a music teacher, and to do this to him! Healthy and whole, and they had destroyed his future. He couldn't make a living and returned to Teotepec. But as he liked to look for trouble, he continued in his old ways there, and they killed him.

Anyway, this son-in-law of Samuel Saldivar came and went. They tried to kill him, but didn't, and they killed one another. And on one of these occasions, this kid went to Tututepec. The Cruz family learned of it—that he had gone—and went to spy on him. They saw how he came and went. So when he left, they were waiting on the path, and they killed this kid and came back to Yaitepec. They walked all night so they could be back in Yaitepec in the morning. They are great walkers. So it was that the feud continued, and the fight with the Cruz family took on more flesh. Then they killed a son of the Cruz family, and the fight gathered more strength. Then they killed another of Samuel Saldivar's sons, a musician named Fidel. Well, these "friends" grabbed him at a *mayordomía*, behind a fence where he was playing, and put a bullet into him there. They continued to fight. They killed another son of Sabino Cruz, and then Sabino Cruz himself.

This started a brutal feud in repayment. Samuel Saldivar had at least fifteen men sleeping in his house at night, and another fifteen would go and shoot at them. It happened that a Darío Kwine' ("baby Darío," they called him) had gone to the house of Samuel Saldivar to drink. He didn't worry about sleeping there and stayed the night. In the night, someone fired a shotgun through the door and killed him. He was a relative of theirs, a cousin of Agustina, Samuel's wife. Then they killed Samuel near the cross that is on the path as you enter town. The brother of a woman named Consuelo, who still lives in Juquila, killed Samuel Saldivar. But her brother didn't last long. They killed him too.

The feud continued. Killings multiplied until they wiped out all of Sabino's sons. But the damage was done. Others had been drawn into the feud's tangle. And even after all the men in the Cruz family had been killed, it continued until it had engulfed almost the entire town. It was congested with criminals. The situation was so grave that they didn't even respect their mothers or fathers. For example, a boy who used to be a good kid killed his own father, Baltazar León, a humble man. His son hit him, and his head hit the corner of a table, and he died.

Many people have come to Juquila from Yaitepec because of the killings, and not only from Yaitepec, but from Ixpantepec too. People are continually leaving Ixpantepec. Ixpantepec was the town that was the most humble, the most peaceful. There were no feuds. But now they, too, have become embroiled in conflicts and are killing one another. Ixpantepec was the most humble of the pueblos. When they begin to have difficulties, they leave Yaitepec to go to Zacatepec, Nopala, or Panixtlahuaca. Others go to the finca La Soledad or to La Aurora. They go to earn money, buy arms, and return to the pueblo for vengeance. In Juquila, it is the same fiesta, to seek revenge for everything and anything.

In Panixtlahuaca it has been the same thing: coffee, greed, and violence. In one year, 1973, they killed two presidentes and twenty-five people. There was one poor man named Saúl Olivera y Olivera. He was an old man, to be respected. He was just about my age. That poor man traveled back and forth between Juquila and Panixtlahuaca. He would take goods and bring things back. He worked for us as a hand for a year. It is said that they had a deep-seated grudge against him, but not that deep-seated. Well, they killed him, and then another man, and finally they killed Benjamin Olivera. I think he was the presidente of Panixtlahuaca.[4]

When they killed Saúl, my compadre Don Pepe Flores left the village. Well, overnight a mob burned his house down and took a crowbar to it. They stole everything in his house. They knocked down about five houses he had on two or three lots. One was on the lot that belonged to him, the others on lots that belonged to his sons Domingo and Humberto.

Don Pepe had provided for all of his sons, so they wouldn't be left out and would have a place to build houses for their sons. What is more, he had already fenced a big field over there in Agua del Encino and one at Cerro Tigre, where he has some coffee. Well, damn, it was one of those things where they went after him in earnest. They went over there one time wanting to kill him, and they fired a shot at him that just missed his head.

All of the people who live in the countryside are friends of my compadre Don Pepe. That is why my compadre is still alive. The problem was that they wanted to take his land away from him and divide it up. That is what the priest had instructed them to do, to divide his land up among the people of the town, because he didn't deserve to be there. Then my compadre made all of his appeals. He informed the state and national officials about the boundary lines of his land and that he was working it. Finally they gave him papers authorizing him to continue working there, and that is how it was.[5]

He told me, "They fired a shot at me, compadre, but I had some boys out there who fired back and went out to chase them." Seeing that he stood up to them and didn't let them dominate him, they haven't come to show their faces around there anymore.

Afterward, the mob went to the house of Rebeca Guzmán's son, from Panixtlahuaca. She had two sons, and they were quite vicious. They were friends of my compadre Don Pepe, but they turned on him. Then these sons of Rebeca went to shoot up Aunt Carmen's house, my compadre Miguel's home. But I think they were sort of drunk when they went. They really wanted to kill that woman and her children, because the man who started the feud over there in Panixtlahuaca, who began to stir things up, was Miguel's son. This kid was my godson of confirmation, but he was venomous.

Anyway, my godson began to stir things up, giving advice to people and having this one and that one beat up. And they started killing each other over there because of him. Then they found out where all that was coming from, and they killed him. At the time, his father was a síndico, so things went up to another level, and the enemies who had had their sons killed became furious. Since Miguel was the authority, he was saying that he was going to do this and that. One night, Miguel got drunk and lay down in a hammock outside his house, and Rebeca's sons caught him asleep. They put a shotgun in his mouth and pulled the trigger, and that was the death of my compadre Miguel.

Afterward, Rebeca's sons killed another man. I think his name was Ezequiel. Later on, Rebeca's sons went to attack a house that is over there on El Cerro Tigre, and a little twelve-year-old boy stood up to them. From inside the house he saw where they were firing from, and he shot one of the most fearless of Rebeca's sons. They carried him back to Panixtlahuaca, but they couldn't do anything to save him.

Finally the government decided to calm things down, because there had been so many complaints from both sides. It stationed a detachment of soldiers there and sent in the state police. Oh, the state police ate and lived with the criminals. They were well paid, that was known; so were the federales. They had definite orders to liquidate those killers if they struck for any reason.

So then the killers picked up and went to Masaquesla. They are over there now. Some of them were even cousins of Arturo Guzmán, whom they had already killed.

Two of Arturo Guzmán sons were killed, but three or four of them are grown men. When they were young they came to Juquila, fleeing from the trouble, and they didn't go back to Panixtlahuaca. Their very own cousins, Rebeca's sons, wanted to kill them, so they went to El Cerro Tigre. That is where Arturo's sons work now, but the killers who committed that crime don't show their faces. Their cousins have gone to look for them, but they are on their toes.

One day, Arturo's sons spied the man who had killed their father when he was coming back from Huaspaltepec. They lived up the arroyo. So much for those who said that those boys weren't going to do anything. One day, it happened that they saw him coming. Their house is on the other side of the arroyo, so they went along in the streambed and came out ahead of him, since he was walking slowly. They were running at full speed, armed, and they came out ahead of him. They are very good at running through the countryside.

"How good did it feel when you killed my father?" one of Arturo's sons asked him.

"Me?"

"Yes, you," he said. "It felt real good, didn't it? Well, now you're going to find out what it feels like." And, bam! Arturo's sons shot him right in the forehead and left him there dead.

It was greed over coffee land that also led to the death of my compadre Emiliano in Yaitepec. After the price of coffee went up a lot in 1950, my compadre Emiliano began to plant a lot of coffee on the land he had in Las Placitas. It was land that his father had left him. He had already taken possession of it. His father had already shown him where his was. Emiliano's father must have got it from his father. Soon after, a woman called María del Refugio Rojas from Juquila, the widow of a Rogelio who had died in jail and who was the uncle of Saúl Amado Ríos, Yaitepec's presidente, sold Emiliano the land Rogelio had had in Las Placitas.

This Saúl Amado wanted to grab the land that his uncle Rogelio had left. But as María del Refugio had sold it to Emiliano, a hatred entered him. He said that Emiliano hadn't bought it but had just grabbed it.

"Of course I bought it," Emiliano told me. "I have the papers in which she sold it to me." Well, at times even I had doubts about my compadre

Emiliano, but no, it wasn't so. She had sold it to him.[6] But Saúl Amado hated him intensely. It was out of bitterness over this land that Saúl set the people against Emiliano so they would kill him.

I knew that Saúl Amado had a deep hatred of Emiliano, but he couldn't do anything to Emiliano because his attempts to be macho were met with calamity. Just before he left office as presidente he began to mistreat some of Emiliano's compadres up there, sons of the brother of Blas Solis. Well, the sons of this friend are killers, and one of them said, "Because you're the presidente you think you can do anything. You may be presidente, but you are worth nothing." They were standing on the edge of a cliff. They gave him a kick and a shove, and over he went, breaking his tailbone. This blow did him a lot of damage. His hair has turned white. The surprise that they gave him turned him into an old man.

He wanted to be very macho too and came away with his tail between his legs. They put him in his place. He still wanted to get Emiliano, but Emiliano wouldn't let him. When he heard that Saúl Amado was going around with his lies, Emiliano armed his supporters out there in the mountains. This made Saúl afraid. I learned this from Saúl Amado. He told me that Emiliano had threatened to shoot him. "This land isn't his," Saúl said. "It was ours, from my father and my uncles, but since my uncle's wife sold it to him, what remedy is there?"

The foundation of all these killings is coffee. All of them were due to jealousy over this land, which Emiliano covered with coffee. Saúl Amado stirred up the people against Emiliano a lot while he was presidente. His word, of course, had power then. He began to influence people. He started to tell lies about Emiliano. He accused him of being a cacique in the pueblo because he didn't hand over the presidente's seal. And that was the reason they began to get stirred up. Yes, he wouldn't give it to them. But then they began to work on him. They told me, "It was his fault. It was because of Emiliano's own politics that he was having problems."[7]

This is what I found out from my godson Antonio Hernández. Sometimes I can dig the truth out of him, and sometimes he denies it to me. Antonio told me that Saúl Amado had made two trips to Oaxaca, trying to get himself re-elected as presidente for another term.

"This Saúl is crazy," Antonio said to me. "What does he believe? Doesn't he know that the law won't allow it? That's why it says there 'no re-election.' Doesn't he know the meaning of effective suffrage? No re-election?"

This is to say that once one has served as the authority, one cannot be re-elected to another term. This came about because in the epoch before they overthrew Don Porfirio Díaz, they put him up as presidente every year or two for thirty-three or thirty-five years. That is why this friend can't stand for re-election.

"But why is he going to go against you," I asked Antonio, "when you have the papers in your hand? He doesn't even know how to read and couldn't if he wanted to."

"True," said Antonio, "but he's making good money there whenever there's a fine and doesn't give a cent to the alcalde, the regidor, the síndico, or worse, to me. He doesn't even take account of me." According to Antonio, Saúl made a lot of money. He took advantage of the people of Yaitepec, so they had to deal him a blow to get even for the money that he had taken from the pueblo. He didn't use it for any public work, he just pocketed it.

Of course, this Antonio Hernández is a real rat too. That is his trade. He has grown accustomed to all kinds of robbery and killing. He had a group that he would send to kill and ask for money. If they paid, they would let them live, but if not, they would kill them. I've spoken to him before, and I've spoken to him even now. "If you can control the people, Antonio," I said to him, "why do you let them do these deeds?"

"I can't stop them, padrino," he replied. "What deeds? I haven't done anything? I can't do anything."

I remembered, and said to myself, Why am I talking to this brute, since it was he who organized a band of thieves there in order to go and kill people and ask them for money? Finally, he even killed a poor pregnant woman.[8]

Well, first they killed Emiliano's son Siriaco. I asked Julia, the killer's aunt, "Why did your nephew do this to his uncle? Why did he kill his cousin? Emiliano is your own family. They say a son of Elvira killed him. Why did he do this to his own family?"

"Ay, brother! It's not true," she said. "This son of Emiliano was going to kill him. Siriaco had taken his rifle and was going to shoot him. He took his rifle away from him and killed him with it. Siriaco was going to kill him, but he turned the tables."

Then, after the nine days of mourning for his son, my compadre Emiliano went to Oaxaca and to Veracruz to leave his other son, Valeriano. My godson Salomón stayed behind. He just stepped aside. He won't get involved for anything. He didn't even go to his father's funeral.[9]

"No," he said to me, "I don't want them to pull me into it, Godfather."

"Don't get involved, son," I said to him, "because they may kill you out of distrust."

"Well, if they want to kill me," he said, "they'll do it, because they like to. But there is God, and He knows that I won't get involved. I don't go with my father anywhere. I don't go around armed. I don't attend fiestas. I'm at my house or at my work, and that's it. I walk on the path, out there in the mountains. I go to my fields with two or three kids and two hands to help me work. I don't like it this way."

"That's all right," I said. "Be careful." He's my godson of baptism. I told him, "Be careful, because things aren't good."

The other day, he came to visit me. "May God protect you," I said to him.

"I'm asking God to protect you that He may deliver you from evil, because you're not a bad person."

"Yes, Godfather," he said, "I don't get involved with anyone. I don't drink. I don't go out in the street. Right now, I'm a godfather of a marriage. Here's a girl I'm taking to be wed. We've already gone to the pueblo, but the fiesta is going to be tomorrow. Only my wife is going to go. I'm not going."

"Don't go." I said, "Because of drink or this or that you might provoke someone into a fight."

"Yes, I know. That's why I'm not going. I don't go anywhere, so no one will pull me into anything."

That's what the poor fellow's doing. May God grant that he is able to, because things are serious, and he has his family to care for.

Then my compadre Emiliano went to Zacatepec. He was on his way to leave his son there one night and came through the plaza in Juquila. He stopped in the shop and said to me, "Compadre, how are you?"

"Fine, compadre, and you?"

"Well, I'm just out for a stroll."

But I was afraid that they were going to ambush him because he walked around with much confidence, so I said to him, "Look, compadre, those people hate and distrust you because they killed your son. They distrust you because there in your pueblo they have the custom that if there are two or three men in a family, they won't rest until they finish them all off. You shouldn't be going around. Moreover, I don't know how you stand with the police here. They might catch you by surprise and put you in jail, and I don't want this. You had better hide yourself for awhile, compadre." Well, that was over. I gave him a shot of mescal, and he set out for Zacatepec.[10]

He lived there for a while, but he must have thought, Why should I be hiding here? I've been powerful there. But I never talked to him again. After that, he went back and forth between Yaitepec and Zacatepec, but he finally returned to Yaitepec. The next thing I knew he was in Yaitepec.[11]

I asked Salomón, "Well, and my compadre? What is he thinking? Why did he go back to Yaitepec again? Isn't he worried that they might try to harm him, that they might do something to him?"

"Ay, Godfather," he says, "it's over. Things will remain the way they are."

"Are you sure, Salomón?"

"Yes, Godfather, it's over."

Little by little, one heard less and less. Things had almost died down completely when suddenly they killed Emiliano. They say that he was lighting a candle at the gate to his house on the side that is above the church. There he was lighting a candle, probably for these devotions they have so no enemy will enter to do them harm. That is what he was doing when they killed him. He died and they buried him. The days passed and Salomón didn't get involved.

A while later, I learned that Emiliano's son Valeriano, who had been in Veracruz, had come back. A short while later he was the comandante, as they say. Antonio told me, "It's a good thing they killed Emiliano's son. He was going around with some fifteen armed men, Godfather. He was frightening all the people. They were hiding in their houses."

His very friends had betrayed him. The day before, they had gone to eat with the son of a woman who lives above the cemetery there. Valeriano was going around with this kid and one of his other followers. The two of them took him one day to drink and the next day to eat over there. Then what happened was that they realized how the land was and everything, and his very friends killed him. They cut out his heart and stuffed it in his mouth. They did it to mock him, because his heart was macho; because he was brave and wasn't afraid. That is why they cut out his heart and stuffed it in his mouth. They say he was very fierce, and I suppose that is why they did it.[12]

My sister Chica, the poor woman, has really suffered. Three hard blows they gave her. They killed two sons and her husband.

Epilogue

The last years of Don Fortino's life, like his first years, were filled with sadness and pain. He was ill, and like King Lear, he felt abandoned. The following is the last letter Don Fortino wrote to me before he died. It is a fitting epilogue for the final chapter of his life.

Dear Compadre,

By way of this present letter, I wish to greet you with my hope that it finds you and your family well. I am still here, thanks to God, but continue to be ill with something I just can't seem to get rid of. As a result, I am in very poor health and am very weak in my lower extremities (my legs). I don't even have the strength to walk from the house to my shop and back. So I don't go out; I am here in the house. I do the little I can by taking some medicine the doctor prescribed. Besides the weakness I feel, I itch all over the trunk of my body. My stomach is upset, and I have pain in my bladder.

My luck has been bad ever since my wife abandoned me when our son died. Today, as always, she is off enjoying herself; my daughters have abandoned me too. They live off me, but none of them will lift a finger to help me. They are all too busy to come see me. After all that I have done for them—wearing myself out with so many sacrifices, never abandoning them—I am worn out after so many years of this. I won't be unhappy when my hour comes. My only regret is that I never was the object of their affection, though I suffered so much for them.

May God grant me life to see you again. With a warm embrace and my best wishes that God may give you the best. That is all your compadre, who holds you in great esteem, says.

Juquila, 28th of February, 1986

Part II

EXPLANATIONS OF

RURAL VIOLENCE IN

MEXICO

Chapter 13

EXPLANATIONS OF

VIOLENCE

The homicide rates in the District of Juquila are among the highest in Mexico and range from sixteen to twenty-nine times the national average.[1] These cold facts, however, only tell the magnitude of the problem; they do not express its human side. Murder is such a common event in the region that it affects everyone. Everyone has lost kin, friends, and neighbors to its deadly transactions. Like cancers, the conflicts that underlie the bloodshed have complex etiologies. Understanding violence is no easy task, even for those to whom it is a fact of daily life. In the heat of conflict, their perception of violence is distorted by denial, ideology, and passion. Even such thoughtful and intelligent native observers as Don Fortino at times offer either simplistic or ideological explanations for the violence in their communities. I should note that the interpretations social scientists provide are often just as ideological or reductionist. Neither Don Fortino's narrative nor the variety of explanations social scientists offer can be taken at face value. To make their biases and limitations explicit, they need to be examined carefully.

Don Fortino's Explanations

When I asked Don Fortino about the causes of violence in Juquila, his answer began with the economic resources people fight over, such as cattle and land, and focused on the problems caused by the introduction of coffee as a cash crop on communal lands. He also pointed out the ethnic and class dimensions of the roles that outsiders have played in the violence dividing these villages: "Native sons are denied lots," he said, "while rich outsiders have the money to grab them." He blamed much of the violence and faction-alism in the district on battles between caciques who are trying to hold onto land or control of the coffee trade. He underlined the frustration Indians and poor peasants feel when injustices cause them to take the law into their own hands. Among the factors he named that contribute to homicide was the widespread acquisition of guns made possible by the money from coffee. Don Fortino also linked alcohol to violence and believed that macho ideol-ogy was a cause of bloodshed in this context. Lastly, he connected character to violence. He saw violence as a result of stupidity or a lack of culture or education. He believed that it stems from a hot temper; from jealousy, envy, or a criminal character; or simply from having become accustomed to doing evil deeds. As this capsule summary shows, Don Fortino's understanding of violence is fairly complex. To explain violence he employs a mix of material, social, political, and psychological factors. If we are to understand the ideo-logical aspects of his account, however, we must examine how he uses them in greater detail.

Conflicts Over Land

Fortino's vision of the violence that afflicts the region begins with the observation that homicide was a rare occurrence before the Revolution.[2] Murders, he states, did not become commonplace until people started to plant coffee on communal lands and greedy individuals grabbed and fenced large tracts of land. To stake their claims, they planted coffee trees around the perimeter of their land. This left others precious little room to plant either corn or coffee, and their reaction was violence. As Fortino notes, the municipal authorities have not been able to make an equitable redistribution of the land, as this would lead to even more bloodshed.

Because the privatization of village land runs counter to communal values of egalitarianism, Fortino uses morally loaded terms to talk about the open-ing of the communal lands to coffee. He regards the resulting land grab as being motivated by simple human greed. In casting his explanation of vio-lence in these terms, he both subsumes a complex process and reduces it to human motivation.

The introduction of coffee, I should mention, did not merely distort the distribution of communal lands; it also led to basic changes in land tenure. Because coffee trees are a long-term investment, coffee parcels have become a defacto form of private property that is bought and sold within the community, although supposedly not to outsiders. Where traditional access to land had been based on usufruct rights and inheritance, this new form of land tenure, where rights could be sold, in effect disinherited large groups of people. As people with money began to buy and accumulate land, the "disinherited" were left with the feeling that the buyers had stolen the land from them. Moreover, boundary conflicts abounded. Since the slash-and-burn techniques used to plant corn require long fallow periods, these new claims inevitably encroached on areas to which other members of the community believed they had usufruct rights.

Ethnic and Class Conflict

Fortino also observes that these conflicts over communal lands have class and ethnic dimensions. As the lands have become de facto private property, the restrictions that limited access to them to native sons have been eroded. In discussing the problems in San Juan Lachao, Teotepec, and Panixtlahuaca, Fortino notes that rich outsiders used their political connections, knowledge, and money to deprive native sons of their communal lands. To deny one access to land is tantamount to depriving one of livelihood. Since Indians lack the political clout and familiarity with the courts to recover their lands through legal means, Fortino argues that they have turned to violence to defend their interests. In painting this as a conflict between poor native sons and rich mestizo outsiders, Fortino not only affirms the egalitarian norms of Indian society but also denies the seriousness of the conflicts among its own members. His picture of mestizo outsiders against native sons also exaggerates ethnic lines of conflict. As mestizos and Indians have migrated to and raised families in Juquila, the distinction he makes between insiders and outsiders has been blurred. The reality is that these categories are manipulated to justify or deny claims to communal resources. Fortino is a good example. Though he says his father was a "rich mestizo," he claims he is a native son, not merely because he was born in the village and because his mother was a Chatino woman, but also because he performed those material services—labor drafts and service in community offices—required of its citizens.

Fortino uses the doctrine of being a native son to legitimize his claims to land as against those of wicked and greedy outsiders. When the people of the Barrio Grande invade his cornfield and cut down the fence, Fortino blames this incident on Lázaro Sánchez, an outsider who stirred up the people against him. By holding Sánchez personally responsible for the invasion, in effect Fortino dismisses the pueblo's interest in defending its communal lands. In justifying the size of his cornfield, he is at great pains to distinguish his claim from the underhanded schemes used by outsiders to appropriate large tracts of communal land for themselves. Fortino claims the usufruct rights of a native son and argues that his field was not really that large. He was not greedy; he had not taken "enough land for five or ten people." He had established usufruct rights by clearing, planting, and fencing the field. He had followed legal precedents, petitioning the *presidente municipal* for a title. It was granted, and his claim was formalized.

Fortino argues that, in contrast, outsiders like Sánchez had grabbed communal lands through chicanery. While presidente, for instance, Sánchez had the municipal archives, which contained all the land records, placed in the prison to be used for toilet paper. Having destroyed the archives, he claimed to have title to El Rancho Viejo. Transformations of land tenure may legally be made on a small scale, but large-scale transformations require extralegal maneuvers and are likely to lead to violent confrontations. So, when Sánchez's son-in-law, a native son, tried to fence El Rancho Viejo (the first step in laying claim to it as private property), the pueblo invaded the rancho and cut the fences. According to Fortino, they would have killed Sánchez's son-in-law had they found him. Fear of violence has had its desired effect. Although they supposedly have a title, as Fortino observes, the owners have not pressed their claim, because they continued to enjoy usufruct rights to the property as members of the community.

Coffee has promoted not just a struggle over land but also, as Fortino contends, a struggle over trade. The coffee trade is unusually lucrative.[3] Even at the local level, coffee buyers amass considerable fortunes. Those who control the coffee trade at regional or state levels are wealthy by any standard in the world. For instance, the wealth of Don Genaro, a major coffee exporter in Oaxaca, includes some seven coffee plantations in the district of Juquila. He has vast real estate holdings in the city of Oaxaca, including the five-story Sears Building. He owns ships to transport coffee to the United States and, until his son was killed in an air crash, even owned an airline. Because great profits are to be had, especially where competition can be eliminated, coffee buyers will literally fight to control local markets. Because peasant coffee growers depend on credit from buyers and land-poor peasants turn to plantation owners for work, the relationship between competing patrons and their clients often splits communities into factions. This is why Fortino contends that the introduction of coffee created the same structural contradictions in every pueblo in the district. Where coffee has been planted, Fortino holds, the attempt by elites to dominate local politics produces the factionalism that ends in the division of these communities.

As attractive as it is to blame the feuding and factionalism in Juquila, Yaitepec, Nopala, Panixtlahuaca, Teotepec, and San Juan Lachao on the mestizo elites, this is a half-truth that minimizes the conflicts that exist among members of the community. To use the example of the conflict over Fortino's cornfield again, even if Sánchez was motivated by personal animosity, his involvement in the movement against Fortino was very likely a response to popular demand. By casting the conflict in personal terms, Fortino deflects our attention away from the tendency of elites to throw their weight behind popular causes to build political support.

Notwithstanding these qualifications, I would argue that to gain and maintain political and economic control in local communities, these competing elites act much like a mafia. Where they are in competition, they are willing to use their money and their business and political connections to back one faction or another in disputes in order to build their political support. Since each dispute is a contest for power, however, if politics fails, caciques are not above assassinating their rivals or others who oppose them. As Fortino holds, splitting villages into opposing groups that orbit competing caciques continually engenders the nasty and long-lived feuds that deeply scar these communities.

The Role of Injustice

Fortino's denunciation of the system of justice is especially virulent. He holds that since people with money can buy and twist the law to suit their purpose, justice is worthless and people have no respect for the law. Since justice can be bought and sold, it has never existed for the poverty-stricken Indian. In an apology for the "criminal" violence in the countryside, Fortino contends that Indians turn to violence out of frustration, because they have no other means of defending their rights and claims. Moreover, he observes, in the countryside the authorities have no power. When crimes are committed, the law cannot protect those who testify against the accused from reprisals, so people are unwilling to become involved, and even authorities who attempt to mete out justice run the risk of becoming targets.

Although there is more than a grain of truth to Fortino's allegations, this explanation contains several oversimplifications. The problem is not merely that justice favors the wealthy but also that various notions of justice are in competition. The crux of the matter is that the state's laws and courts (which have been part of the instrumentality of domination from colonial times) are counterbalanced by indigenous principles of justice and local customs, and the state's definitions of law and crime often run counter to village notions of rights and justice. For instance, though villagers may not consider killing a witch to be a crime, the state would treat it as a homicide. Revenge killings are a similar matter, since they may be considered justified within village society. Not only do definitions of crimes diverge, but many conflicts are created, too, when state law is superimposed on traditional law. Conflicts over land and inheritance are a good example. Some claims to property are based on legal arguments, such as title, adverse possession, or the payment of taxes, while others are rooted in traditional concepts of the right of inheritance, usufruct, or communal tenure.

Finally, there is the question of what is justice. Indigenous conceptions of justice differ radically from those of the state.[4] In the district court, cases are presented according to strict rules of evidence. Judgments not only produce long jail terms and heavy fines but also define winners and losers in the legal process. By contrast, the principal concern of Chatino justice is the mediation and resolution of conflict. Thus the primary concern of Indian authorities is to understand the conflict. They encourage the litigants to re-enact their arguments and express their anger. Yet in the end the authorities seldom favor one side over the other. Instead, like marriage counselors, they attempt to reconcile the two sides. When they impose fines or jail sentences, the fines are never heavy nor the sentences long. Although by definition the state claims jurisdiction over all serious crimes, authorities in Indian communities rarely do more than the legally required minimum to bring even cases of murder to the attention of the state. In part this reflects conceptual differences in defining crimes, but it is also due to structural contradictions created by murders within the community. To act, even in the name of justice, against a murderer is to take sides in the dispute and to continue it. Instead, the position of Chatino authorities is that only God can punish a murderer. Moreover, as Fortino notes, Indians and mestizos do not enter the court on the same footing. This is not simply a matter of money; the social networks of mestizos and their familiarity with the state system give them the advantage.

The Role of Guns

Although his attack on the legal system is ferocious, Fortino is a believer in the system. His position is that of a proponent of law and order who argues that if justice existed, violence would disappear. Consistent with this view of the question, Fortino also blames violence on guns. He reasons that coffee money has allowed people to buy guns and that homicides have increased ever since. Although we must be careful not to blame the instrument for the crime, there is considerable support for Fortino's position. For example, in Yaitepec in the two decades before the introduction of coffee as a cash crop in 1950, homicide as a proportion of all incidents of violence varied between 21 and 22 percent. In the 1950s, as peasants began to buy guns, the total number of incidents remained about the same, but the proportion ending in homicide rose to 48 percent. By the 1960s this proportion had increased to 70 percent (Greenberg 1981:181). In short, although the rate of fighting appears to have been fairly constant,[5] guns have altered the outcome radically.

The Role of Alcohol

Just as blaming violence on guns is often used to avoid analyzing its social or economic basis (although Fortino is not guilty of this), linking violence to alcohol is also often a similar ploy. Fortino sees alcohol as a factor contributing to violence. In recalling how drinking would get him into tight spots, he argues that "shameless men in the heat of mescal reach the point of killing one another." This statement expresses the notion that alcohol diminishes one's inhibitions (i.e., shame) and contributes to violence. But since drinking patterns have not changed significantly, there is no evidence to suggest that alcohol is responsible for the increasing rates of homicide in Juquila. In any case, the question of whether alcohol lowers inhibitions or makes drunks aggressive is almost beside the point. Alcohol provides a culturally accepted excuse for violence. Since diminished capacity is recognized even in law, drinking may be to some extent a deliberate prelude to violence. Moreover, holding alcohol responsible for violence shifts attention away from the history of disputes and away from the substantive issues that lead to incidents, which makes possible the restoration of the status quo ante.

The Role of Machismo

In blaming violence on killers who go around "celebrating this work, saying 'I'm very macho,'" Fortino strongly implies that he sees this behavior as a perverse inversion of the meaning of ritual, work, and manhood. In the context of drinking, macho ideology, with its attendant codes of never "cracking" or backing down, may transform any discord into a matter of defending one's honor and masculinity (Paz 1961:30). In order to restore one's tarnished honor the adversary must be humbled, so a confrontation between "machos" leaves little or no alternative to violence. As romantic as it may be to personalize violence in this way, this explanation functions much like blaming violence on alcohol. It serves to distract attention from any substantive issues that may underlie conflict.

The Role of Human Character

In this sense, blaming violence on machismo is a species of psychological reductionism that seeks to condense the various dimensions of conflict to basic feelings like jealousy or envy. Fortino invokes "criminal character" or "habit" to explain the organized violence of groups led by Lázaro Sánchez, José Próspero, Gustavo Venegas, Angel Aguirre, and Antonio Hernández. By saying, as Fortino does of Sánchez, "He became accustomed to doing evil deeds during the Revolution and continued to do them afterward," he reduces the complex issues behind conflicts to individual deviance. Another form of reductionist explanation often invoked by mestizos to explain violence is the racial stereotype.

Although Fortino does not resort to them, these racist interpretations hold that Indian blood is violent. Accordingly, Indians are said to be capable of greater feeling and more passionate hatred than non-Indians, or their violence is explained as being due to their stupidity or lack of education (Romanucci-Ross 1973:101). Again, I would note that if conflict can be blamed on the feelings or deviant behavior of individuals, then nothing need be done to alter the fundamental social or economic structures that determine the status quo.

The Role of Egalitarian Ideology

Among the recurring motifs expressed in Fortino's thinking about violence is an egalitarian ideology that consistently downplays the disjunction of the interests and inequalities that exist within the community (see Jayawardena 1968). Such egalitarianism continually declares "We are all poor, humble people here," and emphasizes themes of cooperation, reciprocity, sameness, and "brotherhood" (Greenberg 1981:198). This doctrine repeatedly distorts Fortino's perception of conflict. Seen from this perspective, his blaming violence on rich outsiders or on individual deviance, greed, envy, and jealousy is an egalitarian denial of internal struggles. It is an assertion of village solidarity. By overdrawing the ethnic and class lines in these struggles (that is, by saying that the problem lies with the rich mestizo outsiders, who have taken advantage of the poor Indian native sons), attention is directed away from the extent to which villagers' interests often radically diverge. Rather than admit the seriousness of internal conflicts, which would undermine the basis of cooperation within the community, Fortino underplays the substantive issues dividing people and instead invokes specific agents such as alcohol or guns as being the cause of violence. Even when he talks about factionalism, he will not admit that these struggles reflect real divisions within the community. Rather, he portrays these battles as a result of a cult of personality. Although the political battles between elites often take the form of contests between political parties, Fortino does not talk about struggles between competing parties or political ideologies. He talks of fights between caciques. In essence, he sees them as nothing more than reflections of personal conflicts between members of the elite. Since admitting that groups within the village have radically divergent interests would seriously erode daily social interactions among them and further polarize the community, Fortino repeatedly looks to individual motivation or deviance as a means of dismissing violent acts.

Although this ideology distorts Fortino's vision of current conflicts, in a larger sense his insights are a fairly accurate reflection of the historical advance of capitalist forms of investment: in this case, the problems within the community stem from mestizo-dominated activities.

Social Science Explanations

The factors that social scientists have proposed to explain the homicide and violence in rural Mexican communities include many of the elements that Fortino employs in his own reasoning and so are prone to the same criticisms.[6] Even more fundamental biases arise from the social scientists' methodological approach and choice of units of analysis.[7] These methodological biases lead many social historians to dissect history or the social body into separate economic, political, religious, ideological, psychological, and structural parts. Rather than seeing these as aspects of complex historical processes unified in the actions and relations among people, they tend to reify these categories. Too often they treat them as if they were concrete entities that may be analyzed separately. Unfortunately, once dissected, the living society cannot be resurrected from the corpse. The relations among its parts—for instance, among the political, religious, and ideological aspects of economic relations—are easily lost. For example, investigators who use social psychological theories of criminality or psychoanalytical approaches commonly try to explain violence in terms of individual deviance (see Fromm and Maccoby 1970). They usually blame deviance and crime on broken homes, troubled families, child abuse, lax discipline, or alcoholic parents (Bacon, Barry, and Child 1963; McCord and McCord 1959). These investigators, however, seldom ask the larger question: Why are these families' relations pathological? Often they ignore factors such as class, interethnic relations, or glaring differences in wealth, all of which may be important in determining deviance. Since they believe that the roots of deviance lie within the family, it does not matter to them if an individual is a Zapotec, a Hindu, or a Bushman. It is irrelevant whether he or she lives in a capitalist or a socialist country. The ideological implications of this approach are that if deviance is caused by a pathology within the family unit, then society is not at fault. And even if society is not entirely blameless, no social reforms are required. Rather, it is the individual who needs help in adjusting.

Psychological Approaches

In Mexico this kind of approach has been used by a group of social scientists interested in the question of why some Zapotec communities in

Oaxaca have high homicide rates. In their studies they characterize some towns as violent and others as antiviolent.[8] Typically, these studies assume that the towns, aside from their contrasting homicide rates, are comparable. The investigators argue that since the villages "share biological inheritance, culture, language, climate, ecology, poverty, boundary disputes, and abundant use of alcohol with their neighbors, such factors may be disregarded as determining either violence or antiviolence" (Paddock 1975:217). These assertions of sameness, however, are never tested. For instance, the authors do not look carefully at the correlation between homicide and man–land ratios or the quality of the land; they do not examine whether their participation in the market economy is really equivalent; and so on. Instead, they are intent on relating differences in homicide rates to differences in child-rearing practices between communities. The evidence for this argument, however, is weak. Even in towns classified as non-violent there are dramatic shifts in homicide rates over time (Kappel 1978; Paddock 1982). If differences in violence were related to child-rearing practices, then one would expect differences in homicide rates between them to be constant. If anything, these authors have the causal arrow backward. If there are systematic differences in child-rearing practices, it is more likely that they are reflections of different levels of violence due to stresses caused by changes in the politico-economic niche of these communities in the region rather than the other way around.

Structuralist Approaches

One alternative is to explain conflict and violence in terms of the social structure of the community.[9] From this perspective, according to Selby, society rather than the individual "is seen as the 'villain' in the sense that it is set up so as to produce conflicts between certain categories of people" (1974:96). The problem of explaining violence becomes one of simply understanding "how customary arrangements in society may themselves generate tensions and conflict" (Selby 1974:96). For instance, Romanucci-Ross tries to show how conflict, violence, and morality are woven into the village social structure (1973:viii). Similarly, Nash (1967) tries to explain the increasing homicide rate in a Mayan village in terms of changing social structures within the community. She notes that new enterprises have caused a shift in power in the community away from the old curers and toward young, literate civil authorities. This has generated conflicts between them. As interesting as these works are, their decision to focus their analysis within the community means that their explanations of violence are too narrow. They tend to neglect the complex set of relations and processes that link the village to the wider society and so downplay the often-contradictory pressures on the community.

Cultural Idealism

Cultural idealists, who seek to explain violence in terms of cultural values, also concentrate their attention on the community or group. George Foster, a leading proponent of this approach, proposes that conflict among Mexican peasants flows from an "image of limited good" that they have "in their heads." This notion leads them to assume that "all good things in life exist in limited and unexpandable quantities" (1967:12). Since in their view of the world "all desired things in life such as land, other forms of wealth, health, friendship, love, manliness, honor, respect, power, influence, security, and safety *exist in absolute quantities insufficient even to fill the minimal needs of villagers. . . . [I]t follows that an individual or a family can improve its position only at the expense of others*" (Foster 1967:123–124; italics are Foster's). In other words, Foster contends that conflict follows logically from a cultural set of understandings that sees the world as a zero-sum game in which one person's gain is another's loss. He goes on to argue that this view has led peasants to adopt an egalitarian ideology that "limited goods" should be equitably shared. To insure this, they have evolved a set of mechanisms to maintain the status quo in balance or equilibrium by pulling back to the level of the rest those individuals who acquire more than their share of "limited good" (Foster 1967:12). These "leveling mechanisms," which ensure shared poverty, include forced participation in fiesta systems, gossip, envy as a symbolic form of aggression, and witchcraft. Ultimately, homicide is the final sanction. Since to stand out from the crowd, Foster argues, invites attack, the ideal man or woman avoids drawing attention to any betterment in his position by simulating continued poverty, "lest envious people be tempted into aggressive acts" (Foster 1967:13).

The biases in Foster's rendering of the "image of limited good" are not confined to his narrow focus on a community or group. They also flow from his projection onto peasants of a capitalist model of extreme individualism as a zero-sum game. This model distorts the character of the indispensable cooperation among them. It implies that cooperation is only motivated by individual self-interest. As Taussig notes, asserting that Mexican peasants believe that all good things in life exist in finite and short supply "is nothing more than the assertion of the principle of scarce resources, incorporated as an axiom in modern economic theory originally developed in and applied to capitalist organization" (1980:15). Part of the problem with Foster's analysis is that he confounds the clash of two socioeconomic orders in his unitary model of "limited good."[10] The problem is not one of an "image of limited good" in the heads of peasants. Rather, the problem is that a capitalist order based on private property, individualism, and accumulation is intrinsically incompatible with a more indigenous order based on cooperation and communal property, in which coalitions between peasants underwrite individual and family security by emphasizing obligations of reciprocity (Gregory 1975:83). Although Foster links the "image of limited good" historically to colonialism, he fails to understand that the behaviors he describes are responses to the expansion of capitalism per se, that "the two orientations involve completely different sets of values" (Gregory 1975:83). Foster's analysis confuses the egalitarian aspects of behavior as a defense against capitalism with individualism appropriate to the market economy. He fails to recognize that in the context of the larger capitalist economy, opportunities come to individuals, not to communities or classes. So, despite the defensive values of the community, as more and more men choose these new alternatives, which violate communal norms of cooperation (namely generosity and reciprocity), conflicts erupt within the community.[11]

Historical Approaches

In sharp contrast to the cultural idealists, writers who apply historical approaches commonly talk about violence in the Mexican countryside in terms of the penetration of capitalism and class conflict.[12] In broad terms, this thesis, which has many variants, argues that although Indian communities may be mere cogs within a national and even international capitalist system and although they may have been profoundly transformed by their relationship with capitalism, they are not themselves replicas of that system (Taussig 1980:183). Instead, the argument goes, conflict in these communities is grounded in a clash between the trajectories of two distinct civilizations. It emanates from their attempt to defend a whole way of life from the ravages of capitalist trade and labor relationships, which threaten to alienate their lands and atomize the very social ties on which they depend for survival. During the colonial period, Indian communities erected sets of social and cultural barriers to inhibit capitalist forms of investment and social differentiation (Wolf 1955, 1957; Carrasco 1961). Accordingly, both collective and individual forms of violence are responses to the fissuring of these defenses by an unceasing capitalist assault. Historically, where these threats are clearly perceived as emanating from the outside, communities have responded with protests, riots, and revolts to defend their interests. Similarly, homicides, blood feuds, and factionalism from this perspective are the outcome of external pressures, which introduce contradictions that produce conflicts within the community.[13]

The biases in historical interpretations arise from differences in the stress placed on the process of capitalist penetration. To the degree that external factors are held to be responsible for violence, the role that internal factors play in conflicts is denied or ignored.[14] At a deeper level, these prejudices lie in the various visions authors have of the historical process itself. On the one hand, some authors are inclined to see this process as being fairly slow. They see "traditional" Indian societies as having been pushed into isolated "regions of refuge," where they survive until forces of modernization pull them into the mainstream economy.[15] Other writers interested in the evolution of world systems push this process back to the conquest and argue that capitalism rapidly transformed the entire indigenous world (Frank 1969, 1978; Wallerstein 1974, 1979). In this view, little in Indian society is "traditional." Even the so-called defenses against capitalist penetration are cynically seen as primarily colonial devices that suck labor and capital out of these communities and into Spanish enterprises (Harris 1964). The issue, however, is not simply when Indian societies were transformed but how profoundly.

I have my own ax to grind in this regard. If one views the historical expansion of capitalism as a uniform process, then one is likely to sin in the direction of a complete and utter transformation. If one approaches it piecemeal, looking just at its local manifestations, one is likely to overestimate its indigenous content. My own view is that the metal of indigenous society has been repeatedly heated and reformed into new shapes on the anvils of the colonial and capitalist systems. In the following chapter I argue that although the expansion of capitalism has fundamentally altered many aspects of Chatino culture, the Chatino effort to cope with the unaccustomed varieties of exploitation implicit in the new socioeconomic order has not been passive. In this process, although the Chatino have repeatedly altered colonial and national institutions to meet such needs, their "defenses" have been only partially successful. Each defensive accommodation made to the dominant society only temporarily mediates the fundamental conflict between the two systems. In the end, each new compromise has generated new contradictions within the community, deepening its conflicts.

Chapter 14

THE HISTORICAL

DIMENSIONS OF

CONFLICT

The high rates of homicide in the district of Juquila are not simply the result of interpersonal squabbles, sexual jealousies, or drunken brawls —though these make their contribution. Instead, they are the product of a variety of conflicts that exist in the region, including boundary disputes between communities, struggles over communal land between communities and private landowners, fights over land inheritance between individuals and families, conflicts caused by cattle invading fields or being stolen, ethnic tensions between different Indian groups or between Indians and mestizos, various class conflicts and factional struggles among local and national elites for political control and economic power, protests of the abuse of power by authorities, and bitter divisions among the barrios of a community.

Many of these conflicts are reactions to the penetration and development of capitalist formations. This is not to say that pre-Hispanic states were any less conflict-ridden. Rather, it indicates that the historical roots of these conflicts often lie in the confrontation of two cultures with dissimilar political and economic premises. In the pre-Hispanic world, survival was a corporate enterprise. Access to land, labor, and goods was locked up in social relationships and was distributed through elaborate state-administered systems of tribute and redistribution. As the Spanish and Indian worlds collided, the essential premises of the mercantile world turned all things—resources, land, and labor—into market commodities that could be individually owned and appropriated. Inevitably, the lines of strain between and within institutions of pre-Hispanic and colonial origin generated conflicts. In Oaxaca, for example, conflicts between local communities and ethnic groups are in part a legacy of warring pre-Hispanic states and in part the result of Spanish colonial policies of indirect rule. To segregate and separate Indian communities as political entities, the Spanish recognized their often-overlapping territorial claims and set them against one another. In this process, although the Spanish colonial system introduced new forms of government and economy, older forms were not completely destroyed. Thus in the district of Juquila there is a long history of confrontations between the Spanish colonial concepts of private property and law, and indigenous notions of communal property and justice, which play themselves out in land disputes within and between communities.

Preconquest Forms of Domination

Among the lasting legacies of the pre-Hispanic states is Oaxaca's political and ethnic fragmentation. With 572 municipios, or counties, Oaxaca has both the largest Indian population and the greatest number of municipios of any state in Mexico. There are some fifteen families of languages spoken by Indians in the state. Each is in turn divided into several mutually unintelligible languages or distinct dialects. Chatino, for example, includes three languages, within which each village speaks its own distinctive dialect. Although this fragmentation is due in part to colonial policy, its origins lie in the nature of pre-Hispanic states.

Pre-Hispanic States

At the time of the Spanish conquest, Oaxaca's fractured landscape of mountains and valleys was the home of numerous petty warring states. These states were typically ruled by a head town or city surrounded by its various subject hamlets in a single valley. A few powerful states, however, held dominion over several adjoining valleys. The body politic was governed by a hereditary lord, whose lineage not only furnished a corps of noble retainers, advisors, and assistants but also controlled the best lands.

At contact, the Chatino were subject to the coastal Mixtec kingdom of

Tututepec, one of the most powerful pre-Hispanic states in Oaxaca. Tututepec's domain spread along more than 200 kilometers of the Pacific coast of Oaxaca, from the frontier of Guerrero to the port of Huatulco. Under its control were not only Chatino but also Amuzgo, Mixtec, Nahua, and Zapotecan communities. Despite the number of groups under its sway, however, Tututepec could hardly be called a nation. This was not the kind of unitary political entity found in Europe. Instead, like the Aztec, Tututepec's tribute domain was composed of several semiautonomous petty states that either had been conquered by Tututepec's rulers or had formed alliances with them through marriage (Flannery and Marcus 1983:318).

Pre-Hispanic Systems of Production

Tututepec's wealth and power lay in tribute wrested from peasant farmers, who served in its armies, labored on public works, and produced in their swidden fields the staples that fed the empire. Not surprisingly, several features of slash-and-burn agriculture have a direct bearing on pre-Hispanic land tenure, social organization, and economy.

The Mixtec system of stratification had three primary ranks: noble, priest, and commoner. Each of these was linked to a different type of estate. Native lords, whom the Spanish called *caciques*, inherited not only rank but also landed estates, their *cacicazgo*. Similarly, the native nobility (*principales*), officials, temples, and religious cults were all provided lands (worked by peasants) and tribute. So long as they paid tribute, commoners had access to communal lands. Outside of the estate system there existed two other groups: serfs or tenants, and slaves. The former appear to have been landless laborers who worked on the estates of the elites. The slaves included those captured in battle and destined for the sacrificial knife, those sold into slavery for debt, and those born into the households of aristocrats (Spores 1967; Whitecotton 1977).

Before the introduction of European domestic animals, the only power that was available to plant fields, transport crops, or build anything was human labor. The cost of transporting tons of corn, for example, was high in human terms. This encouraged communities to be self-sufficient and affected the way tribute was extracted. Rather than move tons of corn long distances as tribute to native lords, labor was moved instead. The lord's lands, not only in Tututepec but also in his subject communities, were managed by *tequitlatos*, who acted as overseers for the system of rotating labor drafts that provided peasants to work the land (Martínez-Gracida 1907:84).

Because each community had to grow corn, beans, and squash for its subsistence, specialization in other kinds of crops or products was always a secondary affair. What specialized goods were produced usually were those required as tribute. Although each community provided for its own subsistence, the risk of crop failure was high. Not only were there the usual plagues of insects and the predation of animals, which might affect an individual field, but along the coast drought might destroy the entire crop. Similarly, a hurricane or simply too much rain in the mountains periodically destroyed the crop or drastically lowered yields. Because of the difficulties of transportation and the substantial risk of crop failure, pre-Hispanic communities were compelled to evolve cooperative mechanisms to share risks and redistribute goods. For instance, even though each married man had his own fields, the hard work of clearing trees, burning brush, and preparing fields required teamwork. Patrilineally extended families often shared a single large house or clustered into a group of dwellings. These extended households functioned as a cooperative economic unit, not only in normal production but also in times of stress, when the family members shared their stores with one another to reduce the effect of crop damage.[1]

The community also served as a kind of mutual insurance company designed to spread the risk of calamity more evenly among its members. One way it did this was through a communal system of land tenure, which gave peasants usufruct rights to communal lands. These rights were allocated to families for as long the field continued to yield. In farming systems based on slash-and-burn agriculture, however, yields drop markedly after the first year. After two or three years, fields must be abandoned and must lie fallow for periods of from ten to thirty years before they can be replanted. Under these conditions, there is little advantage, and considerable disadvantage, to private property. Instead, communal tenure allowed officials to reallocate land yearly to families according to their needs.

Although most of the land within the boundaries of a community was held in common, elites seem to have had private property. Native lords, nobles, officials, temples, and religious cults were allocated specific parcels of land, which were worked by peasant laborers under a system of labor drafts. The indigenous conception of private property, however, differed markedly from European notions. Tracts of land as such were not owned. Instead, one owned what was worth owning on them—wells, streams, quarries, salt beds, fishing lagoons—or any improvements to them, such as houses, cacao orchards, or fruit trees.[2] This property was not a commodity. It could not be freely transferred to another party. Rather, it was inherited along with a title or an office. Moreover, since nobles owned the valuable resources on the land rather than the land itself, the boundaries of these claims were vague. The imprecise way in which boundaries were defined was to become a problem that plagued Spanish colonial administrators, to whom such things mattered.

Pre-Hispanic Religious Systems

At an even more fundamental level, Indian attitudes toward nature and the land diverged radically from Spanish ones. Unlike European notions of economy, in which land, labor, and natural resources are merely factors in a system of production, the central premise of Tututepec's economy was that nature is a sacred, living entity. In this worldview, gods, animals, human beings, and ancestors formed an interdependent whole. The relations among them were projected onto nature, so that the mountain they climbed to bring the rains not only was thought to be the house of the rain god but also an extension of the god himself.

The ardor with which Indian peasant communities defended their land was based not merely on its economic value. For the peasant, land was more than a means of making a living; it was part of a sacred negotiation. His labors on it, and his rituals for it, were part of the reciprocities with the gods and the living forces that provided for him.

In this animate world, the active forces of nature were seen as alive and omnipresent, and being alive, they demanded careful and continuous attention. Balance in this world was precarious, and it depended upon maintaining the proper set of relations between gods and mortals. Every fifty-two years, when the cycles of the solar and ritual calendars repeated, "the universe reached a cosmic crisis which threatened its survival, and men waited with bated breath to see the sun rise again in the continuation of a new cycle that might yet guarantee life to mankind for another 52 years." (Wolf 1959:88–89). Ritual specialists were required to guarantee that reciprocities expressed in ritual between men, ancestors, and supernatural beings would be correctly fulfilled. Priests controlled the religious calendar, which translated cosmic movements—upon which the use of the environment, and life itself, depended—into social time. Control of the calendar gave the priesthood certain economic functions. They set the time for clearing new land, for planting, for weeding, and for harvest. By holding rituals to ensure a good harvest, each of these tasks was allied to religious activities. In a regime of slash-and-burn cultivation on communal land, priests probably played a part in assigning land to farmers and in regulating its reuse. Priests served not only as organizers of agricultural efforts but also as servants of the gods. They also administered the many offerings made by the faithful (Wolf 1959:81). The picture of Tututepec that emerges from this is that of a theocratic state in which priest-rulers and priests not only served their gods but also were "devotees of power, power over men, . . . capable of exacting labor and tribute, as well as worship from the mass of men" (Wolf 1959:78–79).

Pre-Hispanic Political Organization and Exchange

To offset the risks of agricultural failure, pre-Hispanic states also evolved a complex set of institutions, which redistributed goods within communities, tied them into a regional system of periodic markets, and linked states together through long-distance trade networks. The state played a central role in these systems of exchange. It collected the tribute, stored surpluses, and organized the religious rituals and festivals for the gods that underwrote redistribution. In the periodic markets, its judges ruled on exchanges. Its wars and elite marriages guaranteed the kingdom access to resources not available locally.

The system of tribute and redistribution was organized around the state's basic political units: the barrio, village, and state. Each barrio and village was ruled by a set of officials drawn either from the ruler's own lineage or, where subject states were ruled indirectly, from the ranks of the local nobility. The lords of Tututepec, for example, exercised three methods of political control over their domain. First, near Tututepec, the throne controlled a nucleus of villages directly. Second, some tributary states retained a certain degree of political autonomy, with hereditary rulers, governors, or tax collectors (Gerhard 1972:379–380). In these statelets, Tututepec's method was based on indirect rule. In such towns, the lords of Tututepec named the governor from among the town's highest nobility. The governor, in turn, placed a *principal* in each of the town's wards to govern the commoners and directed the collection of tribute (Paso y Troncoso 1905:243–244). The Chatino communities, whose ruling lineages had a long history of intermarriage with Tututepec's Mixtec rulers, almost certainly were governed in this fashion. Under the third form of political control—used in areas subjugated by force—Tututepec also appointed a member of the native elite to rule, but in addition it sent a nobleman to live in the town, and he collected the tribute and administered justice (Paso y Troncoso 1905:239).

In principle, the lord of Tututepec was the ultimate authority governing the community. He supervised labor, collected tribute, oversaw warfare, and administered justice. In practice, however, his power was limited by various aides, counselors, nobles, and priests, who helped govern the communities in the realm (Dahlgren de Jordán 1954:149–159).

The politico-religious hierarchies that governed these communities consisted of age-graded ladders of office. In these hierarchies, certain posts—such as principal, judge, governor, temple novice, priest, and head priest—were restricted to members of the nobility. In this theocratic society, the religious hierarchy was the key to advancement in other hierarchies. Children of the nobility entered temples or monasteries as novices at from five to seven years of age. There they observed the same rules as did priests:

chastity, abstinence, and long fasts before fiestas. At puberty they entered the priesthood as junior priests, presumably serving one of the lesser gods. After a period of service, they returned to normal life for a time before being recalled. At the top of this hierarchy, serving major deities, were the senior priests, who were so esteemed that the lords did nothing without their advice (Herrera y Tordesillas 1729:3:99). In fact, service as a priest was a basic prerequisite for all high posts, including those of the lord and his counselors (Dahlgren de Jordán 1954:230). The lord's counselors were old men who had served in the priesthood and also in a stipulated set of other public offices. This position was the last post in their ladder of offices, and they were highly respected and were consulted in all important matters.

Although tribute extracted from the peasantry supported these officials, their temples and palaces were not merely focal points where the costly goods and produce accumulated; the offices had redistributive functions as well. The ritual calendar scheduled a series of annual, or calendrical, fiestas, through which at least a portion of this wealth found its way back to the populace. There were also celebrations for special occasions, such as for victories, marriages, funerals, the recovery of the lord from an illness, and so on (Dahlgren de Jordán 1954:257–259). Wide distributions of goods are a feature of all the descriptions of these festivals and celebrations. The cost of these rituals, however, was not borne entirely by institutional coffers. Individuals sponsored certain fiestas, at least in part. Warriors, officials, merchants, artisans, or householders came to the ceremonial center to reside in the temple for a limited period and bore a major portion of the cost of the fiesta. They provided, among other things, slaves for sacrifice, contributions of pulque, copal, feathers, precious stones, and diverse animals (Dahlgren de Jordán 1954:240–259).

The major calendrical fiestas were important economically and politically. Because they were timed to coincide with stress points in the agricultural cycle, they afforded peasants the occasional luxury of eating meat and going to sleep on a full stomach. The fiestas were even more important politically, because they were a means of legitimizing the wealth and power of the elites who organized them.

The prestige of elites rested in part on their control of the system of redistribution, with all its sacred connotations, and in part on their administration of local marketplaces. It also rested on their ability to obtain, through either tribute or long-distance trade, resources not available locally. In fact, the problems associated with access to resources go a long way toward explaining pre-Hispanic warfare.

Pre-Hispanic Wars

Although wars were usually precipitated by ethnic slurs, the taking of women, insults to masculinity, or the killing of merchant-traders, warfare played an important role in a political and economic system of redistribution. In a landscape of mountains and valleys that was both politically divided and ecologically diverse, warfare furnished tribute and guaranteed access to the distinctive resources controlled by each subject community. Unlike European warfare, pre-Hispanic wars were seldom fought for land. In a system predicated on human labor for power, where labor was more valuable than land, the goal was to extract labor and tribute.

In these complex agricultural societies, tribute was a double-edged sword. It was both the economic base of systems of redistribution that unified states, and the object of conflicts between them. Tribute not only provided wealth that underwrote the system of redistribution that the native elites controlled, it also furnished the peasant-soldiers they used as pawns in their deadly games of shifting alliances and internecine warfare among states.

In the pattern of endemic conflicts that developed, the clashes were not only between neighboring states; royal marriages and webs of alliance also led to wars with distant states. For instance, at contact Tututepec was waging war with the Zapotec kingdom of Tehuantepec and was attempting to extend its empire into the Mixteca Alta. Since the Aztecs were also expanding into the Mixteca Alta, this brought Tututepec into repeated conflict with them. Shortly before the arrival of the Spanish, the armies of Tututepec halted an invading force to their north led by Moctezuma II (Gerhard 1972:163). Since warring states constantly vied with one another, few maintained supremacy for very long. Hostility was the rule rather than the exception, even among peoples speaking the same language.

If tribute was the basis of Tututepec's power, it was also the principal flaw in the web of its theocratic society. Towns subject to Tututepec often paid onerous tribute. In addition to labor and military support, they were compelled to provide foodstuffs such as corn, beans, chile, and honey, and such luxury items as gold, feathers, firewood, quail, copper bars and axes, jewels, cotton cloth, raw cotton, cochineal, and cacao. The burden of tribute in this loose-knit kingdom led to periodic uprisings by subject states. The Zapotec of Coatlán, for instance, repeatedly rebelled against Tututepec's rule (Berlin 1947:22). Because status and descent were the basis of access to land, labor, and tribute, the distribution of tribute not only bred resentments between communities but also may have sown the seeds of class antagonisms within the kingdom.

Although some of the tribute funneled into Tututepec from its subject towns was redistributed, most of this wealth remained there. What wealth did flow back benefited primarily the elites of the satellite communities. Although subject communities grew and prospered through their relationship with Tututepec, the center grew more quickly, more opulently, and more obviously. As the gap between Tututepec and its hinterland continued to widen, the very acts that guaranteed Tututepec its wealth and power generated profound internal contradictions, which it could only manage through coercion. In the end, the constant need to resort to force bred the deep internal tensions and rebellions upon which the Spanish conquistadores so readily capitalized (Wolf 1959:108).

Colonial Forms of Domination

The Initial Impact of the Conquest

In 1521 (two years after Hernán Cortés landed his small army of 555 men on the coast of Veracruz), Tenochititlán, the capital of the Aztec empire, fell. Playing off ancient enmities and pursuing the game of intrigue and alliance, Cortés's armies then moved south. By January 1522, Pedro de Alvarado had formed an "alliance" with Cosijopi, the lord of Tehuantepec, who furnished him with 24,000 warriors to move against Tututepec, Tehuantepec's old enemy up the coast. On March 4, Alvarado entered Tututepec (Cortés 1942:2:60). Events followed a familiar pattern. Alvarado discovered a plot to kill him and captured the lord of Tututepec, Coaxintechtli, and his son. Holding them for ransom, Alvarado obtained 25,000 pesos in gold before Coaxintechtli died in prison. During these events the lord of Tututepec died, which led some of the surrounding pueblos to rise in rebellion, though Alvarado soon restored the peace (Romero-Frizzi and Olivera B. de Vásquez 1973:232–233). Alvarado then managed to exact even more gold from the lord's son and heir, Ixta Quinutzin, whom he later baptized as Pedro de Alvarado (Smith 1973:83; Berlin 1947:42).

As in other parts of Mesoamerica, the conquistadores placed themselves at the apex of pre-Hispanic states by exploiting well-developed native institutions such as slavery, indirect rule, and a system of serfdom in which commoners paid tribute to local nobles and caciques in the form of goods and personal services, and did *tequio* work on community projects (Chance 1978:50). To divide and rule, the Spanish imposed the *encomienda* system, which partitioned and subdivided states into smaller and more easily controlled units. Following the subjugation of the Mixteca, Cortés divided the indigenous population into encomiendas or trusteeships to be administered by his companions and himself. As Gerhard points out, "Each native lord was placed with his subjects under the 'protection' of an *encomendero*, who was supposed to see to it that his charges became Christians and vassals of the Spanish king, in return for which he was entitled to their services and tribute" (1972:9).

As reward for his conquest of Tututepec, Cortés granted Alvarado a large encomienda there. Alvarado immediately began to collect tribute from the surrounding pueblos. His exploitation of the native populace, however, was so intense that a year after the conquest the Mixtec and their Chatino allies rose in rebellion. In Teotepec, the Chatino captured and killed forty Spanish soldiers (Martínez-Gracida 1907:30). Alvarado brutally suppressed this rebellion in 1523, again showing that his reputation for unlimited cruelty was well deserved. Pedro de Alvarado, however, did not enjoy the encomienda for very long. By 1526 Cortés was listing it among his own encomiendas. He also noted that the province of Tututepec rendered an annual tribute of 2,000 pesos in gold from its mines (Berlin 1947:26–27). In 1528 the Crown reclaimed Tututepec, almost certainly because of its famed wealth (Berlin 1947:26–27). Sometime between 1534 and 1544 the encomienda was assigned to Don Luis de Castilla, a kinsman of Cortés.[3] Such a reshuffling of encomienda grants was common. Each *audiencia* redistributed encomienda grants as part of a well-established system of patronage. Gerhard concluded that in the colony's first decade "most of the native communities changed masters at least two or three times" (1972:10). As there was no guarantee of how long a holder might enjoy an encomienda, each tried to maximize the amount of tribute extracted while it was in his possession.

Tribute was not only heavy, it required Indians to provide goods they did not possess, which forced them to sell their labor to the Spanish haciendas, mines, and cattle ranches in the region. Indian communities also continued to pay their native lords. Even in 1572, fifty years after the conquest, the lord of Tututepec still received a tribute of 300 pesos a year in gold, forty Indians to work for two days three times a year in his cacao orchards, and Indians to plant, weed, and harvest some four hectares of chiles, twelve hectares of cotton, and twenty hectares of corn (Berlin 1947:39–40). What this meant for small villages may be seen in the *relación* of Temaxcaltepec, a Chatino hamlet of sixty-seven households. Temaxcaltepec was not only forced to pay its Spanish masters fifteen pesos in gold every eighty days, each *tributario* also had to provide the lord of Tututepec an *almud* (4 kg) of corn and twenty cacao beans every eight days. In addition, tributarios had to work in the cacique's cacao orchards eight times a year and provide him at such times a load of firewood and chickens (Paso y Troncoso 1905:1:248). The tribute rates reported in the relaciones, of course, are official rates; the actual tribute required was likely much higher.

Although the conquest brought new masters, a new god, and heavier tribute, the blood spilled by the conquerors was but a minor consequence of the imposition of the new order when compared to the decimation of the native population by European diseases, the real conquerors of the New World. At contact, New Spain had a population estimated at 22 million. By 1532 the population had fallen to 16 million. By 1570 there remained but 2.6 million people. The plague of 1576–1581 reduced the figure to 1.8 million, and the population declined further in the late sixteenth and early seventeenth centuries (Gerhard 1972:23–24). The precontact population of Tututepec's empire may have been more than 250,000. After two epidemics—of smallpox in 1534 and of measles in 1544—Tututepec had only 7,000 tributarios, or approximately 35,000 people. The number of tributarios continued its downward slide—to 4,900 in 1570, to 3,775 in 1597, and to 2,500 in 1650 (Gerhard 1972:381).

The constant exploitation, oppression, and humiliation that the Indians suffered at the hands of the Spanish sparked numerous revolts. In 1525 a rebellion blazed across the whole sierra when false news arrived of the death of Cortés. Another rebellion erupted in 1531 in Analco, and it forced the Spanish to establish a presidio in Villa Alta to battle the unruly Indians of the zone (Romero-Frizzi 1973:234). In 1545 the Zapotecs of Mixtepec and the Chatinos of Zenzontepec, Juquila, and other pueblos took up arms, killing the Spanish in the vicinity.

The Reform Laws of the 1540s

Although the encomienda system initially served the Crown's purposes of subjugating labor and Hispanizing and Christianizing Indians, the abuses of tribute, rapid depopulation, and numerous revolts (as well as agitation by the Dominicans) moved the Crown in the 1540s to pass new laws to protect its Indian subjects. These reform laws, which were generally enforced after 1550, were passed not merely to protect the Indians. The Crown feared that the encomenderos were developing a separate base of economic and political power greater than its own, so it sought to limit their power. The new laws and later legislation denied the encomenderos their right to Indian labor, prohibited them from residing on their encomiendas, and limited an heir's succession to one lifetime. This last provision, however, was soon repealed. Tribute, which had been whatever the encomendero could wring from his charges, became subject to uniform assessment. After 1550 encomenderos were entitled only to a standard yearly head tax, which was fixed by a Crown inspector. Because these head taxes had to be collected from a diminishing native population, by the late sixteenth century most of these grants were of greater value for their prestige than for the money they generated (Gerhard 1972:9–10).

Economic Transformations

The effect of the Spanish conquest on the economy of New Spain was not limited to taking control of aboriginal tribute systems and markets. It also involved the introduction of a European system of mercantile capitalism, which transformed many aspects of the economy. Although common cultural traditions (language, elite class marriage alliances and kinship ties, local and intraregional commercial networks, and a ritual pilgrimage complex) continued to integrate dozens of communities in the Mixteca (Spores 1975:28), these pre-Hispanic mechanisms of socioeconomic integration were overlaid and superseded by this new economic system—with its new plants, animals, and technology—based on new concepts of property and of exchange for profit, using coinage. Even though Indian communities continued to plant subsistence crops, assign land according to clan or community membership, and work their fields through patterns of reciprocity, the conquest introduced a new system of land and labor that was integrated into the Spanish market sphere. In this European "sector," in order to produce crops desired by the Spanish, land and labor became cash commodities. Work was organized by cash payment rather than reciprocity. Similarly, in this new market world, an individual could buy land as a commodity without being a member of a group or community. With the spread of this regime of private property, the lands most suited to the production of cash crops became increasingly concentrated in Spanish hands. In this new environment, the shrinking Indian population not only had to pay tribute, but because the Spanish occupied the better lands, they had to derive the funds from a contracting resource base.

With the rapid decline of the native population, the tribute derived from it plummeted. The indigenous population's catastrophic crash affected all concerned. Since encomenderos relied on tax farms for their revenues, the ebbing Indian population made their encomiendas increasingly unprofitable, and since encomenderos paid the salaries of the clergy on their encomiendas, as the revenues dropped, local priests were forced to turn to other means of gaining revenues, and indeed were often accused of abuses or became impoverished (Takahashi 1981:47–48). The situation of local colonial administrators was similar. The low salaries that *alcaldes mayores, corregidores*, and their lieutenants received from their offices encouraged ever wider abuses as they attempted to compensate for their meager salaries by using their positions to start commercial enterprises. Large cattle ranches, for example, owned by local Spanish bureaucrats and clergymen, were formed along the Río Verde and the Río de la Arena. The estates ranged up to 17,000 hectares, and some herds were as large as 12,500 head. The introduction of cattle caused endless problems. Ranches pushed back the boundaries of Indian communities and took their lands. Cattle were permitted to wander without restraint, and they invaded fields continually, eating or destroying Indian crops. The administrative solution to these problems, as often as not, was to order the Indians to move their cornfields so that the cattle would not damage them (Spores and Saldaña 1975:72).

Conflicts and Changes in Land Tenure

All such enterprises depended on unlocking land and labor. The Crown's recognition of various types of land tenure played an important role in opening lands to Spanish exploitation. The Crown recognized the lands of the native nobility as private property, and under colonial law each Indian town also was entitled to its *fundo legal*, or townsite, in which only Indian commoners could cultivate plots. Theoretically, communal lands could not be bought or sold, and individuals held only usufruct rights over them. The fundo legal was meant to guarantee that Indian communities would have a subsistence base in communally held lands by stipulating that no ranches could be within a kilometer of an Indian community. In reality, limiting the community's lands to its fundo legal potentially opened vast areas to Spanish occupation. The long-term effect of the Crown's granting lands differentially to Indian communities, to Spaniards, and to Indian elites was to pit these groups against one another.

Rapid depopulation also encouraged the Crown to resettle remnant populations. Bitter and often violent disputes resulted as many towns were consolidated into single entities and as other towns were created that had no pre-Hispanic antecedents. In these land disputes, larger communities often expanded at the expense of smaller ones. These land problems were further exacerbated by their vague boundaries and unclear titles. Indian communities soon learned to use legal procedures to argue that their land was held in "primitive patrimony" from pre-Hispanic times. Although colonial authorities considered this a strong argument, many communities still lost their lands. As well, throughout the colonial period violent conflict and litigation often erupted between Indian communities when subject communities, which objected to the rule of their *cabecera*, petitioned for head-town status (Whitecotton 1977:193–197).

The Impoverishment of Native Elites

In the latter half of the sixteenth century, several factors combined slowly to impoverish native elites and induce them to sell land to the Spanish officials and clergy residing in the area. Since the colonial administration held native elites financially liable for the collection of tribute quotas, native rulers, faced with a declining native population, were increasingly forced to make up the difference out of their own funds (Paso y Troncoso 1905:4:200). The Church, too, looked to native elites to help finance its rituals and fiestas. So, in 1561, when Don Domingo Cosumatl, the cacique of Pochutla, one of the communities subject to Tututepec, sold 1,120 hectares to Don Melchor Mejia for one hundred pesos, he declared that the motive for the sale was "to pay the tribute levied and buy wax and other things necessary for the church" (Takahashi 1981:10–11). As well, the economic position of native elites was further eroded when colonial policies shifted the production of cacao—the basis of native wealth on the coast—to Venezuela. Lastly, under the Pax Hispana, what had been pre-Hispanic wars of succession or bound-ary wars between hostile communities became expensive legal battles fought through the Spanish court system. This situation was further complicated since the cacicazgo lands had not had the status of private property in the pre-Hispanic system that Spanish law accorded them. Instead, the lands of the nobility were inherited together with the office of cacique. Similarly, the barrio's lands were considered the collective property of the community (Carrasco 1949:17). Because many caciques used the new Spanish juridical norms to sell property and make out their wills, in long and bitter conflicts with commoners and noble creditors they were often accused of having com-mitted fraud (Romero-Frizzi 1973:278). In theory, the Spanish administrator (the corregidor) would only approve such sales if he were satisfied that the seller was the legitimate owner, that there were no inhabitants on or near it, that the sale and subsequent use would not affect their livelihood, that the sale was of a "voluntary nature," and that the seller had not been induced to sell it under threat or duress. In practice, because sales were almost invariably to members of the local Spanish administration and often to relatives, few sales met with any legal obstacles.

The Repartimiento

Despite the Spaniards' considerable success in acquiring land, labor short-ages persisted. The propensity of Indian households for autarchy—that is, working only enough to satisfy their own needs—posed special problems for the colonial regime. The solution Spanish ranchers and plantation owners found is evident in the kinds of companies and contracts they made with the encomenderos and the administrators of the repartimiento, or labor draft. For example, although possession of an encomienda did not give Don Luis de Castilla (1502–1587) ownership of any land or direct jurisdiction over the Indians, by forming a company with a local entrepreneur who had acquired land near the area of his encomienda, he was nonetheless able to exploit the

Indian labor at his disposal on sugar plantations and cattle *estancias* (Takahashi 1981:70). The company was still short on labor, however, so it imported Negro slaves to work on the plantations.

Even after the New Laws of the 1540s stripped the *encomenderos* of their control over labor, little changed. Under provisions of the New Laws of the Indies, Indians became subject to a royal head tax. To gain tribute money, Indians were forced to grow cash crops and to seek wage labor in European haciendas, plantations, and mines. In addition to these taxes, Indians had to tithe to the Church and perform forced labor imposed by the corregidor on public works such as roads and church constructions.

Integration of the Economy Into the Colonial Empire

The transformation of the economy, however, went far beyond changes in land tenure and the exploitation of labor. The Spanish held an effective monopoly of both state administration and trade. Royal patents and exclusive rights geared the economy of New Spain to the requirements of the mother country and essentially guaranteed its steady slide toward underdevelopment and dependency. Wolf describes the economy as

> circumscribed by royal regulations, to fit it as one component into the larger empire. The Crown frowned on the production of goods in the colony which could compete with products of the mother country. The production of olive oil, wine, silken goods, and textiles was therefore forbidden or inhibited. Single colonies might receive exclusive rights to the production of certain crops; but these rights were frequently reallocated to the detriment of established plantings. Thus in the course of a century, cacao production in New Spain was halted and transferred to Venezuela. This was done in spite of the fact that Middle America was the homeland of cacao.... From then on, New Spain had to export silver, flour, sacking, tableware, and copper goods to acquire Venezuelan cacao.... New Spain thus took its place in a planned economy in which its economic decisions were subject to revision and censorship by a superior authority thousands of miles away. (1959:188)

In this planned economy, Spanish and Indians basically specialized in different types of agricultural production. Along the Oaxacan coast, although Spanish enterprises initially produced aboriginal crops—cacao, corn, and cotton—when they found themselves faced with chronic labor shortages, they turned increasingly to large-scale operations such as cattle ranching that required relatively little labor. Although Indians continued to plant their subsistence crops, in order to meet their tribute obligations they were forced to produce labor-intensive cash crops.

The Indians in Oaxaca took their place in this planned economy as producers of subsistence goods and cochineal, a scarlet dyestuff extracted from grana, insects that live on a species of cactus. During the colonial period, cochineal was second in value only to silver among New Spain's exports, and Oaxaca was the largest single producer of cochineal in New Spain. The richest sources of cochineal in the state were apparently in the Sierra Madre del Sur. Valley cochineal was considered inferior in quality (Brading 1971:99; Taylor 1972:94). The production of cochineal involved the careful nurturing of grana, which involved small-scale intensive cultivation rather than large-scale extensive techniques. So, although hacienda labor produced some grana, the principal producers were Indians working their own lands (Waterbury 1975:419–420).

Merchants, however, used the rapartimiento system, legally and otherwise, to obtain these valuable commodities from the Indians (Waterbury 1975:420). The repartimiento system was a classic colonial tool. In its basic form it was used to draft Indians to serve on public works projects, in the mines, and on haciendas. In each district an *alcalde mayor* was appointed to administer the repartimiento. In Oaxaca, however, rather than distributing labor itself, *repartimientos de comercio* (forced sales paid for with cochineal) were used to distribute the products of Indian labor to Spanish merchants.[4] Repartimiento agents, however, never offered Indians the market price for their goods. Indeed, as Farriss notes, "they invested the motto 'buy cheap and sell dear' with a special meaning" (1984:44). Although before 1751 alcaldes mayores were prohibited from employing repartimientos de comercio to trade with the Indians in their care, the practice was common and was openly acknowledged. Scandalous abuses of the system soon generated complaints from many quarters. Although the repartimiento system was officially abolished in 1786, in Oaxaca analogous practices continued long afterward.

In Jiyacán, the district to which the Chatino were subordinated during the colonial period, the scale of these repartimientos de comercio was remarkable. In the three years between 1781 and 1784, the alcalde mayor of Jiyacán dispersed 400,000 pesos in cash. Backed by Pedro de Alles, a merchant in Mexico City, the magistrate supplied several shops with merchandise to exchange for cochineal with the Indians of the province and for the cotton grown by the local mestizos and mulattos. The profits from this enterprise, which were split between the alcalde mayor and his backer, came to 20 percent (Brading 1971:99).

Not only did Spanish colonial policy create a system of vicious monopolies, it was also responsible for fundamental changes in the settlement pattern. Between 1575 and 1742, for example, pirates harassed the Pacific coast of Mexico with little opposition because the only fortifications along it were at Acapulco. This repeatedly led the viceroys of New Spain to issue orders that the whole Pacific shore for several leagues inland should be kept free of Spanish settlements and cattle, on the theory that this would make pirate raids unprofitable (Gerhard 1960:95, 208). As the result of these edicts, many coastal ranches and plantations were abandoned. Over the course of a century, the edicts forbidding colonization of the coast, coupled with the Spanish monopoly on trade, reduced Tututepec—one of the richest and most powerful states in preconquest Mexico—to a dependent and impoverished satellite of the Spanish empire. By the beginning of the eighteenth century, Tututepec had become a sleepy coastal village. A depopulated empire, with its seacoast deserted and much of its fertile territory untilled and abandoned, Tututepec had become a classic area of refuge for Indians and runaway slaves.

Religious Transformations

If the Spanish attempted to accommodate native political and economic institutions, at least in part, they viewed native religion and cosmology as the work of the devil, to be destroyed. Idol smashing was, of course, "merely one of the more spectacular ways of trying to extirpate idolatry, that world enemy of Christendom" (Taussig 1974:68–69). If the New World held out the promise of gold to conqueror and king, it also offered a new continent filled with souls hungry for salvation. "The shock troops of the new faith," Wolf observes, "were the friars, members of monastic orders" (1959:165). Even though the outward conversion of Indians to Christianity was accomplished rapidly, at first they simply placed the Christian God in a native pantheon of deities. It must have come as a great shock when they realized that what the Church wanted was for the Christian God to replace their gods, not merely to be given precedence over them (Farriss 1984:287). Christianity presented the Indians with a dilemma. If they continued to worship their deities, they faced Spanish wrath; if they did not, they feared they might provoke the even more terrifying consequences of offending the gods, who provided them with the necessities of life. The Church's efforts to stamp out the native religion and cosmology gave rise to a seemingly endless confrontation between Spanish authorities (backed by physical force) and the power of indigenous tradition, which repeatedly found expression in various messianic movements and attempts at syncretism.

One of the earliest of these messianic movements to affect the Oaxacan coast occurred in 1545. It was led by a Zapotec priest from Ejutla named Pitio. He claimed that Petela, the great prophet and emperor, had appeared to him in a dream. He told him that they must "take up arms and fight the Spanish that had come to take away their gods, their lands, and their treasures" (Martínez Gracida 1907:74). Pitio's message raised Coatlán, Ejutla, Miahuatlán, and Ozolotepec to arms, but the weight of the Spanish administration came down on Pitio's messianic rebellion almost immediately. Pitio was apprehended, and he and five hundred prisoners were sent to Mexico City to await the justice of the viceroy (Martínez Gracida 1907:75). Only two years later, a native lord of Titiquipa led a second messianic uprising. The Indians killed a cleric and other Spaniards and refused to pay service and tribute to the Crown. The native ruler sent a messenger to Miahuatlán and other towns nearby, saying:

> Let it be known that three Lords have been born: a lord of Mexico, another in the Mixteca, and another in Tehuantepec. These three lords have as a kingdom the whole earth, and to them we must pay tribute. They shall rule the land as it was before the Christians came. Because we know that if the Spanish come to kill us, we shall kill them, but we shall not have to fight with them, rather there will be eight days of earthquakes and great darkness and in these all the Spanish will die ... and with them their laws ... and we will not have to serve their God but return to our religion as it used to be. (Paso y Troncoso 1939–42: 5:36–41)

To use Aberle's term, these messianic rebellions had the characteristics of a transformative movement. They involved a radical rejection of things as they stood. They sought to transform the social order both through ritual and force to restore their world. Often, the confrontation between Spanish and Indian worlds was manifested in "redemptive movements," whose aim was the "search for a new individual state" rather than any transformation of the entire social order (Aberle 1966: 320–322). The redemptive movements, although syncretic, usually rejected Spanish values and society. Salvation, the leaders claimed, lay in adherence to the obligations and responsibilities preached in their collectivist ethic, in continuing the system of reciprocities between gods and mortals that had always maintained the balance between the social and natural orders.

The cult of the Virgin (among the Chatino) was one of the earliest of such movements. It paralleled a similar movement about the Virgin of Guadalupe in the Valley of Mexico. Historically, the image of the Virgin was given by Friar Jordán to his Indian servant, who accompanied him during the conquest of Villa Alta. As Ruiz y Cervántez notes, "Upon returning to Amialtepec Fr. Jordán's servant ... placed our queen in the house of the saints, *Santocale*, as they say in Mexican. The fame of her miracles spread and soon people from distant places came to find her" (1786:27).

Although this account is probably accurate, Chatino tradition is more interesting and informative. As the Chatino tell it, the Virgin was "born" from a "cave" (really a crevice) in the rock face of the falls behind the church in Amialtepec. The Chatino called her y'o, "mother," and also equate her with ho'o ko', "the moon god." Similarly, God-the-Father is equated with ho'o kwicha, "the sun god." The Virgin offsets the dangers of the sun's heat, being strongly associated with water. Like the Virgin of Guadalupe, who appeared in 1531 to an Indian convert, Juan Diego, at the shrine of a fertility goddess, Tonantzin, the Virgin of Juquila, is simultaneously the Virgin, the earth mother, and the moon goddess, who oversees production and reproduction.

Despite its efforts, the Church did not succeed in completely eradicating native religious systems in Juquila. Instead, the Chatino incorporated Catholic saints into a pre-Hispanic layered cosmos oriented to the world directions that, by equating places with gods, used nature to map out an ancient pantheon. What emerged was a syncretic blend of Catholic and Chatino belief and ritual. Idols peek out from behind altars. The indigenous gods of the sun, moon, mountain, rain, wind, corn, and earth were equated with Catholic saints. Pre-Hispanic rituals to bring rains from the house of the rain god and return them to it were performed on mountaintops side by side with masses, rosaries, and prayers. In this new blend, Spanish and Indian interpretations of the saints commingled, and in this cosmological framework, each human being had, as animal spirit companions, *tonales*, whose life was joined with their own. Moreover, places, gods, and saints had tonales of their own, which also could be tonales for human beings. Indigenous belief, ritual, and cosmology infused Catholicism with an indigenous content that continued to emphasize reciprocities among man, animals, and gods— reciprocities needed to maintain ecological and cosmological balance.

Just as Indian communities tried to protect their lands from the encroachment of the new mercantile system by limiting membership in their communities to native sons, they also attempted to shut out the values implicit in the new order. In this, redemptive movements were the key. By rejecting the "evils" of Spanish society and emphasizing traditional values, they provided a framework in which Catholicism could be resynthesized in terms of the content of the preexisting religious system. Although Chatino and other Indian communities reinterpreted Catholicism and achieved some degree of closure, this does not mean that they were not fully integrated into the colonial structure. Rather, such strategies were responses to the colonial structures that enclosed Indian communities and denied Indians access to the sources of power and wealth in the wider society. As such, they represent an accommodation to Spanish exploitation. Though they afforded some measure of protection and continuity, they did not totally prevent the Spanish from leeching the lifeblood from the community.

Colonial Transformations of Indian Communities

The colonial policy was explicitly segregationist, discouraging Spanish settlement in native communities. Much like South Africa's current system of apartheid, Indian communities were treated as "homelands." Under this regime, they were defined by law as discrete political units, *repúblicas de indios*. In theory, each Indian republic was a self-governing and self-supporting unit, with its own land base and its own *cabildo*. In reality, the republics were administratively and economically subordinate to Spanish towns. By defining each community as an independent unit and dealing separately with its ruler, the Spanish undermined the hierarchical chains of command between communities that had integrated them into pre-Hispanic states. In effect, this policy isolated Indian communities from direct access to power and guaranteed the paternalism that allowed economic exploitation to continue with little interference from higher levels of government.

Essentially, the Spanish superimposed on the pre-Hispanic political system a Castillian *municipio* system of town government that effectively restricted the power of indigenous elites to the local level. In key provinces the Spanish established provincial capitals to integrate each region administratively as never before. Although native kingdoms continued to exist, they existed alongside a new administrative organization, the Spanish cabildo, as a parallel but interrelated traditional arm of native government. In the early stages of its evolution, the highest offices within the cabildo were generally occupied by the native nobility. The native ruler was given the title of *gobernador*. Nobles served as *alcaldes*, "judges," for minor crimes and civil suits and as *regidores*, "councilmen," who passed local ordinances. The cabildo also included a number of lesser posts. Among these were *mayordomos*, who supervised the communal lands that were worked to provide funds for the cult of saints, scribes, police officers, janitors, errand boys, and church cantors. These positions were usually assigned to commoners through a system of rotation. Through its cabildo each community, each kingdom, was tied to an *alcaldía mayor* or *corregimento*. Each of these was in turn linked to a provincial capital, to the viceroy and *audiencia* in Mexico, and ultimately to the king and the Council of the Indies in Spain (Spores 1975:19).

As colonial forms of exploitation—with their insatiable demand for labor, tribute, taxes, and land—made the lives of Indian peasants ever more precarious, the need to maintain systems of mutual support and redistribution became stronger than ever. Native lords, though their power had been reduced to the local level, continued to play a key role in organizing and maintaining systems of redistribution within the community. Although nominally Catholics, native elites used the cult of the saints to replicate "the same corporate bond with the supernatural that their ancestors had sustained" (Farriss 1984:320). Because *cofradías* (lay brotherhoods dedicated to particular saints) sponsored religious fiestas for the community, control of the confradías allowed elites to mobilize and channel the community's surplus wealth and "in so doing represent themselves as the source of all the material goods

they offered on the community's behalf" (Farriss 1984:339). Although elites
furnished leadership and dipped into their own pockets—though not to the
bottom—to support the saints, a variety of other means were also used to
raise funds (Farriss 1984:350). To finance these celebrations, saints were en-
dowed with treasury boxes and lands. The elites also raised revenues by
venturing into the very untraditional but profitable pursuit they had learned
from the Spanish: cattle ranching. Members' contributions to a saint's treasury provided cash to pay for masses, candles, fireworks, and mescal. Worked
by the members of the cofradía, the saint's land and cattle furnished corn for
tortillas and meat for fiestas. In this process, the cofradías were transformed
into corporate enterprises in Indian communities. They not only sponsored
fiestas for the saints but also provided for the sick and helped those in ex-
tremis to die properly. In time of need, they reduced the effects of famine by
distributing their stores of maize and beans within the community.

The native elite's domination of the Indian cabildo was but a transitional
phase. Although the native nobility persisted in Tututepec into the latter
half of the eighteenth century, their hold over cabildo posts waned. Several
factors were involved in the eventual democratization of the Indian communities. First, depopulation made it increasingly difficult for the nobility to
fill all the required offices. Second, the rapid Spanish acculturation of Indian
elites led to increasing abuses and turned their people against them. Lastly, as
the colonial bureaucracy consolidated its power, the native nobility became
less and less necessary, and the prerogatives accorded to them decreased.
For instance, in the 1560s the native elites' tribute rights were reduced. This
impoverished many of them and ultimately blurred the distinction between
noble and commoner. In the seventeenth and eighteenth centuries, as the
power of native elites waned, disputes between townsmen and the nobility
were frequent. In some towns nobles were barred from holding any cabildo
post; when they attempted to usurp offices, violence often erupted (Whitecotton 1977:189–191). Resentments of the nobility bred a fierce egalitarianism, which manifested itself in a cultural complex of envy and witchcraft.
This egalitarian ethic was deeply suspicious of marked differences in wealth
and contained an implicit criticism of the new economic order. Conspicuous differences in wealth could only be explained by witchcraft. The rich
were accused of making a pact with the devil, usually described as being a
rich Spanish hacendado. They were accused of selling their souls or those of
others to him, of being nahuales, "transforming witches," who in animal form
attacked people or stole their goods. To protect themselves from envy and
witchcraft accusations, peasants either hid their wealth or used it in socially
approved ways, such as in support of the saints.

By the eighteenth century, "because of the growing pressures and responsibilities on gobernadores and cabildo members to meet Spanish demands for

tribute and labor, the once-prestigeful posts in civil community government had become a burden to be avoided if at all possible" (Helms 1975:198). In the 1780s the Bourbon rulers of Spain passed an extensive series of reforms that not only reorganized the colonial bureaucracy but also attacked the political autonomy of Indian communities. The reform divided New Spain into *partidos*, or districts. It also created a new set of officials, *subdelegados*, between the Indian community and the central government. Their administrative authority reached directly into the repúblicas de indios. Under these reforms, control over the *cajas de comunidad* (the public revenues that had paid the costs of civil administration) passed into the hands of the subdelegado (Zavala and Miranda 1973:154–157). Deprived of funds to pay town officials, these offices, called *cargos* (literally, burdens) became exactly that. Service in civil offices after this was unpaid and time-consuming, and the cargoholder was required to meet any expenses that might be incurred out of their own funds. Almost concurrent with the appropriation of the cajas de comunidad, the Church moved to take control of the cofradías. As a result, cofradia members were also required to pay almost all the expenses of a saint's fiestas out of their own pockets. This system rapidly leveled any remaining differences in wealth within the community, and it spelled the end of native elites. Since these fiestas had become the major community expense, in order to spread the burden of these offices, all men were required to serve. In the course of a lifetime, men served in a series of *cargos* of increasing prestige and responsibility. Whitecotton has summarized the situation at this time:

> By the end of the Spanish Colonial period, the Indian *cabildo* had taken a form that was neither distinctively Spanish nor like the government of pre-Conquest times. Instead, it represented an adaptation of Spanish town government to local conditions—conditions that made the holding of political offices less a right that could bring wealth and power to a privileged nobility than a duty designed to preserve and protect a local Indian community of peasants. In this system, prestige became synonymous not with wealth and power but with their antithesis—poverty and service. (1977:191)

In these egalitarian Indian communities, even though the ranks of the civil-religious hierarchies were now filled by age cohorts, they continued to organize a system of redistributive exchange within the community. Furthermore, service in civil and religious offices came to define the boundaries of membership in Indian communities. Because access to communal lands was limited to native sons who served the community as officeholders, these offices became one of the principal mechanisms through which Indian villages defended their lands against Spanish encroachment. Since officeholders had to pay their own expenses, one argument holds that the *cargo* system inhibited individuals from undertaking capitalist forms of investment that would increase social inequality. Moreover, as these expenditures often required cash to buy goods in Spanish-dominated market systems, these *cargos* also served to pump goods and labor into the market, and ultimately into the hands of Spanish merchants (Wolf 1955, 1957; Harris 1964; Greenberg 1981).

Late Colonial Indian Rebellions and Insurrections

The Revolution of Independence that swept Mexico in 1810 had been building within Indian communities as their conflicts with the wider capitalist society grew steadily deeper, and it was not without its precursors: Chiapas in 1712, Yucatán in 1761, and Petén in 1775 all experienced revolts. Most of the uprisings in Oaxaca, however, had a very local character. Between 1680 and the beginning of the Revolution, more than fifty Indian communities in Oaxaca rose in rebellion against the excesses of the colonial administration (Taylor 1979:114). As Taylor notes, nearly all these local uprisings "were short-lived armed outbursts by members of a single community in reaction to threats from the outside. They were 'popular' uprisings in which virtually the entire community acted collectively, and usually without identifiable leadership" (1979:115). Typically, at some commonly understood signal, usually the ringing of church bells, townsfolk assembled with whatever weapons were at hand. Spanish militia men were likely to encounter nasty mobs of men, women, and children, brandishing spears, knives, and rocks.

Despite their impressive violence, most of these uprisings were less revolutionary acts than protests to a colonial government whose legitimacy was still unquestioned. They were protests against new taxes or against abuses by local officials who made greater demands on their labor than allowed, forced the sale of their stored corn, or tampered with their communal lands. Reflecting this, the targets of violence were almost always a colonial official or priest, or a building identified with outside authority, usually the jail or the government offices. Although these rebellions were set off by seemingly minor changes, more was at stake for the rebels than a nominal tax increase. Any new demand had a greater impact on the local economy than merely the extraction of another increment of the community's production. As the demands usually required cash, they forced villagers to look for additional sources of cash through wage labor, the sale of produce, or land rentals. Such minor changes were often seen as direct threats to the villagers' livelihood and to the community's independence (Taylor 1979:133–143).

Since colonial militias were small, poorly paid, and often ill-equipped, the Spanish response to these uprisings was a calculated blend of mercy and punishment. Because Indian villages were the primary source of agricultural goods, taxes, and labor drafts, colonial officials were anxious to end revolts by negotiation rather than force of arms, especially if this would prevent them from spreading. "As long as the violence had not spread to neighboring communities," Taylor observes, "colonial magistrates were inclined to conciliatory verdicts in which village loyalty to the Crown was reaffirmed. Generally, a few local rebels were singled out by the judge as leading troublemakers subject to exemplary punishment: whipping, labor service, exile, occasionally execution, whereas the community at large received a pardon, tempered with a threat of harsh punishment for future violence" (1979:120–121).

Although few uprisings in Oaxaca were class wars on the rich or against the colonial system, unrest was widespread, and several of the revolts became regional insurrections. For instance, the constant abuses of forced sales and tribute by the alcaldes mayores, who administered the repartimiento system, led to a regional insurrection in the Sierra Zapoteca Alta in 1660 and 1696 (Huerta and Palacios 1976:100–113; Taylor 1979:114). About a century later, in 1774 and 1796, the coercive methods of the repartimiento system used to force production of cochineal in villages in the Mixteca and Sierra Zapoteca again caused brief regional uprisings.

The War of Independence

The War of Independence is usually discussed in terms of middle-class Creoles, unhappy with Spanish monopolies on trade, using the upheavals in Europe (which placed Napoleon's brother on the Spanish throne) to advance their own interests. Among the masses, however, the rebellion had a messianic character. Hidalgo's cries for "land and liberty" and "death to the Spanish" had special meaning for the Indians, who rose up in rebellion. Marching under a banner of the Virgin of Guadalupe, they saw this as a holy war to regain their lands and free themselves from Spanish domination.

In the district of Juquila, Chatino participation in the War of Independence was brief and tragic. In November 1811, Antonio Váldes, a resident of Tataltepec, raised a small army composed of Chatino Indians from Tataltepec, Tepenixtlahuaca, and Panixtlahuaca, and Mixtec Indians from Jamiltepec and Pinotepa. They proclaimed their independence by killing eleven Spaniards. Royalist troops led by Don Juan José Caldelas, along with Negro slaves from the coast, pursued Váldes and defeated his poorly equipped and inexperienced Indian army at Hornos de Cal. Their defeat was a bitter affair. The royalists captured many Indians, and as a reprisal burned their houses and forced them to deliver up their leaders. Although Váldes escaped to joined Morelos, two of their leaders were handed over. One was taken to Juquila, a royalist stronghold, and shot. The other was sent to Oaxaca to meet his fate

(Gay 1881:2:386–387; Esteva 1913:226–227). Whether this fiasco was responsible or not, after this the Chatino refused to fight the Spanish, or at least there exists no other mention of their participation in the war.

Postcolonial Forms of Domination

Independence

Mexico was singularly unprepared for independence. Overnight, the traditional institutions of colonial rule vanished, leaving a vast, loose-knit nation. The early decades of the republic's history were a sad time of internal decline and humiliation at the hands of foreign powers. The nation's economy was substantially weakened with the departure of the Spanish, who took their "monies" with them. Internal and external trade stagnated. The frequent changes in government (almost invariably by unconstitutional means) left the nation with precious little purposeful direction of policy and no continuity. Moreover, the new republic was saddled with debts incurred by previous governments, and it faced a major budgetary crisis. Income from all sources amounted to only half of expenditures, much of which was spent on the military. To raise funds for internal purposes, the government mortgaged the nation's assets to Mexican financiers and further impoverished the state. For external finances, Mexico turned to Great Britain. Two loans, totaling 6.5 million pounds sterling, were floated with British bankers at a high rate of interest (Cheetham 1971:137–144). This indebtedness to Great Britain was the first in a series of claims that helped to exhaust the young republic. The westward expansion by U.S. interests forced Mexico to surrender over half its territory between 1836 and 1855, receiving only 25 million dollars in compensation.

The Economic Impact on the District of Juquila

Like that of the nation as a whole, the economy of the coast was left a shambles. Although cochineal continued to be produced, only small quantities were harvested because, after the withdrawal of Spanish capital, few lenders were left to support its production. Similarly, with only a local market, cattle production declined. Many Spanish cattle ranches were apparently abandoned: in 1826 only three ranches were in Spanish hands, with no more than 800 head of cattle among them (Bartolomé and Barabas 1982:36–38). Where in the sixteenth century, single herds as large as 12,500 head could be found in the district, in 1827 there were only 7,770 head of cattle in the whole district (Florescano and Sánchez 1976:309). This statistical impression of collapse is confirmed by a German traveler, Eduard Muhlenpfordt. Between 1827 and 1835 he visited the Chatino villages of Juquila, Ixtapan, Quiahije, Zacatepec, and Jocotepec, noting that commercial production in the region was very scant and that most villages produced just for their own consumption (Lameiras 1973:128–129).

Postcolonial Reforms

The newly independent republic tried to cope with these problems by reorganizing the countryside both politically and economically. What followed was a series of transformations as massive in scale as any introduced by Spanish colonialism. Liberals, inspired by the Enlightenment ideals of equality and freedom, targeted the system of castes. Their constitutional reforms granted Indians "full citizenship" before the law and abolished the repúblicas de indios, which had for so long separated them from the rest of society. As Indians were to be equal citizens in the new republic, paternalistic colonial laws for the protection of Indian communities were repealed. As Taylor points out, "non-Indians were no longer forbidden to reside in Indian communities, and the special Indian courts, such as the Juzgado de Indios, were disbanded, and the special protection of community property afforded by the colonial judicial system, and the Indian's right to legal counsel, fell into disuse" (1977:146).

Since the state's political control over Indian communities was weak at best, the state government moved toward a more centralized form of administration. In 1826 the political divisions of Oaxaca were reorganized into twenty-six departamentos, later called distritos. The partido of Jamiltepec on the coast was split in two. Juquila, which had been subject to Jamiltepec since 1700, became the seat of a new district comprising sixteen municipios, or counties, within which another fifteen agencias, or townships, were defined. These new centralized districts were administered by jefe políticos, "political chiefs." As agents of the state government, they were named by the governor of the state and were responsible only to him. The jefe político ruled on all political matters, passing, for instance, on the suitability of men elected to civil posts in municipios and agencias, and the acceptability of any actions taken by local governments.

In an effort to solve its financial problems, Church and Indian lands came under scrutiny. Political struggles pitted conservatives, defenders of the Church who wished to return to the order of the Spanish monarchy, against liberals, who espoused a philosophy of growth and progress. Between 1856 and 1859 the liberal government passed legislation designed to confiscate the estates of the Church, the largest landholder in Mexico. The Liberals hoped that the impoverished Indians and mestizos would buy up small pieces of land when Church property was auctioned off. In this way Mexico would become a nation of small landowners. At the same time, the government would fill the state's impoverished coffers by taxing each transaction. In theory, everyone would benefit. In practice, this legislation was an utter fiasco. Few Mexicans, and still fewer poor Indians or mestizos, could afford to buy land. Instead, when the Church's lands were sold, one set of landlords was exchanged for another. Rich mestizos and foreigners—French and Germans especially —bought the land at ridiculously low figures and became the new class of large landowners (McHenry 1962:122). Worst of all, because these laws were framed to include all corporate bodies, countless Indian villages lost their lands. The revenue accruing to the state from this colossal rape was a disappointing 3 million pesos, and this was almost completely dissipated by 1860.

The Effect of Reform Laws on Juquila

Although initial expropriations in the district of Juquila were not immense, Tataltepec, Tepenixtlahuaca, Zenzontepec, and Santiago Minas lost their best lands. Since the cofradías that survived from the colonial period were considered to be corporate bodies, they lost both their land and cattle. In the district of Juquila, the holdings of cofradías were extensive. In 1826 in the tiny Chatino village of Tlapanalquiahuitl, with a population 145 souls, the Cofradía la Purísima managed a communal ranch that had some 170 cows, 45 bulls, 22 mares, 21 stallions, 5 colts, 11 mules, 1 donkey, 10 sheep, and 16 pigs. San Juan Quiahije's cofradía had a communal ranch with 110 head of cattle. Tataltepec's cofradía had 250 head. Even poor cofradías like that of Temaxcaltepec had 20 head (Bartolomé and Barabas 1982:37–38). Not only were these properties alienated, but another of the enduring consequences of the reform laws was the reorganization of the way fiestas were financed. Where previously brotherhoods had sponsored fiestas, in order to insure the revenue from them, priests now fostered a system of individual sponsorship of saints' fiestas by mayordomos, who, rotating yearly, bore the burden of their cost out of their own pockets.

The Porfiriato and Laissez-Faire Development

The early abuses of the liberal reform laws were minor compared to the damage done by their cynical application between 1880 and 1910 by the new generation of leaders who came into power with Don Porfirio Díaz. These new leaders, disciples of positivism and laissez-faire, argued that development could be achieved by fervently exploiting Mexico's natural resources and by relying on foreign capital to furnish the country with the technology of the industrial revolution (Cheetham 1971:197). Although foreign capital gave Mexico the symbols of the industrial revolution—an efficient banking system, some heavy and light industry, electric power, railways, the telegraph, and telephones—this "development" was paid for many times over in the countryside, both financially and in increased human suffering. There was a heavy flow of capital into the extractive industries: mining, oil, and agriculture. To attract investors, enormous tracts of officially "empty" land were sold on easy terms to individuals and companies in Mexico and the United States. It has been calculated that during the Porfiriato no less than 50 million hectares of "national" property were disposed of to private interests. Peasants were methodically and callously dispossessed as their lands were gobbled up by large estates. Conditions in the countryside were abysmal. Wages were low. Disease was rife. On haciendas, corporal punishment of *peones* was routine, and debt slavery flourished. Although there was some resistance, especially from villages whose land titles had been honored throughout the colonial era, peasants had little chance against chicanery and brute force. Where occasional agrarian revolts occurred, they were put down with pitiless severity by the *rurales*, the corps of police with which the dictatorship kept the peace (Cheetham 1971:198).

Economic Transformations in Juquila

The changes in the postcolonial regime brought a similar restructuring of political and economic relations along Oaxaca's coast. With independence, the bottom fell out of the cochineal market. Although some cochineal continued to be produced, the development of cheap aniline dyes between 1858 and 1884 destroyed what was left of the market (Brand 1966:81–83). Merchants in Miahuatlán, a neighboring district, were especially hard hit and began to cast an eye toward coffee as a substitute for the sagging cochineal market. In 1868 they asked Don Basilio Rojas, a schoolteacher and businessman, to study the possibility of cultivating coffee in the region. Rojas reported that "the district of Miahuatlán had no suitable lands except in small quantities along its boundaries with Pochutla and Juquila." Rojas also reported realistically that in Pochutla and Juquila, "the only obstacle that exists for the development of the project is the love with which the Indian takes care of his land, making it untouchable although unproductive, defending it from outsiders with a jealous fervor although he cannot exploit it, fighting for a piece of it, though it be the most miserable, with a devilish fervor; this being the case, the study of the forms of acquisition of appropriate lands, without injuring the sensibilities of its Indian proprietors, is required" (1964:49–50).

In 1875 he took his own advice. Rojas, who spoke Zapotec, went to the authorities of Santo Domingo Coatlán, and petitioned them to grant him a small parcel of land on which to grow coffee. By requesting land from the Indian authorities in the traditional manner, Don Basilio was able to establish a 25-hectare plantation in Coatlán. His success was an example to others who wished to gain access to Indian lands. In 1878 Rojas, along with various acquaintances and friends, went to Juquila to establish coffee *fincas* (Rojas 1964:65–69).

After 1880 what had been a trickle of coffee speculators coming into the district became a torrent as the flood gates of the land grab were opened by the cynical application of the liberal reform laws of 1855 and 1857. Where the early *finqueros* had established moderate-sized plantations of about 25 hectares by claiming rights to land as "sons of the pueblo" either through descent or marriage, the new wave of land speculators grabbed huge tracts of land, gobbling up Indian lands indiscriminately. A partial list of the larger plantations in the district established during this period shows the scale of the invasion. In San Gabriel Mixtepec, the fincas La Aurora and La Virgen grabbed 843 hectares, El Jazmín had 638 hectares, and the Santa Mariana enclosed 342 hectares. In Juquila, La Esmeralda sprawled over 2,170 hectares. In Nopala, La Petra covered 243 hectares, and El Sinaí and La Profeta together had 341 hectares. In San Juan Lachao, the San Rafael spread across 1,065 hectares (Esteva 1913:32–33). By 1892 the finqueros in the district were so rich that "they drank French champagne and smoked cigars rolled in bank notes" (Rojas 1964:72). Indians, however, did not share in this prosperity. Communal land on which they had planted their cornfields had suddenly become private property. Since only a small fraction of the estates were suitable for coffee, the finqueros were willing to rent lands to Indians as sharecroppers. The rent on these desperately needed lands, however, was half the harvest. Then, too, it was not just large plantations that threatened Indian lands. Many smaller fincas were also established by mestizos who poured into the region in search of land and wealth. Between 1880 and 1900 the influx of mestizos doubled the population of the municipios of Juquila, Nopala, and Zenzontepec.

Chatino Armed Struggles in the Nineteenth Century

Between 1821 and 1880, Oaxaca, like the rest of Mexico, was in political turmoil. The political vacuum left after independence led to a new form of violence: factional struggles between liberals and conservatives. As these factions, which competed on the national level, used patronage to mobilize support at the state and local levels, their political struggles frequently led to armed clashes between local *caudillos*, petty warlords. As a result, there were armed confrontations in Oaxaca in 1828, 1834 to 1837, 1855, 1857 to 1860, 1871 to 1873, and 1876.

Since Chatino communities emerged intact from the colonial period as corporate units capable of fielding small armies, factional leaders sought alliances with them. Although the Chatino participated in various factional conflicts, their involvement was usually in response to economic, political, or territorial threats to their communities posed by one or another of these competing factions. In other words, Chatino villages reacted defensively to what they perceived to be external threats, but in so doing, they often backed factions that had interests that were the opposite of their own because they considered them the lesser of two evils. This tendency is clearly seen in their participation in the political struggles of 1860 and 1871.

The nationalization of ecclesiastical properties by Benito Juárez in 1859 precipitated the War of the Reform, a bloody and destructive conflict that pitted Liberals against Conservatives. Chatino involvement in the political events of the Reform began in October 1860, when the Liberal leader José García ambushed the Conservative leader Blas Quintana on his way through Juquila (Jijón 1883). In this encounter, although the defeated Conservatives fled, the Liberal leader did not remain in Juquila. He retreated with the guns and horses he had captured from Quintana toward the pueblos of Panixtlahuaca and Quiahije, where he had supporters. Shortly after this, Quintana's troops, in reprisal, tried to force the Chatino of Panixtlahuaca to hand over two months of head tax due the state, threatening to burn the town on his return if they refused. This threat alarmed the populace, who turned to the Chatino of Quiahije for help. On Quintana's return, the Chatino, allied with García's Liberal troops, surprised him on the pastures of La Cruz, causing him two casualties and forcing him to retreat to Tututepec (Bartolomé and Barabas 1982:39).

In 1871 the Chatino again became embroiled in national politics when a factional split among the Liberals led to an attempt to usurp the presidency from Benito Juárez. The national elections in June were marked by violence in Oaxaca. When Benito Juárez was elected president, the governor, Félix Díaz (a brother of Porfirio Díaz) claimed that there had been election irregularities, declared Oaxaca an independent state, and assumed virtually complete military and political control (Spores 1984:165). In November the district judge, Victoriano Martínez, went to Panixtlahuaca and Quiahije. Claiming to have an order from Benito Juárez, he asked them to help him arrest the jefe político, Juan Rubiera, a Díaz supporter. Making infinite promises, Martínez convinced the Chatino to march on Juquila and capture Juan Rubiera, which they did. In response, the Díaz forces sent Colonel Mauro Vásquez to occupy the plaza of Juquila. Martínez withdrew, leaving the Chatino to confront Vásquez. Even so, Vásquez's troops soon abandoned the plaza too, intimidated by the hostile populace, which laid siege to them for three days. Pursued by Indians and fighting frequent skirmishes, they retreated to Jamiltepec. The Juárez forces, under General Ignacio Alatorre, then gathered all the pueblos to march against Vásquez's forces in Jamiltepec. The rebels were quickly defeated, and the state was brought back under federal control. Although Félix Díaz fled the state, he was soon captured and executed (Spores 1984:165; Jijón 1883; Bartolomé and Barabas 1982:39).

Since Chatino involvement in national struggles did little to curb abuses by jefes políticos, stop the imposition of heavy taxes, or halt the expropriations of land, the Chatino responded to these threats to their communities with repeated uprisings.

In 1875 the district judge in Juquila jailed the Indian authorities of San Juan Quiahije for failing to deliver the head taxes. Quiahije's inhabitants gathered threateningly, "as they are accustomed to do every time they rebel," said Jijón (1883). The judge appealed to the jefe político, Octavio Jijón, for help in maintaining his authority. Taking advantage of state troops passing through the district on their way to Jamiltepec, the jefe político called on them to confront the rebels and managed to prevent an insurrection. In 1879 Quiahije and Juquila again rose up against the jefe político, this time because a petition concerning jurisdictional titles caused them to fear for the security of their lands. The jefe político, Octavio Jijón, again managed to smother the uprising, again by calling on the state's armed forces. Shortly afterward, the leaders of this rebellion were captured and were treated as criminals (Jijón 1883; Bartolomé and Barabas 1982:42).

By far the most serious insurrection occurred in 1896, when the state passed a new tax law, which raised the monthly head tax from 25 to 50 centavos. Because this was considerably more than peasants earned for a day's work, it sparked a class war, the "War of the Pants," as the Chatino refer to it. Although the insurrection apparently began in the Zapotec community of Zimatlán, it soon spread to Chatino villages when Indians from Zimatlán, pursued by federales, took refuge among them. On April 9, Chatino from Panixtlahuaca, Yaitepec, Zacatepec, Juquila, and several other towns, led by Indians from San Juan Quiahije, attacked Juquila and attempted to wipe out the literate mestizos (the new landowners and merchants), whom they identified as "wearing pants," as opposed to native dress. Screaming "Death to the pants!" they burned public buildings, cut off the head of the telegraph operator, stuck it on a spiked pole, and paraded with it through the streets, killing all the officials and mestizos they could find, including the jefe político, Sebastian Núñez, and his children; the former jefe político, Octavio Jijón; the district judge; and a teacher. Federal troops were called in, and the leaders of the revolt were caught and executed. To prevent any recurrence of the War of the Pants, the new jefe político of Juquila forced the Chatino to adopt the mestizo costume of the period. The costume is still worn today (Esteva 1913:228; Basauri 1940:501–502; Carrasco 1949:7; DeCicco 1969).

The defensive stance of Indian communities runs through these events like a thread. As growing outside pressures impinged on their ability to survive, the intensity of their reactions became ever more violent. Increasingly, despite boundary conflicts fostered among them throughout the colonial period, class alliances were forged among Chatino villages to combat these threats.

The Mexican Revolution

The War of the Pants was symptomatic of the tensions building up in the countryside under the Díaz regime, tensions that made the Revolution of 1910 inevitable. During the revolution, political factions in the district lined up as they had in 1896, along the lines of class and ethnicity. In the rural countryside of Juquila there were two phases to these struggles. In the first phase, a series of competing factions—which from the peasant's point of view were not much different one from another—fought for control of the state and for power: the Maderistas, the Huertistas, the Carranzistas, and the state militia.

During this phase of the Revolution, one army after another mounted campaigns in the district, taking the plaza in Juquila and holding it until forced to abandon it. First the Maderistas fought the state militia that had been organized by Félix Díaz, the dictator's nephew and governor of the state. About 1915, José Luis Dávila, who was then the governor, declared Oaxaca "a sovereign and free" state in an attempt to keep Oaxaca out of the Revolution. He organized a state militia, the Serranos, and sent them to defend the plaza in Juquila. The Carranzistas attacked the Serranos and forced them to flee by setting fire to the Loma de Toro, burning its houses.

After the defeat of the Serranos, the second phase of the Revolution pitted the old order, represented by the Carranzistas, against the Zapatistas' promise of "land and liberty." In this contest, the Chatino and the poor mestizos in the villages surrounding Juquila supported the Zapatistas, while the mestizo elites in Juquila, fearing a repeat of the War of the Pants, backed the Carranzistas. Juquila was again the battleground. The Carranzistas and the Zapatistas repeatedly fought for control of Juquila's plaza. Generally, when the Zapatistas won such battles they occupied the plaza for a few days and then abandoned it before the Carranzistas could mount a counterattack. In 1918, on one of the many occasions that the Zapatistas attacked the Carranzistas in Juquila, they burned part of the town. In retaliation, the Carranzistas attacked and burned the Chatino village of Panixtlahuaca, claiming that the village supported the Zapatistas. Although the revolutionary violence that swept Mexico generally subsided after 1920, in the district of Juquila, Zapatista guerrilla bands continued their struggle until at least 1927. They were ultimately defeated when the Indians began to view them as little more than bandits because of their constant and finally intolerable demands for food and money. In the end, the last such band, led by José Próspero, was betrayed and massacred at a feast held for the band by the Chatino of Teotepec.

The Postrevolutionary Period

Political Changes

The Revolution is credited with bringing about sweeping reforms in land tenure and social structure. In Juquila, however, little or nothing changed. The large estates in the district were unaffected by the land reform program. Debt peonage, outlawed in the Constitution of 1917, continued to be practiced. The hated system of jefes políticos was abolished by the constitution, and Article 115 provided that a directly elected government would administer "free" municipios directly. But the colonial system of head and subject towns remained essentially intact, allowing mestizo elites to retain either direct or indirect control of Indian communities. Elites have used two strategies to this end. First, few Chatino communities were granted "free" municipio status. Instead, following the ancient pattern, the vast majority were still defined as *agencias*, or townships, and were subordinated to mestizo-dominated head towns. In formal terms, township status means that the civil officials elected by the community must be confirmed by the presidente of the municipio's county seat and are accountable to him. Frequently, to guarantee the township's "cooperation," the presidente municipal names a non-Indian secretary for the township. The secretary ensures that legal formalities are observed, at least on paper. He also sees to it that in all important matters the officials in the county seat remain the township's judges and arbitrators.

This arrangement, in other words, creates a closed circuit between the county seat and its townships, which places substantial obstacles between townships and the state and federal governments. Even in those Indian communities that are "free" municipios, the civil officials are legally accountable to mestizo authorities in Juquila. Any real attempt at autonomy would likely lead to their removal from office, their imprisonment, or as occurred in several cases, the suppression of the Chatino community's status as a "free" municipio. The close ties between the district capital and the "free" Indian municipio creates another closed circuit, similar in form and content to that between the municipio and its townships. Between Juquila and the federal government there is yet another closed circuit, the government of the state, which further insulates Chatino communities from contact with the central government. Because Chatino communities remain three or four levels removed from the federal government, they are held politically almost in-communicado.

Economic Transformations

Since few of the tensions that led to the Revolution have been resolved in Juquila, violence has continued unabated. In fact, since peasants began to grow coffee as a cash crop, the increasing rhythm of capitalist development has generated whole new sets of conflicts within peasant and Indian communities, markedly increasing the level of violence in the region (Greenberg 1981; Bartolomé and Barabas 1982).

Peasants were induced to grow coffee in the mid-1930s because at that time the demand for coffee in the United States was on the rise at the same time that its major coffee supplier, Brazil, was undergoing a production crisis. Looking to Oaxaca, North American buyers promised coffee entrepreneurs interest-free loans to help them to increase their exports. Although Oaxaca's coffee plantation owners had managed to prevent expropriation of their lands by allying themselves with the national ruling party, the PRI, and by arguing that such land reform would lead to the collapse of the coffee industry, pressures for land reform during the Cárdenas regime prevented them from expanding their operations directly. Instead, coffee entrepreneurs, backed by North American capital, organized a system of highly usurious loans to peasants (reminiscent of the colonial repartimiento de comercio system) to induce them to grow coffee on their land. Among others, Genaro Ayuzo, a kinsman of Basilio Rojas and owner of some seven plantations in the region, became a coffee buyer. Ayuzo began to make loans to peasants in Juquila who would plant coffee on their land. Peasants needed not only start-up capital but frequently also a loan before the harvest season. Coffee buyers then extended credit to the peasants if they agreed to sell them their crop at a price fixed well below its value on the international market and to pay high rates of interests on these loans. Under these arrangements, the credit extended is often for the goods sold at exorbitant prices in the buyer's general store. Obtaining loans and credit, moreover, is often contingent upon being a good customer. Because of their cash needs, peasants are at a disadvantage when it comes to selling products. They can seldom wait for better market prices and are forced to sell cheap and buy dear. The peasant no sooner sells his coffee and pays off his debts than he must turn around and buy the few things he needs from the coffee buyer.

Because Indian communities feared that coffee would turn their communal lands into private property, they forbade its cultivation. Initially, most of the peasants who planted coffee were mestizos who owned small pieces of private property. As a result, despite the coffee buyers' efforts, in the district of Juquila only 900 more hectares of coffee were in production by 1940. A short ten years later, however, their policies began to pay off.

By 1950 population growth, which had followed an exponential curve since 1900, had begun to exceed the capacity of Indian communities to subsist solely on corn farming. Coffee prices on the world market had reached an all-time high, and community pressures finally forced the Indian authorities to allow coffee to be planted on communal lands.

The shift to coffee as a cash crop marked a radical departure in production strategies. Whereas the generalized pattern of subsistence corn farming handed down from pre-Hispanic times had given the local peasantry a large measure of autonomy and independence from the market, the scales of production that coffee demanded to be profitable radically altered this subsistence orientation. It transformed the local economy into a highly dependent and specialized cog in the machinery of the world market. The effects of this transformation were multifaceted. Although the land is still technically communal, coffee parcels—because of the capital invested in them and the longevity of trees—became de facto forms of private property. The introduction of coffee created a market for land within these communities, and not just for coffee parcels. Although peasant coffee growers put their best lands into coffee, they still wanted to buy cornfields. As a result, land ownership became concentrated in fewer and fewer hands. Moreover, as communal lands were divided between barrios, some barrios had more coffee land than others, and bitter conflicts erupted between them in many Chatino villages: Yaitepec, Teotepec, Lachao, Panixtlahuaca, and Juquila, to name a few.

Conflicts

As privatization engendered conflicts between claims to land based on "sale" and those based on traditional rights of inheritance or usufruct, the fuel of envy and witchcraft accusations was added to the fires that produced homicides. As privatization proceeded apace, many villagers were reduced to landless rural proletarians. Witchcraft accusations soon gave way to killings and vendettas, until blood feuds tore the Indian communities apart.

The present pattern of peasant violence, however, is significantly different from the violence leading up to the Revolution. When coffee plantations first invaded the district, the violence was directed outward—as a defense against the mestizo elites and plantations threatening the Indians' land. In contrast, the bloodshed accompanying the introduction of coffee on communal lands has been primarily directed inward—at other members of the Indian communities.

As peasants have become increasingly dependent on the market, not only have Indian and peasant communities become ever more violent but also the various coalitions that traditionally served as a base for community solidarity have become harder to sustain. In Indian communities these coalitions are maintained by reciprocities among kin and fictive kin, such as compadres, by actively participating in the community's civil-religious hierarchy. These coalitions, and many other superficially odd village practices are forms of social insurance. As cash becomes an ever more essential tool of production, households that grow coffee become less and less willing to distribute their wealth in religious offices. As a result, *cargo* systems have begun to atrophy, and in Panixtlahuaca they have been abolished altogether. The gradual weakening of fiesta systems and of the Indian communities' defensive solidarity has not lessened the exploitation of such communities; it has merely changed its form. Whereas in the past, goods and labor were pumped out of Chatino communities by the fiesta system, now they are extracted by a system of usurious loans from buyers to peasant coffee growers.

Despite the internal conflicts tearing apart the fabric of Chatino communities, when threats are made to the villages' territorial claims, they are still capable of uniting in common defense. Territorial battles continue to be fought between Yaitepec and the neighboring communities of Juquila, Yolotepec, and Temaxcaltepec. Yolotepec continues to defend its lands from San Juan Lachao. Ixtapan and Santiago Minas are still engaged in a prolonged and bloody war. Tataltepec and Tepenixtlahuaca also continue to dispute a boundary area between them. Similarly, communities have continued to defend their interests against attempts by plantation owners to expand or solidify their claims to land through political chicanery. In recent years, peasants in Juquila have invaded Rancho Viejo and have torn down its fences when its owners threatened communal lands. Indians in Yaitepec, attempting to recover communal lands leased in 1899 by the plantation La Constancia have invaded it several times. On at least two occasions they have killed members of the owner's family.

Political Factionalism

Although the Revolution did away with the hated system of jefes políticos and their monopoly over local politics, their demise was not without its price. Its cost was greater factionalism as local elites vied with one another for political and economic power. In what might be described as a power vacuum following the Revolution, these factions, led by local strongmen—merchants, plantation owners, and even priests—behaved much like the classic Sicilian Mafia (Hobsbawm 1959:50–56). Local caciques surround themselves with men who need their political protection—frequently because they have killed someone in their home community. Caciques use these men as thugs and killers to protect themselves both from their political rivals and from the general populace, whose interests they have repeatedly frustrated by preventing land reform or substantial political change. Since the power of rival strongmen also rests on supporters, these *políticos* used patronage and *compadrazgo* (ritual coparenthood) to recruit peasants and Indian followers. Conflicts between political rivals invariably drew their followers into them, frequently with gory results. Political struggles between the elites have been particularly bitter in mestizo-dominated centers such as Juquila and Nopala.

Since the establishment of the PRI in the 1930s, these feuding factions have taken on political masks. For more than fifty years, one Mafia-like faction, whose public face is the PRI, has been headed by a group of businessmen, coffee buyers, and plantation owners. Several groups in Juquila have opposed this faction. The most enduring of them, however, has been an equally Mafia-like faction, whose political face has been the Partido de la Auténtico Revolución Mexicana, PARM. Until they were overthrown in a violent confrontation in 1982, this faction was led by a priest (who was a local cacique) and by the head of the communal lands office in Juquila. The struggle between PRI and PARM factions was particularly bitter, because the priest and his mistress were the principal competitors of the coffee buyers of the PRI faction. As the scale of the coffee trade grew, the rivalry between these two factions became increasingly intense and bloody.

The Police and the Army

The principal weapons the state uses to control violence are the army, the police, and the court system. It has had only limited success in controlling violence in Juquila, however, because of several structural contradictions.

Although there exist local and state police and federal troops, the government's distrust of Indian communities—whom the government fears might use weapons in revolt or against other Indian communities—has meant that their local constabularies are unarmed. Moreover, the police force in Chatino communities is usually made up of young boys aged thirteen to eighteen, who serve as *topiles*, errand boys, for the civil authorities. When violence occurs, unarmed topiles are extremely reluctant to attempt to arrest armed culprits. Although in theory Indian communities can call upon state and federal troops to make arrests, in practice Chatino authorities almost never do. In part this is because underpaid police forces are notoriously corrupt. But more than this it is because a homicide, in which one villager kills another, creates a deep schism in the community. Any action against offenders would constitute taking sides and would invite reprisals. Given the constant threat of violence, the understandable attitude of Indian authorities is that "Only God can punish a murderer." Although by law civil authorities must investigate homicides and report their findings to the district court, reports most often read "Killed by a person or persons unknown." Because witnesses cannot count on police protection, and because testifying invites reprisal, few are willing to become involved. Even when arrests are made, few result in a conviction. Because vengeance is left to God's will and the victim's family, blood feuds fester. Despite government attempts to control violence through stringent gun-control laws and periodic raids by the state police and the army on Indian and peasant communities to confiscate weapons, the level of violence in the area has created a lucrative black market in arms, and many confiscated weapons eventually recirculate.

Justice

The reluctance of Indians to take cases to the district court in Juquila goes beyond a fear of reprisals. It also stems from a fear of the power the court wields. Unlike Indian municipal courts, which settle disputes through mediation and consensus, the district court is dominated by mestizos and its legalisms are alien. Moreover, its justice is often influenced by the politics of patronage. Since in court a person's economic status and political connections often determine the outcome of a case, Indians, peasants, and the poor are at a distinct disadvantage. Despite peasants' and Indians' fear of Juquila's justice, the perception that justice is for sale and is arbitrary leads them to take matters into their own hands.

Primitive Political Movements

As long as homicides are directed at other Indians and poor peasants, violence poses little threat to the state, and little effort is made to apprehend murderers. In fact, since the schisms engendered by blood feuds in Indian villages erode the community's solidarity, the violence is to the advantage of the state, as divided villages are more easily manipulated and controlled politically. The reaction to battles between villages, invasions of plantations, and homicides directed at elites, however, is much more vigorous. Battles between villages over boundaries invariably result in the state asserting its authority, first by sending in troops to guarantee the peace and second by taking legal steps to resolve the problem. These legal measures, however, rarely decide anything; they merely set the stage for the next round. Similarly, the invasion of plantations by peasants calls for the state's response. Finca owners typically obtain injunctions against the peasant community, and troops are called in to evict the peasants, often by force of arms (Greenberg 1981:75–81). The state also uses its power to quell the violent demonstrations that have often followed the fraudulent election of PRI candidates in Juquila. The use of force to defend the status quo is not, however, without danger: each time it is employed, class conflicts are reinforced.

The sundry conflicts present in the region are, broadly speaking, reactions to the penetration of capitalistic forms of economy. Even conflicts rooted in the pre-Hispanic past have survived and continue to bear their deadly fruit, because they were carefully nurtured by the colonial administration. Until now, the response to capitalist development has been manifested in what Hobsbawm would term primitive rather than modern forms of social protest: movements, banditry, Mafias, blood feuds, mob violence, and village insurrections. While these reactions have often been misdirected, more revolutionary and politically based forms of class struggle are likely to arise because repression is a continuing feature of the political landscape.

Chapter 15

THE IDEOLOGY OF

CONFLICT AND VIOLENCE

I n Juquila, two moral orders, one Indian and one mestizo, compete with one another. Although both claim to be Catholic and they use many of the same symbols, Indian folk Catholicism is rooted in a preexisting native religion, and it entails a fundamentally different set of premises from mestizo Catholicism. Chatino folk Catholicism promotes values of equality, reciprocity, and cooperation. In contrast, the Catholicism of mestizos is a state religion that justifies the individualistic values and inequalities of capitalism. In this bicultural community, the differing moral claims that the two cultures make often generate conflict. They not only give rise to conflict between Indians and mestizos, but since many individuals (such as Don Fortino) have a foot in both worlds, these conflicting moral systems may lead to inner turmoil as well.

The differences between Indian and mestizo moral universes are profound, entailing antithetical sets of beliefs and norms and radically different notions of good and evil. On the one hand, the Church offers a vision of the universe split into two opposing camps: the pure good of God and the malice of the devil, who rules this pervasively evil world. In this world, all people are by definition sinners. They are condemned to perdition unless they "individually" embrace Christ, who is a forgiving but distant God. Christ, the supreme judge, applies an absolute moral code, passing judgment on every act. Sinners, however, dare not appeal to Christ directly. They must pray to his intermediaries, the saints, to intercede on their behalf. In a world in which access to wealth often depends on personal relations, the saints idealize the system of patronage. Moreover, church doctrine presents alienation as part of the natural order, the result of sin. Since the wages of sin is death, in this simple catechism one atones for sin by suffering and finds redemption in the faithful performance of one's duties to saint, Church, God, and state. In short, in an evolving market economy in which peasants as a class are alienated from power and abundance, this orthodox view offers redemption in this world through personal relations with a patron, and in the next life through personal relations with a patron saint (Greenberg 1981:45–46).

On the other hand, Chatino folk religion is based on the indigenous vision of the supernatural realm. The Chatino cosmos is a layered universe, like a cosmic egg, in which the earth sits in the middle of a sea. On the other side of the sea is the first concave layer of the underworld: the land of the dead. Beneath it is a second layer, inhabited by the devil and his minions. The heavens are like a set of inverted bowls: a layer of air in which the moon and stars travel. The shell of this cosmic egg is circumscribed by the sun in its daily journey through the heavens and the underworld. Holding this egg in his hands, God sits in the company of the saints. This cosmos is conceived of as a kind of ecological system. In it human beings, to maintain the universe in equilibrium, reciprocate with God, saints, pre-Hispanic deities, animals, tonales, nahuales, ancestors, demons, witches, and even the devil. In this complex cosmology, each being is a complex entity, a microcosm of the universe, linked to other beings. For example, human beings have multiple souls: a heart or living soul, which is immortal, and a tonal, or animal spirit companion, whose fate is inextricably linked to their own, so what happens to one, happens to the other. Tonales not only tie humanity to nature, but because gods, saints, and geographical places also have tonales, they connect us to the supernatural. Moreover, these gods, places, and saints may be tonales for individuals as well as for other beings. So, for instance, a person might either have the rain god, ho'o ti'yu, or its mythical flower serpent as a tonal.

Unlike the Cartesian dualism of Spanish Catholicism, in which the irreconcilable opposition of good and evil locks them in a universal contest, Chatino folk Catholicism does not bifurcate good and evil into separate spheres. Instead, it expresses such dualities in metaphors of sexual union or marriage as being essential to the equilibrium of the universe (Taussig 1980:161–163). Chatino saints and deities can be both malevolent and benevolent at the same time. For example, Christ and the devil are brothers; both are sons of the Virgin of Juquila. As a result, the devil is capable of "good," just as the gods and saints can do "evil." For instance, the "holy spirit" of a household saint is its owner's guardian angel and will send all manner of harm, or even kill, if asked to do so (Greenberg 1981:96). Moreover, the Chatino conception of sin is quite different from the Church's universal definition of morality. Theirs is a normative definition that becomes less and less stringent as it radiates away from the family circle to kinsmen, villagers, and outsiders.[1] Again, in contrast to the Church's view, in which individuals are held personally liable for their sins, the folk religion sees many infractions and crimes—such as carelessness in ritual—as disturbances of the universe at large, which might threaten the future of crops and imperil the whole community (Taussig 1980:176–177).

The Native Critique of and Resistance to Capitalism

In the confrontation between these two moral orders, the Chatino folk religion and belief have come to express a searing critique of the unbalanced exchanges essential to capitalism, portraying them as a diabolical form of cannibalism. For instance, in the symbolic landscape in which Indians express their experience of Spanish greed, mastery, and violence, the mountain god is equated with the devil, who is described as a rich hacendado in constant need of workers and pack animals for his many enterprises (Taussig 1980:184). A thoroughly evil spirit, he is described as a fat, greedy mestizo dressed in European garb who with promises of wealth lures Indians to his abode to devour them. These metaphors of cannibalism are also extended to foreigners. The Chatino, for example, believe that gringos live across the sea (that is, are members of the underworld) and eat children.

Among the consequences of these beliefs is the fact that chicanery is suspected if one suddenly becomes wealthy. Hard work does not lead to sudden wealth; sudden wealth comes from making a pact with the devil, the real owner of all the riches on earth. Reputedly, witches and *curanderos* also gain their power to change themselves into *nahuales* (human-animal doubles who attack people or eat their tonales) not only by selling their souls to the devil but also by promising to deliver the souls of others.[2] The money gained from such pacts is not only dangerous but sterile. It brings little or no benefit to those who take or have it. It is most often squandered on drink and women. As Fortino's narrative indicates, there is a deep-seated fear of ill-gotten money, buried money, or money that is not earned. For instance, Fortino claims that the money the presidente stole from the Church would not let him sleep and finally killed him. Fortino, consequently, always gave any money he found to the saints.

Rich mestizos are automatically suspected of having made pacts with the devil. For instance, I was told by a number of Chatino that Don Genaro Ayuzo, a rich coffee buyer and plantation owner (and father-in-law of Fortino's son) had such a pact. The proof they offered is that he never seems to grow old and has survived several attempts on his life. Because the Chatino, like other Indians, believe that the rich have a pact with the devil, they consider it dangerous to work for them (Flanet 1977:92). These beliefs, of course, reflect the conditions on mestizo ranches and plantations, where low wages make it hard to make ends meet, and the arduous work consumes one's health.

The Personal Face of Class Conflict

These conceptions do more than encourage Indians to avoid relationships of dependence through which they are exploited; they influence their re-actions to the inequalities generated as these relations penetrate the heart of the community. In the late 1940s and early 1950s, when peasants in the region began to specialize in coffee as a cash crop, the inequalities created by changing land tenure violated village norms of sharing, cooperation, and reciprocity. Instead of casting these conflicts in class terms, people personal-ized them. They blamed their misfortunes on the greed, envy, and jealousy of evil people. They explained these changes as witchcraft and saw them as personal attacks. Villagers began to suspect one another of witchcraft, and as Fortino notes, started killing witches in great numbers.

Although not all those killed are labeled witches, the evaluation of char-acter plays an important role in social relations. Within the moral universe that sustains reciprocity and cooperation, two opposed archetypes guide the judgment of an individual's actions and moral reputation. On one end of the continuum are *gente humilde*, ideally humble, good people. They are consider-ate, generous, respectful, honorable, serious, hardworking, and trustworthy. This is an expression of the way people would like to live their lives. Humility implies a pervasive sense of egalitarianism. It is the absence of selfishness and the presence of an altruism that puts the desires of others ahead of one's own immediate welfare or self-interest (Selby 1974:23). At the other end of this continuum are the *egoistas*. These are selfish, evil people who pursue self-interest to the detriment of the common interest of the group (Romanucci-Ross 1973:94). Such people are reputed to be lazy, untrustworthy, greedy, envious, petty, unruly, disrespectful, and shameless. Within this moral frame-work the difference between the gente humilde and the egoistas is generally explained in terms of *envidia*, or envy. Witchcraft is invariably ascribed to envy, as it expresses the dark side of human character and the possibility of evil in social relations (Selby 1974:29–30). As among the Zapotec, "envy is a style, a way of coping, just as humility is. The envious man is ... forever making invidious comparisons between himself and others" (Selby 1974:28–29). Unlike the humble man, whose character is changeless and who is there-fore trustworthy, the envious man is a political creature who changes like a chameleon. His often sudden and erratic shifts in behavior mean that he cannot be taken as a constant in the social equation or safely ignored. Because one does not know "what is in his heart," he cannot be trusted (Selby 1974:25–26).

In contrast to moral codes that underwrite reciprocity, the system of values supporting the individualism inherent in the commercial world sees egoism as rational economic behavior. Those who are successful in this competitive world are described as being sharp or as having good business sense.

As people often use and manipulate these two opposed systems of values to justify their actions, exploitive relationships may often be disguised in an idiom of friendship, compadrazgo, and even generosity. For instance, although taking in children is phrased in terms of love and charity, Fortino's description of these relationships makes it clear the children are a source of cheap and obedient labor. Since personal relationships often disguise exploitation or make it more palatable, the social evaluation of people as good or bad depends not on whether they exploit other people but on the idiom and style in which they do it. Since patrons, at least symbolically, use an idiom of personal relationships and reciprocity, false consciousness often surround exploitation. For example, even when Fortino speaks of the hard work and low wages he received while working as a blacksmith, he gives no indication that he felt exploited. Similarly, his apprenticeship with the beltmaker, initially unpaid work, is wrapped in personal affection and gratitude for this man's patience in teaching him a trade.

Because exploitive relations are ordinarily disguised by personal relationships, class conflicts have a personal face. They are cast in terms of bad people who are disloyal, abuse confidence, betray trusts, and injure one out of envy, jealousy, or greed. Since conflicts are personalized in these terms, class struggles tend to focus on individuals instead of groups.

Egalitarian Ideology and Conflict

The personal cast to relationships, even those of exploitation, tends to submerge the disparities that exist within the community in an egalitarian ideology that emphasizes sameness (Jayawardena 1968). Its basic premise, that "We are all equal," is proclaimed daily as villagers address one another as brother, paisano (countryman), friend, or compadre. This egalitarianism, however, is not based on equal rights but on certain empirical facts perceived through the experience of deprivation, such as common residence and descent, common subordination, relative absence of differences in wealth, and feelings of powerlessness. Egalitarianism takes these facts and makes them the basis of norms of interpersonal relations. Generally expressed in terms of brotherhood, these norms take the form of obligations of reciprocity or fiesta sponsorship. As long as these traditional obligations are met, individual differences in wealth, power, and prestige may be disregarded and subsumed in notions of brotherhood.

Egalitarianism, however, is a two-edged sword. The same norms that stress friendship and brotherhood may be turned against one if a favor is refused. As a result, among the hardest things to do is to say no. Any denial of reciprocity is problematical. Even a "No, thank you" is often seen as a rejection of a favor and may be keenly felt. For instance, to refuse a drink is considered a personal insult and often leads to a bitter argument or conflict (Flanet 1977:176). In such circumstances, friendship turns to hatred and even murder. Because the communities' relations with the wider society have become increasingly capitalistic, it has become more difficult to meet the traditional obligations of reciprocity with kin, compadres, and neighbors. Although men feel compelled by the expectations of reciprocity to accede to the demands of kinsmen and friends, they are often forced to deny these demands by the facts of the marketplace. In the face of this no-win situation, men often lie. To illustrate, when a compadre asks a man for a loan, since he cannot simply say no, he invents a story: "I can't just now, but I'll be glad to in a couple of weeks." Because each lie erodes trust, he can only put off his compadre for so long before he risks making an enemy. Even if the loan is made, it may be made grudgingly and the borrower resented. In this process, the inevitable conflict between the individualism of the wider society and the egalitarian ethics of the community creates frequent, spasmodic, and sometimes violent interpersonal quarrels.

As Jayawardena has observed, when egalitarian norms are violated, the resulting gossip, envy, slander, and violence, though not always successful in resolving conflicts, indicate the strength, not the weakness, of community bonds (1968:441). In fact, since capitalist relations of production erode peasant strategies of subsistence, thus placing households at greater risk, such bonds are not only needed but, when threatened, may lead to serious confrontations. Such conflicts are a defensive response to the inroads of capitalist development and serve to inhibit the free accumulation and use of capital to alienate land and labor.

The Defense of Communal Rights

Egalitarian responses are particularly strong where capitalist forms of investment threaten communal rights and lands. In such instances, every possible means, including violence, is considered honorable and justifiable, as Fortino's description of such events shows. Even so, while "fighting for the pueblo" may be honorable, individual disputes that lead to violence are condemned. These egalitarian ideals also extend to politics, especially in Indian communities. The egalitarian notion of politics, as expressed by Fortino, is that one should serve the community and not use one's office for personal advantage. These ideals motivate men not only to serve in civil offices but also repeatedly to sponsor the saints' fiestas, which make men rich in sacred experience but poor in earthly goods. This is exactly the opposite of the politics of patronage in the mestizo world, in which politics is routinely used for personal advancement.

Mechanisms of Social Control

Egalitarian norms and values are premised on reciprocity and mutual trust. As such, reciprocal exchange does more than distribute goods and services; it establishes the foundation for trust and shared confidences. Any change in the frequency and quality of such exchanges transmits important information to participants about the state of relations with their kinsmen, friends, and neighbors. Reciprocity establishes a system of checks and balances, which, as long as balance is maintained, supports mutual trust. Distrust emerges where unbalanced exchange or unequal power defines relationships. In short, reciprocity tells a person whom he or she can trust and how far. One's honor and reputation, in other words, stem from one's record in such relationships. In small communities any infraction affecting such relations is soon public knowledge.

Reputation plays an important role, of course, in establishing mutual trust. Unless a person is trustworthy, one cannot assume he or she will reciprocate or have any commitment to continuing the relationship. As people never forget any rejection or wrong, great care is taken to be correct in such relationships. One outcome of such concerns is that bonds of mutual trust are not just between the two parties in an exchange relationship. They are a good that is distributed in a network of social relationships and that may be affected by the behavior of others for whom one has assumed responsibility (see Vélez-Ibáñez 1983). Because such bonds depend on the good will of others in one's social circle, people will "smile through their teeth" and show elaborate formality and politeness even to those they can hardly stomach.

Trust and distrust are not merely moral indicators of the status of relations of exchange; trust is often an economic necessity. Simply put, in a milieu of corruption, transactions based on trust are preferable because state mechanisms to enforce contracts are unreliable. For instance, when Fortino bought a *cafetal* from Ricardo Velasco and arranged for his father to look after it for him, he told him they didn't need a contract, because he trusted him. Plantation owners, coffee buyers, and other patrons also use social relations to tie peasants to them as *compadres* whenever possible. Coffee buyers, for example, in order to buy cheap and sell dear, use the idiom of trust as a social guarantee for the credit they extend to peasants. Because exchange often depends on trust, in many transactions price is not determined strictly by market forces but also partly by one's social obligations. A coffee buyer may give a peasant compadre a break on the price of goods he sells in his store. Although the exchange is not truly balanced, this obligates the peasant compadre to sell his coffee to this coffee buyer rather than to one of his competitors, who might actually pay more.

Because exploitation and unbalanced forms of exchange are often disguised as social relations premised on trust, there is a curious contradiction in these relationships, in which giving is valued but taking borders on the immoral. For example, Fortino persuaded his brother-in-law to buy him barber's clippers, promising to cut the family's hair in return. When his sister found out about it, however, she accused Fortino of being lazy and forced him to return the clippers. This is not just an illustration that it is better to give than to receive; it is a demonstration that delayed reciprocity in the context of capitalist forms of exchange seems to be just another form of unbalanced exchange.

In this context each transaction, each exchange, is a moral statement that must be weighed on a scale of egalitarian norms. Where the transaction is found wanting, a variety of mechanisms, such as gossip and shame, are employed to persuade people to conform to the norms. Since the trust essential to social and economic life is based on reputation and honor, these are powerful mechanisms of social control. Transgressions of norms are not only the immediate subject of gossip, they are stains that are not forgotten.

Envy also plays a significant role in enforcing reciprocity and compliance with egalitarian norms. Although envy is often expressed in the form of compliments, these compliments hide thinly disguised feelings of hostility and carry an implicit threat of aggression. For example, when one admires an animal and asks the owner to sell it, if the owner refuses, it is commonly believed that the animal will die. As Flanet has observed, "The person who compliments is, in fact, guilty of aggression. He is saying the other has some trait or quality or possession that he would like himself . . . or he is telling the person he compliments that he has risen above his proper level, and that his behavior may trigger sanctions" (1977:156). As so many live at the margin, even the most minuscule differentiation evokes petty resentments, ill will, malice, and actions to censure the upstart's status or cancel the gains (Romanucci-Ross 1973:96). Envy also provides a convenient explanation for a history of bad dealings between parties which often obscures the wider class bases of conflicts by reducing them to human passion or deviance.

It is but a small step from envy to accusations of witchcraft. Such accusations are the outcome of a labeling process in which an individual's actions are judged against egalitarian norms and deemed immoral. As reciprocity is built on trust, so too are such accusations. Not only do they indicate that the accused has broken the bonds of mutual trust, but, as Selby notes, "To communicate the identity of a witch is a singular act of trust. To believe the news is equally an act of inclusion.... As the news passes from household to household, ... the boundary between insiders and outsiders is affirmed. The acceptance of the witch accusation is tantamount to denying that the accused could be a member of the inside group, and as a result the bonds that bind the insiders are drawn ever tighter" (1974:93). As a mechanism of social control enforcing conformity to egalitarian norms and values, charges of witchcraft either discourage antisocial behavior or (because their behavior creates dangerous conflicts among its members) end in the expulsion of deviant individuals from the inner group.[3] As previously noted, folk beliefs make it abundantly clear that it is the abandonment of reciprocity in the pursuit of wealth that gives rise to such accusations. Such a strategy is tantamount to a pact with the devil. Although this strategy may bring individuals money and wealth, it is often at the expense of the rest of the community. Laying the blame for illness, crop failures, and disasters at the feet of individuals who have made a pact with the capitalist devil is both an explanation of misfortune and a political statement. Since "the money economy imposed from the outside is a disruptive influence in the village community, creating conflict within it, or the loss of land to outsiders," such witchcraft accusations "can be seen as a defense of the Indian way of life" (Wolf 1957:48).

The Ideology of Individualism

The ideology of individualism is founded on a capitalist ethic that holds that individual responsibility and effort should bring personal reward. This ideology not only provides private property with its sacred aura, its basic premises are encoded as a set of legal fictions that grant individuals exclusive title to and ownership of property. The fetishism of saints is particularly interesting in this regard. The Virgin of Juquila, for example, is given the legal status of a person. Her crown is her personal property. By endowing an inanimate but sacred object with a legal personality that can own things, the respect of private property (a basic premise of capitalism) is shown to be sacred too. When, as Fortino recounts, thieves stole her crown, people considered this a crime not against the Church but against the Virgin and wept bitterly at the lack of respect it showed. If private property is sacred, then respect for private property is a virtue. For instance, although Fortino invested fifteen years of time and sweat in working on his brother's ranch, he showed his respect for his brother's property by taking nothing when he left.

Individualism and Honor

Since respect for private property rests on a person's legal or moral claim to it, many cultural preoccupations and disputes revolve around the nature of transactions. These cultural concerns are expressed in terms of legitimacy, honor, and reputation. For example, to provide legitimate heirs, the concept of family honor requires virginity, proper marriage, and chastity among women. Since the inheritance of property depends on a woman's virtue, the rules governing her behavior are as strict before marriage as after. For instance, a good woman does not go into the street alone but "stays at home unless some domestic necessity brings her out.... Visiting and socialization not incidental to household duties are considered to be wasteful, indolent, or immoral habits" (Romanucci-Ross 1973:79). God forbid that her brother or father should see her talking to a man alone; they would probably drag her away or even beat her for it.

Since family honor turns on the reputation of its women for morality, their every move may become the subject of village gossip. Because the women's stock in the village rises and falls accordingly, they have a vital interest in attacking or defending one another's reputations. This clear double standard not only places the burden of family honor on women but imposes an absolute moral dichotomy that turns them into either saints or whores. Since a man's legitimacy depends on his mother and that of his children on his wife, they are like saints to be respected and their honor defended. Any woman who enters into an illicit relationship is by definition a fallen woman. Since the worst thing a man can do to another is to defile his family, men jealously guard the fidelity of their wives and react severely, even violently, to anything that damages the reputation of the women in the family (Romanucci-Ross 1973:106). Insults that question a man's legitimacy or his wife's chastity are likely to lead to violence.

Although the family honor rests on sexual behavior, a man's personal reputation, his "good name," does not. Instead, the respect he may enjoy hinges on his track record for honesty and fairness. The measure of a person's good name is his "word." It is his good name that insures relations of trust essential to economic transactions, and good will and support in political matters. A man will try to protect his good name by honoring the trusts not only of the property placed in his care but also of the confidential information imparted to him. A man who does this consistently is both respected and trusted.

Individualism and Machismo

The ideology of individualism finds its most extreme expression in *machismo*, or manliness. As a popular saying defines it, "To be a man, one must drink, have passed at least one night in jail, and have been shot once." It is through machismo that men defend their honor and reputation, and that of their family. The language of machismo is often sexual. A man can accept almost any kind of insult except one to his mother, as this is a direct questioning of his family's honor and his legitimacy. As capitalist relations of production and exchange come increasingly to define social relations within the village, competition over resources makes people sensitive about their status and about insults. Where honor and reputation are at stake, despite moral teachings about turning the other cheek, the code of manliness requires that one should not yield or give in but be willing to fight. For example, when Don Fortino confronted the public prosecutor at a dance and took away his gun, he sought to provoke a fight by questioning his manliness: "Are you a real man or not? I'm more of a man than you. I'm brave. I don't need a gun for courage."

The ideology of individualism associated with machismo defines life as a struggle, *una lucha*, in which a man "must use whatever resources he has to 'defend' himself" (Foster 1967:135). In this sense, being macho is simply defending oneself against economic disaster or social compromise. It is the struggle to maintain one's independence by not being in anyone's debt or under anyone's power. Dependence is demeaning; it replicates the position of women and children. In the language of machismo, it is castrating. In contrast, machismo means having the wit, knowledge, and resources to take the right step at the right time, to remain on top of the situation. Nevertheless, being manly and being macho are two different qualities. Being manly implies living up to one's obligations to others and implies taking responsibility for one's actions. To some extent, being macho is a perversion of these values. Ultimately, if violence does not get one killed, one may be forced to flee. In either case, it is a man's family who will suffer.

Individualism and Compromisos

Entailed in the ideology of individualism is the principle of being in debt to no man. A man who has no economic or political debts is said to be *sin compromiso*, or uncompromised by anything. Such a man may do as he pleases (Flanet 1977:179). To the villagers, the notion of being *sin compromiso* entails a strategy of avoiding entanglements in conflict, which are considered dangerous compromisos. They are appointments with death.

Since involvement in conflict may lead to compromisos, the primary rule guiding most people in their relations with others is to avoid trouble at almost any cost (Foster 1967:105). This strategy is summed up by such important phrases as *evitar dificultades* (to avoid difficulties) and *de no meterse* (not to involve oneself). To do the opposite is to become a troublemaker (a *pleitista* or *revoltoso*) or a *metiche* (one who sticks his nose into other people's business).

Villagers have well-developed strategies to avoid being compromised. Don Fortino, for example, recommends that if one wants to avoid problems, one should not carry a gun or go out alone, should stay out of politics, and must remain uninvolved in conflicts. He emphasizes that in politics or conflict it is important to remain neutral and "not to define one's position as against them." One must also be careful not to form too close a relationship with people. One must be particularly careful not to fall under others' mandate by accepting favors that put one in their debt. So that people won't feel envious, he counsels, one should not be conspicuous with one's wealth or take advantage of people. Since drinking is often the occasion for violence, he advises one not to drink, attend fiestas, or go to cantinas.

Remaining uninvolved in conflict, however, is not easy. It is a matter not only of avoidance but also of impression management, of hiding feelings of hostility. People often go to great lengths to deny feelings of hostility (O'Nell 1981:360). Similarly, it is dangerous to know certain things, because such knowledge may be compromising. Where serious conflicts are concerned, there is a law of silence. Typically, people pretend ignorance of them, refuse to talk about them, or downplay their seriousness, a tactic that is especially common in factional conflicts.

Individualism and Distrust

Since the prevalence of conflict forces people to hide their thoughts behind a mask of dignity, harmony, and courtesy, the result is that except in one's immediate family, distrust is the rule. Because people are afraid to express their true feelings, one cannot know what is in others' hearts, and one can never be sure who can be trusted. Suspicion, timidity, and fear mark everyone's behavior. People are inordinately sensitive to real and imagined slights, insults, and criticisms (Foster 1967:96–103).

The sensitivity and concern people show over small slights or other details of behavior stem from the extraordinary amount of information these signals convey. Since people are distrusted if they become unpredictable, small changes or inconsistencies in their behavior may signal important shifts in attitude. Since even people who try to avoid conflict may be compromised when kinsmen or friends become embroiled in conflicts, the consistency of their behavior is a public signal of their intentions. For example, even though Salomón's father and brothers were murdered in a feud, he managed to stay out of it by his unwavering avoidance of the conflict. When his father was killed, as a sign of his uninvolvement he did not even attend the funeral. Fortino did much the same thing in distancing himself from his brother Timoteo's battles. He avoided his brother and advised his son, Nico, to do the same.

Machismo and the Compromiso

A compromiso is not a private affair. Once a man has been compromised by an ongoing conflict, he is a marked man. He lives on borrowed time. He is in a war, playing a game of hide-and-seek with death (Flanet 1977:203). He must take care or he may be killed right off. His *credo* becomes extreme individualism. He lives on the defensive for days, months, years. As Flanet describes it, "He trusts only his pistol. He stops attending fiestas, going to bars, going out at night. He shuts himself up at night. He is afraid of his own shadow" (1977:203–204). Only if luck is with him will he live to old age. As Flanet notes, the tragedy of this game is that hiding from one's enemies means giving up a measure of self-respect and manhood. In the end, many men choose to live the life of a *valiente* and go looking for death (Flanet 1977:204). The valiente lives his tragedy. When he feels his end is coming, he goes to find death on his own terms. He wants to die honorably, bravely, heroically. He will face his enemy and with exaggerated machismo tell him, "Pull your gun. I want to die with you" (Flanet 1977:205).

Most violence, however, is not heroic. People are often ambushed or set on by a group of killers. As Foster notes, "An opponent or enemy may be accused of being egotistical, abusive, treacherous, quarrelsome, or dishonest, but he is unlikely to be accused of not playing fair. . . . It is assumed that opponents will use any means at their disposal. A murderer hopes to shoot from ambush; surprise is one of his resources" (1967:110). Often the surprise comes as a betrayal. Each new killing engenders new enemies. Because allegiances may shift, each murder forces everyone to sort out a tangle of loyalties to kinsmen, friends, and compadres. Inevitably, some supporters become enemies who, like Judas, betray one. In the nastiness of blood feuds, revenge, like hunting a cattle-killing jaguar and its cubs as well, seeks not just to even the score but to go one better by eliminating friends and kinsmen whether they were involved or not.

False Consciousness and Individualism

The ideology of individualism, like that of egalitarianism, disguises social realities and produces a false consciousness of the world. It directs attention away from the material underpinnings of contention by transforming conflicts over the right to the use and distribution of resources into sexually charged matters of manhood and honor. In this respect, the ideology of individualism bears a formal resemblance to the ideology of capitalism, of which it is an integral part. Where capitalist ideology mystifies the social relations that separate people from the products of their labor by reducing land, labor, and everything else to commodities exchanged in a magical matrix of things, the ideology of individualism transforms the conflicts over commodities into phantasmagoric sexual competition among men. In so doing, the real nature of conflict is not just disguised but is lifted off its material base so that even men who possess nothing but their manhood can fight over women and honor.

Although both egalitarianism and individualism mystify certain aspects of social relations, the ideology of egalitarianism is itself a reaction to individualism and contains a critique of it. As relations with the wider society become increasingly capitalist, Indian communities have come uneasily to contain these two contradictory ideologies within themselves. As a result, every social act requires individuals to choose between the alternatives the ideologies present. Friction and violence not only hang on their choices, but each of these ideologies generates its own form of turmoil and mayhem.

Chapter 16

DISPUTING AND FORMS

OF CONFLICT

Capitalist development puts all social relations in a pressure cooker. The way conflicts are expressed, however, and the forms they take are just as complex as their causes. Although all social groups contain their own peculiar conflicts, the processes that lead to the conflicts are often external. This is because each group—whether large or small, formal or informal, local or regional—has its own niche in the political economy.[1] As a result, each group, depending on its composition, size, and political weight, has its own proclivity for particular forms of violence, and each uses distinctive arenas for settling disputes. For example, in political and economic struggles between Indians and mestizos, Indians are often unable to influence external powerholders, so when their interests are threatened they usually have little choice but to take the law into their own hands. In contrast, because mestizos generally have greater access to patrons, they are more likely to use legitimized forms of violence by calling on the court, the army, or the police to fight their battles. The point is that within larger political and economic entities the specific location occupied by families, communities, political parties, and ethnic groups not only gives each a distinctive set of structural problems and conflicts but also constrains their choices, making certain forms of violence more likely than others.

Conflict Within the Family

Capitalist relations of production and exchange, besides generating struggles between classes, cause significant conflicts that corrode the social bonds within classes. As capitalist forms have expanded and have rationalized systems of production and concentrated wealth in fewer and fewer hands, households and families in Juquila have come under growing pressure.

This pressure makes the relationship between a husband and a wife easily the most fragile within the family. Although social forces may strain marriages, economic pressures are often at the root of domestic difficulties. In part this stems from inheritance patterns. Although, in theory, estates are divided equally among siblings, in practice, because husbands are expected to support their wives, men usually inherit the productive resources, such as land. Because women seldom inherit important sources of income, they find themselves in difficult circumstances when they are widowed or abandoned. Beyond making women dependent on men, this pattern induces wives to put up with their abusive, drunken, or adulterous husbands for as long as they continue to be good providers. Only when a man fails to live up to his economic responsibilities by squandering resources on drink or other women is a wife likely to abandon him. Fortino's mother, for instance, threw his father out because he took money he gave her to support the household and spent it on other women. This, however, is generally a last resort. A woman's first line of defense is to attack her rivals. Because a man's mistress is apt to pressure him to leave his family, conflicts (although not homicides) are more likely to occur between women over men than vice versa. As Romanucci-Ross has observed, "Women make more of a spouse's adultery than do men (though the opposite is supposed to be true), but they do not regard it as a basis for separation unless it leads to nonsupport. Women leave men more often than they are abandoned by them ... to rejoin their families, to go to their lovers, to support themselves alone" (1973:64).

If women depend on men to provide economic support, men rely on their wives to cook, clean, and care for their children. A man expects his wife to fulfill her domestic obligations and to be obedient. For instance, it is in these terms that Fortino explains his difficulties with his wife following the death of their son. According to Fortino, his son died because his wife disobeyed him and did not send the boy to Oaxaca as instructed. Antonia, on the other hand, blamed Fortino for the child's death because he left town when her son was ill. After the death of their son, their relationship deteriorated. She moved into separate quarters. Fortino grumbled that his wife no longer cooked or cleaned for him because she is lazy and uncaring. He also complained that she no longer asked his permission to travel or told him when she left the house. Fortino has repeatedly tried to throw Antonia out. She has remained because of pressures from his children to maintain the family's honor, since if Fortino were to remarry, they would no longer receive support and might be disinherited.

As the above example shows, many of the same issues arise between parents and children as between husbands and wives. Certain conflicts, however, are peculiar to the parent-child relationship. Parents, while loving, are strict disciplinarians who demand obedience. Any deviations from the moral path are taken seriously. Children are disciplined physically, severely, and frequently, especially if they are too young to understand explanations (Romanucci-Ross 1973:66). The authoritarian stance of parents, however, must be understood in economic and social terms. In an economy where households often live at the margin, mistakes can be costly, and poor decisions may have dire consequences. The social context of households is also critical: a child who keeps bad company, drinks, or fights may involve the family in problems that may compromise everyone. An illustration of this is the conflict between Fortino and his son concerning Nico's uncle. As his uncle was heavily involved in village politics, Fortino repeatedly warned Nicolás that he trusted his uncle too much. Since his son was a grown man, Fortino could do no more than warn him about becoming involved in his uncle's problems. When he ignored his father's advice, it nearly cost him his life.

Differing expectations of sons and daughters also shape the conflicts with them. As children approach puberty, parents worry about their sons' drinking, fighting, or keeping bad company, and about their daughters' moral conduct. The tight rein parents keep on their daughters to guard their chastity and moral reputation is the source of constant conflict with them. A watchful eye is kept on their comings and goings. Breaches of conduct are severely punished. Because arranged marriages are still common, and in any case a family has a considerable stake in marriage alliances, parents routinely discourage their daughters from interacting with young men. Merely talking with a young man may be cause for a beating. Parents go to great lengths to discourage unwanted suitors and elopements. If a girl persists in seeing an unwanted suitor, a common strategy is to pack her off or marry her to someone else. Questions of suitability (involving family, class, reputation, and ethnic background) are not the only obstacles to marriage. One cause of parental resistance to a daughter's marriage may be the loss of her labor. Since couples often prefer to set up their own households, this can be an issue in granting sons permission to marry as well. Fortino's mother, for instance, refused to grant him permission to marry until he could prove that he knew how to work and could support a family. He was over thirty before his mother would consent to his looking for a wife. Fortino, in turn, placed such obstacles before his own daughters that one became a spinster and the other eventually eloped.

Because courtship frequently involves delicate negotiations, it is often a source of conflict both within and between families. For example, Nico's first engagement was broken off by his fiancée's family on the grounds that he was an unfaithful suitor. Nor was his courtship of his wife without conflict. Her father objected to the marriage: Nicolás was the son of an Indian barber, hardly an ideal choice for a wealthy, educated woman. Only when she threatened to elope if her father refused to give them his blessing did he reluctantly consent.

Because of the considerable obstacles—including economic obstacles—that parents may place before couples, elopement is not uncommon. Nevertheless, it is considered a *robo* (a violation akin to rape) and a stain on family honor. The crime involves not just stealing the woman but also depriving her family of the compensations for the loss of a daughter that are ordinarily part of marriage arrangements. Because the family sees elopement as a form of theft, even where the woman is a willing partner, the act of robo can be a dangerous, even violent, enterprise. For instance, Fortino's first plan to steal Antonia included an ambush, guns, and accomplices. It only failed because the *mozo* accompanying her took a different path. Violence may also occur if the eloping couple is caught. Because of the many dangers involved, eloping usually requires the support of trusted friends or kinsmen, who, beyond helping the couple to elope, can help reconcile both families.

Courtship itself may be fraught with danger. A woman may have other suitors who may be tempted to violence. For example, when Fortino began to court Dominga, his rival, a silversmith, hired two soldiers to kill him. Similarly, when Nicolás had problems with his fiancée, Catalina, Fortino cautioned his son not to act crazy or go around with thugs, because of the danger his rival presented. The potential for violence is particularly acute when the suitor is an outsider. Women are expected to marry within the village. Local rules of endogamy equate women with communal property. Within the framework of this ideology, violence against outsiders coming to steal village women is socially approved. For instance, Fortino justifies his eloping with Antonia on the grounds that she had suitors in her village, so he was afraid to come there and court her openly.

Relations among siblings are a particularly contradictory mix of rivalry and cooperation. This is because as children, despite sibling jealousies, household chores and enterprises demand their cooperation. After marriage, however, they are expected to establish independent households. Moreover, struggles over inheritance often set them against one another. One problem in this regard is that membership in a household does not necessarily give one rights to capital accumulation. Collateral relatives have access to food and shelter but not inheritance or accumulated goods. For instance, when Fortino left his brother's home after giving him fifteen years of his labor, he left empty-handed. Even among lineal descendants, such as siblings, rights of inheritance may be clouded. For instance, although he was legitimate, Fortino received little or nothing from his father, because his father remarried after Fortino's mother left him. Even when his half brother Timoteo tore down his father's house and took the adobes and wood from it to build his store on the plaza, Fortino felt that since the materials had come from his father's house, this gave him the right to set up his barbering practice on the store's porch. Exercising this "right" led him into constant conflict with his brother.

Because rights to inheritance may be based on various moral and legal claims, a wide range of kin may be drawn into conflicts. For example, in his conflict with Serafín over the inheritance of his mother's house, Fortino bases his claim to it on moral and legal grounds. First, Fortino argues that he is a closer descendant than Serafín: Fortino was her son; Serafín was only a grandson. Second, Fortino claims usufruct rights because he, not Serafín, helped build the house and has paid the property taxes on the property all these years. Lastly, Fortino argues that he has a greater moral right than Serafín because when Serafín's mother lay dying he did not even come to her deathbed when summoned, nor did he shoulder the responsibilities of raising his son, Agustino, after his own wife died, but left the task to Fortino. Because moral obligations, not just property, go along with inheritance, this latter issue is often a particularly thorny point. Children who do not inherit often fare badly, as was the case with Fortino's half brothers Berto and Francisco. After their uncle grabbed their father's estate, he treated the boys like orphans. Had not Fortino convinced his brother Teófilo to take them in, they would have continued to have a hardscrabble life.

Conflict with Friends and Compadres

Friendship and compadrazgo hinge on maintaining a delicately balanced set of reciprocities. As the rationality of the market has come increasingly to affect economic decisions, individuals are often forced to choose between self-interest and friendship. Despite egalitarian attempts to mask inequalities and disjunctions of interest, money is often put ahead of friendship. Misunderstandings and conflicts among friends are common. This is especially true among men, because they are more prone to use friendship as an instrument to achieve economic or political ends.

Many of these conflicts arise over drinks. When not working, men spend a lot of time drinking with their companions. Even if they are broke, they may drink, since whoever has money will buy. Abuse of this trust, however, is common. When drunk, men pass easily from exaggerated declarations of friendship and affection to rage and jealousy, and like Fortino, they habitually complain that they only have friends when they have money. Because drinking together is a symbolic idiom to express friendship and mutual trust, men are easily offended if a person refuses to drink with them. Even among long-term friends, such refusals may cause fights, even murders, unless excuses such as "I'm taking some medicine and can't" or "I have some work to do first" are accepted. For example, Fortino, in his efforts to stop drinking, ceased going to fiestas, dances, and other social occasions where he would be forced to drink. Even so, his sobriety at times brought him into conflict with his kinsmen and friends. Indeed, because refusals are a denial of the principle of reciprocity, any refusal, even of favors offered, can lead to conflict with friends. For instance, Fortino remembers that when he was young he had many long and heated arguments with Padre Soreano when he would refuse a cup of hot chocolate his godfather offered him because he believed that it had been given to the priest and was not meant for him.

Aside from drinking or a denial of reciprocity, another issue that tears friendships apart, and even leads to violence, is a breach of mutual trust. One illustration of this is the problem Fortino had with Jerónimo Franco after he discovered him making love to the priest's maid in the church. Afraid that Fortino would report them to the priest, they lost faith in him and began to treat him badly. Moreover, as people can be compromised by their friends or kin, loss of confidence need not result from their own actions but merely from their position in a web of friendship, compadrazgo, and kinship. Such a loss of trust may be fatal. In blood feuds, for example, people may be killed simply because they cannot be trusted to stay out of the conflict.

Institutional Expressions of Conflict

Beyond family and friends, an array of institutions are found in the district. These include the Church, schools, municipal government, communal lands organizations, political parties, tax collectors, the army, the state police, and the state courts. The principal complaint about such institutions is that authorities abuse their power and position. Few problems can be solved unless one has connections or cash, or can repay favors in some way. Without these, unless one has a patron who can intercede, little help can be expected from institutions. Not only do individuals become entangled in conflicts with them, but conflicts frequently pit organizations against one another. For instance, in the War of the Cristeros, the confrontation between church and state in the parish took the form of a clash between the priest and the citizen's committee established to administer the Church's property. Not only are national struggles often manifested locally, but since each institution has its own niche in the political economy and its own set of problems, the potential for conflict in each varies accordingly. For instance, one issue in the schools is cruelty to children. Although teachers may be dismissed or transferred, conflicts with schools almost never lead to violence. In contrast, because the Church has often been a platform for political and economic power in the community, struggles with priests have repeatedly led to mass demonstrations and mob violence. In such cases, what begins as a local problem may readily expand to involve the state and national levels of government, as well as the Church's hierarchy.

Because Mexican political institutions rest on a hierarchy of patron-client relations stretching from local communities to the highest levels of government, each change in administration causes turmoil as realignments take place within the system. These changes often cause the political fortunes of local patrons to wax or wane. The constant upheavals caused by the politics of patronage are a well-known source of rancor and violence. In Juquila, for example, as the political patrons (coffee buyers, landowners, or businessmen) try to carve out a bigger slice of the economic pie, they often act like petty Mafias. Since political and economic power—not just political office— is at stake, violent confrontations are apt to occur between their followers, especially around the time of elections. Since Mexican law does not permit the re-election of officials, political bosses seldom run for office themselves. Instead, they seek to maintain their power by running henchmen who will leave important decisions to them. As a result of such battles, the municipal government is under continual siege. As Fortino attests, caciques may fix elections or have them annulled, and not infrequently presidentes are removed from office before finishing their term.

The violence swirling around the caciques is not restricted to clashes between their followers. Like the Mafia, political bosses are not afraid to use violence to remove political rivals or disloyal followers. For example, Don Genaro, a caudillo in Miahuatlán after the Revolution, had Fortino's cousin killed because he refused to carry out an order to kill someone. This assassination is typical of such politically directed violence. Unlike peasants who take the law into their own hands, caciques, landowners, and businessmen prefer to use hired assassins. Such hired assassins are recruited among poor Indians, poor relatives, compadres, or clients who have fled other villages because of their involvement in blood feuds. For instance, when the Muñoz family attempted to kill Fortino's brother, they hired a poor Indian to assassinate Timoteo and trained him to shoot a pistol.

Barrio and Community Conflict

Certain conflicts—such as threats to communal land—may lead to demonstrations, mob attacks, or land invasions. Although patrons may attempt to manipulate these conflicts to gain political support, such manifestations generally reflect a consensus of barrio or community interests. For instance, Yaitepec's conflicts with Yolotepec and Temaxcaltepec over municipio boundaries have caused repeated incidents of violence approaching warfare each time villagers from these towns attempt to plant fields in the disputed areas. Although troops may be called in to keep the peace for a time, usually little if anything can be done to reach a settlement between them. Even where the government steps in to resolve a boundary dispute, the losing side rarely accepts its legal decision. Fortino's account of the war between the Chatino village of Ixtapan and the mestizo community of Santiago Minas is a case in point. Although Santiago Minas prevailed in court because the mestizos have greater knowledge of the political system, more money, and better access to political patronage than the Indians, Ixtapan refused to recognize the legitimacy of the court's decision, and Santiago Minas's legal victory meant nothing on the battlefield.

This type of conflict is not exclusively between communities. As the process of capitalist development has transformed communal lands into private property, conflict within communities has become increasingly common as well. In part, these conflicts reflect ambiguities about land tenure that arise as a result of development. For instance, before the introduction of coffee, the town council granted petitioners usufruct rights to communal land. As long as it was for subsistence, villagers could clear and plant as much land as needed. Because swidden cornfields were abandoned after a year or two, such rights were temporary. When villagers began to grow coffee, they used their usufruct rights to plant, fence, and claim parcels. Coffee trees, however, unlike corn, typically do not begin to produce until their fifth year, so they represent a large investment of both time and capital. Moreover, since trees may produce for more than thirty years, they represent an almost permanent investment. Because of these large investments, planting coffee converts land into a de facto form of private property.

As Fortino's narrative indicates, the transformation of land from communal to private property may be made within the law. Titles may be issued and permissions granted without violence if traditional norms governing community membership and size of holdings are respected. Because large scale transformations usually entail chicanery and extralegal maneuvers, however, they often lead to public outcries and communal forms of resistance. For instance, even though Lázaro Sánchez, while presidente, was able to grab

Rancho Viejo by destroying the municipal archives, when his son-in-law later attempted to use "false titles" to claim the rancho as private property, he provoked villagers to defend its communal status. They invaded the finca, cut down the fences, and would have killed him had they found him. Such conflicts between villagers and private landowners often lead to bloodshed. The conflict, for instance, between Yaitepec and the Valencias over the finca La Constancia has seen blood spilled on both sides.

Capitalist transformations, aside from pitting communal and private interests against one another, have been followed by conflicts that divide communities along barrio lines. As Fortino's testimony indicates, such splits have occurred wherever coffee was introduced—that is, at Yaitepec, Teotepec, Juquila, Panixtlahuaca, San Juan Lachao, and Nopala. Schisms in the community occur along barrio lines for two reasons. First, the barrios are communities within the community. Barrios in Chatino communities have their own rituals and fiestas, and even their own representatives in the town's civil-religious hierarchy. In addition, people often marry within their barrio, creating dense social ties with other barrio members. Second, the rifts follow barrio lines for economic reasons. Prior to the introduction of coffee, the location of one's land did not matter a great deal. Most land was equally unproductive, and swidden cornfields were soon abandoned anyway. Coffee, however, requires special conditions and so can only be grown in certain areas. This puts a premium on such land, and competition for it often leads to violence. Moreover, since communal lands are divided among the barrios, the distribution of such land is very important. Yaitepec, for instance, has been split down the middle by feuds since the introduction of coffee. Just how much this matters may be gauged from the distribution of the coffee lands between its two barrios. Although only 45 percent of the households in the community live in the Barrio Abajo, they have 72 percent of the coffee land in the village. This leaves the 55 percent of the village's households in the Barrio Arriba with only 28 percent of the coffee lands—the cause of much bitterness (Greenberg 1981:196).

Processes of Disputes

Social formations are not like ancient cathedrals built of stone but instead are analogous to legal systems, constantly evolving as they settle disputes. As conflicts are played out, old social orders are reworked and new ones created. Since social relations are shaped and reshaped by conflict, it is essential to understand how conflicts either expand or are resolved.

Individuals and groups in conflict often seek alliances. In Juquila, because many conflicts are intense and violent, such alliances are necessary, not to win but simply to survive. When people are involved in conflicts, they are prone to interpret every gesture as either for or against them and to see people as either friends or enemies. Since neutrality is unacceptable, they construe any association with their enemies as an alliance and any fence-sitting as a betrayal. As a result, conflicts drag individuals, families, groups, and institutions into them, and as they grow in scale, they involve the participants in still other conflicts (Romanucci-Ross 1973:29–32). In blood feuds, for example, disputes between individuals escalate as each killing creates new enemies. As the feuds spread through kinship networks, they take on momentum. Once they begin, they are difficult to end, and many people may be killed as whole towns are engulfed by violence.

Often what starts out as a personal dispute widens, as others are drawn in, to include important leaders, regional political movements, state political parties, and government bureaucracies. In such cases, these disputes become a referendum on issues confronting the community in its relationship with the wider society. As they progress, factions representing all the major components of the village's social universe line up on opposing sides. Such disputes, then, become the focus of gossip within social networks and shape public opinion on a variety of issues (Parnell 1988).

Although social networks may spread blood feuds, the dense crisscrossing of kinship and friendship lines within the village also serves to check their expansion. Social networks often incorporate members who are related to close friends or kinsmen whom an individual can hardly stomach or may even roundly hate but whom he will treat with at least a minimum of courtesy for the sake of others. Because social networks provide offsetting restraints on violence, the families of victims and assassins may hate one another but remain in the village, crossing paths daily. The desire for revenge, however, often lurks beneath the peaceful surface. Since each new killing sees a realignment of loyalties, the potential for violence remains. As nearly everyone in the village is related, when a killing occurs the social restraints on old hatreds may disappear, and blood feuds may flare up again. Because such feuds engender chronic tension and distrust, when social checks disappear or alliances change, people may be killed out of *desconfianza*, a suspicion that they will not remain uninvolved and so must be eliminated as a safety precaution.

Factionalism, Caciques, and Government Involvement

The politics of patronage often has a cyclical quality. Because elites rise to power by providing leadership on local issues, the more serious that conflicts become, the more apt the elites are to become involved. When this happens, what may have been a personal conflict enters a new arena where it becomes part of the factional struggles within the community. The more a patron's personal following and power grows, the more likely he is to resort to force to maintain his power. Moreover, because each battle produces its losers, each increase in his power increases the resentment against him. As violence and his abuse of power increases, people will oppose him by switching their allegiance to another *cacique*. Because this gives the new cacique a free hand to exploit the community, the cycle is likely to be repeated.

Fortino's account of the struggle in Juquila between Lázaro Sánchez and Saúl León Villanueva provides a good illustration of this process. After Sánchez had two of Villanueva's supporters assassinated in 1935 during an Independence Day celebration, the community reacted by boycotting his store, which ruined him financially. Although this finished Sánchez politically, the bitter divisions created in his battles with Villanueva remained long afterward, and the two factions continued to fight and kill one another. As this example shows, the divisions in the community are not simply a matter of personal followings; they follow barrio lines. Hence, after Sánchez's power waned, his cousin Florencio Valencia, the owner of a larger coffee plantation, succeeded him as leader of his faction.

The factionalism in the Chatino village of Panixtlahuaca also had a more profound base than simply a cacique's personal following. In this Chatino village, the rise of *caciquismo* accompanied the introduction of coffee. Fortino's compadre, Don Pepe Flores, came to Panixtlahuaca in 1950 as a schoolteacher. As few Indians were literate, the town officials asked him to become their municipal secretary. Using his position as secretary, Don Pepe established a coffee plantation on over 300 hectares of communal land and made himself a local cacique. During the 1960s, when nearly half the town began to grow coffee on communal lands, he became a rich coffee buyer as well. The process of privatization accompanying the introduction of coffee, however, increased tension. When a Franciscan priest came to Panixtlahuaca in 1968, the tension came to a head. The priest began a campaign against the cacique, pushing for the expropriation and redivision of his lands among the people. At the priest's instigation, the presidente demanded that Don Pepe return the lands he had appropriated from the community. The cacique then appealed to the state and ecclesiastical authorities, claiming that they were trying to dispossess him of his private property. As in many such class struggles between Indians and mestizos, the government sided with Don Pepe. They authorized him to continue working his lands and took punitive action against the presidente municipal, forcing him to resign. In response to this, a drunken mob attacked the cacique's house and burned all his property, forcing him to flee the village.[2] As Fortino's account makes clear, even after the cacique fled, the town remained divided into two warring factions. The consequent violence was truly impressive. In 1973 alone, two presidentes and twenty-five men were killed, and federal troops had to be stationed in the village.

As this case illustrates, when local conflicts escalate they may pit groups against one another at state, regional, and national levels. However, because calling in state or federal troops often turns local conflicts into state or even federal issues, state and federal authorities are loath to become entangled in such struggles. They will only intervene if local officials are unable to deal with them and petition the government to do so. When they do become involved, it often leads to confrontations between the local populace and state or federal troops. Because state and federal intervention often entails a loss of local autonomy, repressive measures by the police and the army, and costly court battles, Indian communities are reluctant to ask the government for help in their affairs. In fact, they will often back down in a conflict if it means the state or federal government's involvement. For example, when the people of Barrio Grande attempted to reclaim Fortino's forty-hectare corn-field by cutting the fences, he sent a letter of protest to the president of the republic. Although the office of the president simply sent a letter instructing local authorities to give him justice, fear of federal involvement was enough to cause them to back down.

Since they lack powerful patrons, the state political apparatus is effectively closed to the common people. So when the interest of peasants and villagers runs counter to that of the elites, forms of mass protest like land invasions or mob violence are the only weapons they have against them. It is more than coincidence that many public protests converge on the town hall or the church, as these buildings are the visible symbols of state and ecclesiastical power in the village. In Juquila, assaults on the town hall by the losing side have become almost a postelection ritual. For instance, when Fortino's election as presidente municipal was annulled due to Florencio Valencia's political machinations, the people of the Barrio de Jesús asked him for guns to kill the new presidente. Fortino refused to become involved in any killings, instead ordering the sergeant not to let anyone into the municipio. In response, Valencia's armed supporters from the Barrio Grande forced their way into the municipio, frightening away the people from the Barrio de Jesús.

As long as such public forms of protest do not get too far out of hand, state and federal authorities will not step in. If they are forced to send in state police or federal troops, however, communities may be punished for rebelling. As happened in the Chatino community of Teotepec (and almost happened in Yaitepec following the invasion of the Valencia's plantation), they may have their political status downgraded from that of a self-governing municipio to that of an agencia subject to another municipio.

Signals and Gossip in the Disputing Process

Disputes broadcast signals to the community that indicate how serious the disputes are at the moment. Homicides, for example, are often preceded by a series of chismes, malicious lies, and gossip. Such chismes are analog measures of conflict: the more people involved and the more often gossip is repeated, the more serious is the conflict. Even silence about a dispute is a signal about its status. When conflict reaches a dangerous level, people become increasingly unwilling to talk about it. A heavy silence often precedes killings (Flanet 1977:175–182). As relations between conflicting parties worsen, a series of incidents and attacks often occurs, taking the form of threats, robberies, vandalism, assaults, and woundings. Such crimes are a signal that conflict is escalating to a dangerous point. Finally, when someone is killed in retaliation, it is a clear sign that blood feuds are imminent.

As it is an appeal to the court of public opinion, gossip plays a crucial role in the disputing process. Gossip has a formal set of rules for developing and evaluating "facts" and hearsay. Because gossip is a labeling process, its standards of evidence are its believability and the probability of its being true. Its believability rests in part on the reputation of the teller as a reliable source, and this is judged in part by how the teller qualifies and narrates the story. If a person claims he saw or heard something, then the more detailed his account, the more likely it is to be believed. If he is only repeating gossip, his reputation as a reliable, careful source is at stake. In that case, his assessment of its source is as important as the tale itself. If the source is of an unreliable nature, it is important to acknowledge this. For example, Fortino, when repeating tales told to him by his godson, Antonio Hernández, carefully adds, "Sometimes I can get the truth out of my godson. Sometimes he denies it to me." If the gossip is to be believed, maintaining one's reputation as a reliable source is of paramount importance. One common strategy speakers use to lend credence to their tales is to specify their personal relationship to the subject. Gossip is often prefaced by a remark to the effect that "Even though he is my (friend, compadre, kinsman), nevertheless I am forced to say this of him."

Apart from the reputation of the teller, judgments on the probability that an account is true rest on how well it accords with the personal histories of those involved. An account is more likely to be accepted if it is in character. As well, how well an account agrees with other versions of the story also influences whether it is believed.

Acceptance of gossip also depends to a large extent on its context. Gossip should be repeated only to the appropriate people (i.e., trusted friends) in a proper context, not in public. The subject must be fitting. As Flanet describes this, "If a poor devil is killed in a drunken brawl, it is fit for gossip; however, if someone important politically is killed or a *valiente* is killed, there may be those who want to take revenge, and one must be prudent" (1977:182). Certain things are just too dangerous to repeat, because such gossip would expose animosities that would make daily life impossible. People who repeat gossip to the wrong people or in the wrong place, or who talk about things that are better left unsaid, are labeled *leperos, revoltosos,* and *chismosos* (lepers, troublemakers, and malicious gossips). Because they have violated the rules for sharing information, much of what they say is discounted.

People defend themselves from verbal attacks by spreading their own gossip and rumors. Women often play an important role in starting, gathering, and repeating the gossip used in the disputing process to assess a person's reputation and shape public opinion. Because women can say things that would get a man killed, men commonly use the hostility and vindictiveness of their women as political weapons in disputes (Flanet 1977:140).

Apart from shaping public opinion in the disputing process, gossip also plays an important role in containing conflicts. As a mechanism of social control similar to public ridicule, shunning, and ostracism, gossip is a means of censuring people. Because it need not be true but merely believed, people fear gossip and will go to great lengths to avoid being the subject of it.[3] What is more, as gossip stains family honor as well as personal reputations, members are pressured to tow the line and avoid embarrassing the family.

The Mediation of Conflict

Conflicts exist in almost every relationship at times which may cause them to lapse or become antagonistic. This is especially true in communities like Juquila where dense, complex, and often overlapping networks divide individual loyalties. On the one hand, this means that as individuals choose sides in a conflict, they alienate friends and relatives who are on the other side. On the other hand, individuals who have kin and friends on both sides may act as mediators even for violent conflicts. Fortino's story of the capture of Urbano Núñez, a Serrano, by Colonel Gustavo Labastida during the Revolution is such an instance. When the colonel's aunt learned that he had decided to execute her nephew Urbano, she managed to convince him to spare Urbano because, unbeknownst to him, Urbano was his kinsman. This form of third-party mediation is common, and generally the more closely mediators are related to the parties concerned, the more likely their efforts as peacemakers are to succeed.[4] For example, when Fortino forcefully took a gun away from the public prosecutor at a dance because he was threatening people with it, and was ready to beat him or worse, the comandante mediated the conflict by approaching Fortino, who was being very macho, in a nonconfrontational, almost womanly manner. He appealed to him to surrender the gun out of friendship rather than because of his authority, saying, "I've always loved you. Please give me that gun."

When such informal efforts at mediation fail, village authorities may become involved. Typically, the town council (made up of the presidente, síndico, alcaldes, and regidores) enters disputes after complaints are made. Although such appeals to the town council are a signal that the conflict is escalating, they also indicate that the parties are still amenable to mediation. In Chatino villages, both plaintiff and defendant are amply plied with mescal and are encouraged to speak from the heart, reenacting their quarrel before the council as the council members examine them. Since the council is composed of fellow villagers, the men who hear a case usually know all the parties well. Because they know the personal histories of those involved, they often use this knowledge as evidence in their favor or to their disadvantage (Nader 1967:124). If they think someone is lying, they may laugh or jeer at him.[5] Since their aim is to mediate disputes, not to punish crimes, the council's main effort is directed toward soothing the two parties (Vogt 1969:280). Because they know a decision for one party would cause the other to continue to bear a grudge, rarely does the town council render a clear-cut decision; instead they often fault or even fine both parties.

By law the town council must refer serious felony cases to the district court to be tried under the state's civil and penal codes. Judges, however, have enormous latitude in the handling of such cases and may choose to mediate rather than try them. A good example of this is the way the judge handled Anselmo's drunken attack on his comadre and compadre with a machete. The judge could have charged Anselmo with felony assault or attempted murder for the machete attack on his comadre and compadre. He also could have brought similar charges against those who later tried to shoot Anselmo in retaliation. Instead, he elected to mediate the dispute by threatening to impose stiff sentences if there were any further violence. Even if the court cannot deter violence, at least the threat posed by long sentences, heavy fines, and the cost of a legal defense may force those involved to flee the village or the region.

Although mediation is an important mechanism for inhibiting the escalation of conflicts, it is not the only way they may be contained. For example, the authorities may define conflicts as private disputes to avoid becoming entangled in them if they believe conflicts are likely to escalate if they do become involved. Or, if the issues involved have public implications, the authorities may simply try to contain the conflict and let the informal mechanisms of social control settle the matter (O'Nell 1981:357). Avoidance and denial, of course, are conflict containment strategies available to all. People often go to great lengths to deny that conflict exists, since admitting its existence may inflame it. Indeed, rather than fighting, people often leave the area to avoid a conflict.

The Effects of Violence

Violence is costly. When men are killed, their mothers, wives, and daughters are often impoverished. For example, with the death of her husband, a widow is not only deprived of his labor and income but also must bear the expense of his funeral, and the division of his estate among grown children may leave her with little to live on and may force her to sell what lands, cattle, or other resources she has left. Even if men are merely wounded, their medical costs may bankrupt their family. Similarly, when men are forced to flee the village, women are often left in dire straits. If perpetrators are so unfortunate as to get caught, their families face legal costs as well as the expense of maintaining them while they are in prison.[6]

Such violence has contradictory effects on the distribution of wealth in the community. At the same time that violence impoverishes some families, it obviously provides the opportunity for others to accumulate land and wealth. By forcing the redistribution of wealth and resources, violence within the community may in fact increase wealth differences within it.

Conflicts are also a source of revenue for the state. As Dennis points out, the government has a vested interest in maintaining the system of continued feuds between villages. The feuds not only serve to divide the villages, making them dependent on the central government for arbitration, but they also provide an endless source of revenue as such disputes are dragged out (Dennis 1976:177–183). Inevitably, litigation pumps vast sums of money out of the community.[7] Aside from filing fees, seals, and stamps, which enrich state coffers, such disputes provide a steady source of fees and bribes for lawyers, patrons, judges, and bureaucrats. As a result, even within the village the attitude of authorities may be, "Well, let them fight. It means more revenue for the village treasury" (Dennis 1976:178).

Capitalist development, by reducing the communal lands of Chatino communities, has forced many villagers to migrate to look for work outside the area, and in addition the deep, vicious blood feuds engendered by development have added to this steady stream of refugees. As of 1980, about 12 percent of the 30,000 Chatino had left their home communities to live elsewhere in the state. Some idea of the destination of these economic and political refugees may be gathered from the 1980 census (Secretaría de Programación y Presupuesto 1983:vol. 20). It shows that some 3,097 Chatino are found in municipios outside of the region. Of these, 77 percent are in the city of Oaxaca or its surrounding villages in the central valleys. Another 13 percent have moved to coastal villages, probably to work on plantations. The remaining 10 percent are spread in small numbers throughout the state.

The social effects of such migrations on the Chatino villages are twofold. First, exposure to the wider society has a strong acculturative influence on peasants. As they return, their home communities are exposed to all kinds of new and often conflicting cultural values, which tend to erode the mechanisms of social control within the village (Restrepo 1970:507–508). Second, violence may follow refugees. Even if they flee to other villages, since both sides of a feud may have their refugees, there is no guarantee that trouble will not follow them. The costs of flight, however, are high. Such refugees must leave their houses, animals, relatives, and social networks of assistance behind them and start over. Because they cannot claim land as native sons in other towns, they must work as peons, or day laborers. As a result, they are often impoverished. In the face of such hardships, even though it may mean death, men like Emiliano may elect to return to their villages and fight.

Perhaps the most pernicious effect of violence is the way it erodes trust. As violence has engulfed communities, the dense networks of kinship, friendship, and reciprocity that promoted village solidarity have given way to a culture of suspicion. Without trust, the ties that build solidarity are the same ones that destroy it. In this culture of suspicion, every association is seen as an alliance, every change as a betrayal. Most tragic of all, although violence rarely settles anything but merely clears the way for more violence, it has become an accepted way of handling disputes.

Afterword

One of the classic problems in science is to understand the relationship between reality and the observer. Simply stated, the problem is: How does theory affect perception? And in the social sciences, such as anthropology, does personality determine which theoretical models an investigator may find attractive? For example, when Redfield went to study Tepoztlán in 1930, he had a romantic vision of the countryside. He was interested in finding a solidary rural community to represent one pole of a continuum leading toward anonymous and conflictive urban places (Redfield 1930). Oscar Lewis, an antiromantic, was interested in class conflict, so when he restudied Tepoztlán twenty years later, he emphasized the conflicts in the community (Lewis 1951). The contrasts between these two studies of Tepoztlán, however, are not merely reflections of the theoretical interests and expectations of each man; historical changes had in fact increased the level of conflict in the community.

I bring up this problem of interpretation and history because things do indeed change. When I interviewed Don Fortino in 1978, I was skeptical—as was he—that any solution to the violence afflicting the region could be found. The weight of history certainly seemed to be very much against the Chatino. The penetration of capital had introduced a series of contradictions into Indian communities which generated violence and led to the slow, and at times not so slow, destruction of the social customs and forms that defined their communities. If there was to be any resistance to this historical process, it could at best be a holding action. For individuals the solution seemed to be to find a means of coping with the violence. Yaitepec's efforts to recover its communal lands from the finca La Constancia which began in 1973 seemed to have failed. The leaders of this movement had been arrested, some villagers had been shot, and some, like Emiliano, had been killed in blood feuds. Moreover, in 1975 Don Florencio Valencia's son Alfonso, who was a member of the executive board of the Departamento de Asuntos Agrarios in Mexico City, obtained a resolution, unbeknownst to Yaitepec, defining the lands of La Constancia as private property and excluding them from the confirmed titles to the village's communal lands. I doubted that there was any solution to the Chatino's plight, and my skepticism led me to underestimate Chatino determination and their ability to respond to problems creatively.

When I returned to Yaitepec in April 1987, I was amazed by the transformations that had taken place. I learned that in 1981 the Chatino had successfully invaded La Constancia and divided the land among the people. Even more astounding, I found out that in 1982, sick of seeing their men killed in blood feuds, the women of the village had organized and had managed to pass an ordinance prohibiting the sale and consumption of alcohol and the carrying of knives or guns. These measures were effective and put an end to blood feuding and factionalism in the village. Although I might have foreseen that women would lead such a prohibition movement, I could not have imagined that in a culture where alcohol had been such an integral part of ritual and social life, it would have occurred without missionary or outsider impetus. Almost as remarkable is the fact that Yaitepec's success has inspired Yolotepec, San Juan Quiahije, and Cieneguilla to pass similar measures.

Yaitepec's Agrarian Struggle

Because Yaitepec's agrarian struggle led to the healing of deep divisions within the community, an examination of the history of these struggles is instructive.[1] Although the Valencias had obtained a resolution in 1975 excluding their lands from the communal lands of Yaitepec, it was not until 1979 that villagers found out about it. When they did, private meetings to discuss what they could do began in the house of Juan Peralta Vásquez, the senior member of the council of elders. These meetings led to other meetings in other people's homes. As a consensus began to build, larger barrio-level meetings to debate the alternatives took place. Finally a general assembly was called in 1981 to discuss the matter. The dominant argument at this assembly was that the village's communal lands could not be protected by recourse to the legal system and that unless they reclaimed their lands by invading the plantation, they would lose them. Not everyone agreed. The village presidente, Santiago Quintas, was of the opinion that such an invasion would probably fail, given their previous experience in 1973. The assembly's response, however, was that they did not have time to remember the past. They were resolved to launch this struggle with or without the presidente's support, and if he did not lend his support, they would declare him a persona non grata in the village. Anticipating the Valencias' reaction and hoping to blunt their acts of retaliation, however, the assembly voted to respect the area the Valencias actually had under cultivation, about 20 percent of the total. They would also offer to allow them to continue to work these "communal" lands as members of the community. Seeing how deep was the community's support for the movement, the presidente decided to support the movement and ordered that the plan be implemented the next day, March 2, 1981.

The next morning the pueblo invaded the finca. Dividing into groups of from ten to twenty persons, each led by one of the village elders, the groups dispersed and moved across the finca. The elders began to assign two pieces of land to each household: one on which to plant from 300 to 500 coffee trees and another on which to plant four *maquilas* of corn for subsistence. Since the elders were familiar with the personal circumstances of each household, if a large family needed a little more land for subsistence, they would assign them more. In accordance with their decision to respect the areas worked by the Valencias, 80 percent of the land, 945 hectares, was divided among the village's 310 households.

People began to plant almost immediately. In less than fifteen days they had planted almost all their subsistence land in corn and had begun to plant coffee trees. By June the villagers had planted more than 500,000 coffee trees.

Acts of Retaliation

Denunciations and acts of retaliation followed swiftly. The Valencias denounced the invasion to the Departamento de Asuntos Agrarios and lodged a complaint with the public prosecutor. In July the Valencias had a villager arrested for trespass as he was weeding his cornfield. When Yaitepec marched en masse to Juquila to protest, he was freed. Not satisfied, the Valencias then let their cattle loose in the waist-high corn in the fields. In October, still looking for a means to dislodge the peasants from their lands, the Valencias had Juan Peralta Vásquez arrested and charged the village elder with leading the conspiracy to deprive them of their private property.

Yaitepec's response to Juan's arrest caught the authorities by surprise. The whole village descended on Juquila. To avoid police repression, the villagers entered Juquila led by children carrying a Mexican flag as a sign that the march was peaceful, followed by women. The men, armed with machetes and ready for anything, brought up the rear. They burst into the palacio municipal, took the district judge and the public prosecutor hostage, and announced that they would not leave until Juan Peralta Vásquez was set free.

Predictably, the authorities in Juquila sent out a call for help, and the next afternoon two hundred state police arrived. Although the police tried throughout the day to intimidate the villagers into leaving the palacio, in truth there was little they could do. If they attacked, they might be hacked to death. Moreover, even if the attack were successful, if any of the Indian women or children were hurt, the incident, which had already made the newspapers, could easily become a national and even international issue. It was a stalemate. About midnight, a commission from Oaxaca arrived to negotiate. The commission, however, was headed by the secretary of state and Alfonso Valencia, who was now the rector of the Universidad Autónoma de Benito Juárez de Oaxaca. Not surprisingly, rather than dealing with the land problem, the commission focused its attention on the occupation of the palacio and on the freeing of the elder, Juan Peralta Vásquez. Finally it was agreed that the commission would pay Juan's bail if the villagers would leave the palacio. Nothing had been settled concerning the status of the land, but after this, acts of retaliation and repression ceased.

The Ban on Alcohol

One spin-off of the crucial role that women played in the vanguard of the demonstrations to protect the communal lands and to win the release of Juan Peralta Vásquez was a growing awareness of their own political importance and power. They blamed alcohol for the internal violence that had claimed their fathers, husbands, brothers, and sons. They also blamed the violence on the many cantinas of the town, where throughout the day drunks would dedicate music and thoughts blaring at full volume to their family, friends, and sweethearts—generally in codes that only they would understand but that on occasion would provoke fights. As women discussed what might be done, a consensus grew that the only solution was to close the bars and ban alcohol completely. They had to prohibit alcohol from being consumed, whether at wedding or funeral, mayordomía or fiesta.

In the beginning of January 1982 the women called for a general assembly to discuss what measures could be taken to curb violence in the community. At this general assembly it was decided that the municipal authorities should not only ban the sale and consumption of alcohol and prohibit the dedication of music by loudspeaker but should also forbid the carrying of knives and guns without authorization. To give this ordinance teeth, it was decided that anyone suspected of violating the ban would be jailed. The ban is, in fact, strictly enforced. It applies not only to consuming alcohol in the village, but to villagers consuming alcohol anywhere. Thus, if a person is seen drinking even in another village, and even though he may return to Yaitepec sober, he is jailed and fined a week's wages.

Since this ordinance meant the closure of cantinas, the assembly named a commission to carry out the ban. This measure, however, affected Santiago

Quintas, the presidente municipal, who owned the largest cantina in Yaitepec. The presidente rejected the assembly's resolution. Arguing that every
citizen was free to work within the law and that no one could stop him, he
refused to implement the ordinance. The presidente and other affected bar
owners went to Oaxaca to lodge a complaint. This opposition, however, did
not change the decision of the general assembly, and when he persisted in
his opposition, the indignant villagers, led by the presidente's sister, used the
same tactic they had used in Juquila: they took over the palacio municipal.
For ten days they tried to force the presidente to come to terms. When on
the tenth day he still refused to recognize the will of the people, the villagers
removed him from office and named his alternate as presidente.

Healing and Empowerment

When Yaitepec began its struggle in 1973, it was exclusively an agrarian
struggle, but in uniting against a common foe, the villagers also laid the foundation for healing the internal divisions within the community. In reclaiming
their communal lands, the community regained more than land. It regained
its sense of sovereignty, it regained its ability to control its internal affairs,
and it renewed the tradition of respect for the will of the people. Through
these struggles the villagers have learned not only how to make the mestizos
respect their rights but also how to fend off the foreign ideas of groups who
want to use them for political ends. The experience the women gained in
these struggles opened the way for their participation in the political process and allowed them, without the destruction of their customs, to regain
control of their lives.

While violence continues to be endemic in most of the villages of the
district, Yaitepec's example offers hope and serves as a reminder that people
are seldom merely the passive victims of forces beyond their control but are
active and creative participants in shaping their future.

Part III

REFERENCE MATERIAL

Appendix

GENEALOGY OF

DON FORTINO SANTIAGO

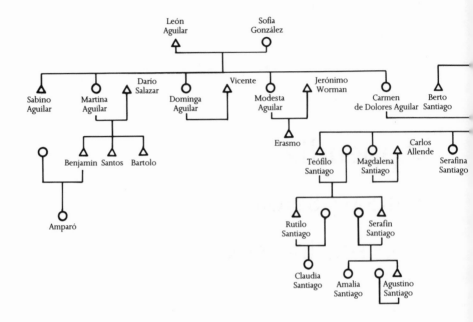

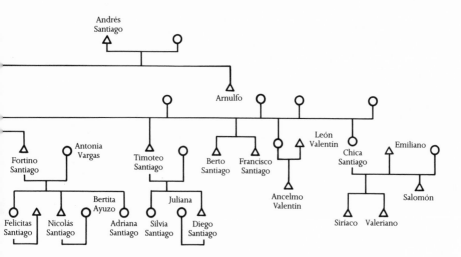

Notes

Preface

1. These figures are from the United Nations *Demographic Yearbook* (1985:Table 31). The national rate of homicide in Mexico in 1981 was 17.7 per 100,000 population.

Chapter 1. My Early Years

1. Fortino uses two dimensions to define his social identity: a dimension of kinship, in which birth order is so important that he mentions his sister Serafina (1896–1900), who died before he was born, to talk about his siblings. His concern for birth order reflects an underlying Chatino rule of older-younger sibling respect. The other dimension he uses to define his social identity is subsumed in the notion of being a native of a particular pueblo. Fortino is at pains to note where not only his father and mother were from but also where his grandfather was born.

2. *Che* is a Chatino word meaning male friend.

3. Fortino defines the music teacher as a good man because he was of service to the pueblo. Elsewhere he says that he liked to get drunk and fight, and that was what got him killed by local residents.

4. Corporal punishment is not unusual in schools, but this teacher's use of it was excessive even by local standards.

5. Todos los Santos, the day of the dead, is celebrated November 1.

6. Although Fortino claims his uncle Sabino grabbed his grandfather's estate and "we got nothing," this is not wholly accurate. His mother got the house in Juquila. But the contrast here is between productive land and simple real estate, and Fortino feels that they were cheated.

7. When Urbano behaved "very *macho*," what was at issue was not political ideology but submissiveness: male pride. The only way that both parties could save face was through the intervention of a third party. The obvious advantage of turning to a woman is that a woman would not threaten their macho stances.

8. Fortino explains the fact that he said nothing about the coming Zapatista attack

to anyone, not even his mother, by saying that the "fight isn't with me." Implicitly, if he were to say anything about it, this "abuse" of Cirilo's confidence could easily have gotten him killed.

9. Whether this detachment had a treasonous "agreement" with the Zapatistas is not important. That such practices were not unknown suggests that even violence on the battlefield may be open to mediation.

10. The notion of making a mockery of the enemy is tied to a complex macho ideology that equates defeat with impotence.

11. Fortino likens his cousin's death, who was murdered on the orders of this caudillo, to the death of Christ, as he was shot standing in a doorway, hands stretched out as on a cross.

12. Reflecting his father's attitude, Fortino personalizes this conflict by casting it in the context of a feudal patron-client relationship in which a disloyal mozo rebels against his master. He fails to see that his father, a rich mestizo from Miahuatlán, was an outsider taking communal lands and was thus a hated enemy.

13. The setting of this homicide in the plaza in front of witnesses is important. As a public execution, it was an appeal for public support for ridding the town of an abusive comandante.

14. Although Berto died of an illness, Fortino—using a medieval notion of body humors—blames his father's death on the Revolution's causing him muina, bitter anger, which is said to produce bile and a bilious fever.

15. This incident, in which Fortino discovers Jerónimo having sex with a woman in the church, reveals the dynamics of confianza. This incident threatened Jerónimo's social face, and despite Fortino's denial and reassurance, he felt compromised because it gave Fortino power over him, and their relationship thereafter was characterized by distrust.

16. What is interesting in this rivalry is the equation that would convert hard work into mother's love. Love is a fetishized commodity that, like other commodities in the market, must be earned.

17. According to traditional rights of inheritance, at his death his father's property should have gone to his sons. Had their uncle made a home for his young nephews, his administration of their father's estate might have been justified, but he just gave them a place to sleep and left them to fend for themselves like orphans. This is why Fortino says their uncle "grabbed" (i.e., stole) everything from them.

18. Fortino's lecture to his brother Francisco is interesting from several standpoints. One theme is that, as far as one is able, one should be willing to help one's kinsmen if they are in need. The second theme is that one has to strive to be independent and not to ask for help. Running in counterpoint to these two themes is the notion of "learning to be a man." Manliness is equated not just with being self-supporting but also with fulfilling one's obligations to others. Implicit in this lecture is the belief that relations of reciprocity are subordinate to a capitalist work ethic, which stresses independence.

19. Since trust is not just a dyadic matter but a good that is distributed in social relationships, it may be affected by the behavior of others for whom one has assumed responsibility. Since Fortino is responsible for Francisco and Berto's being there, he

wants to insure their best behavior, lest their laziness affect his own relationship with his brother.

20. Francisco uses his kinship with Fortino to get a good price on some bulls so that he can sell them for a profit. Price in this instance is not determined solely by market forces but also by social obligations.

Chapter 2. Courtship and Marriage

1. As men have illicit relations and children out of wedlock, one of the inherent problems is that one might not recognize one's kinsmen and either have incestuous relations with them or kill them.

2. If a family does not approve of a suitor, their usual strategy is to send the girl off to live with a relative.

3. A cultural rule defines it as dangerous and almost immoral for unmarried persons of the opposite sex to be together alone. By saying that she would be with a group of friends, not with just him, he defined the context as a safe one, and Antonia's mother gave her permission.

4. Antonia's mother discovered that a woman she considered a whore was going to be in the group, so she came to fetch Antonia to protect her daughter's reputation.

5. Fortino's status as an outsider in Antonia's village, and the presence of rivals, would make such a courtship a dangerous enterprise. Under local rules of endogamy, women are considered to belong to their village and are expected to marry within it.

6. Because family honor entails maintaining a woman's virginity and arranging a proper marriage for her, these being the guarantees of legitimate offspring, Fortino knows that by stealing Antonia he was bringing dishonor to her father's house.

7. The negotiations involved in this transaction illustrate the complex relationship between forms of reciprocity and market transactions. As an inducement, Fortino offers to pay the man but then asks him to trust him and extend him credit. The fellow decides not to charge Fortino, since he is "known around here," which indicates that if Fortino were not part of a local network of relationships, he would have charged him. Although Fortino probably figured that this is what would happen, he had to make the offer of payment to give the man the choice of mode of transaction. When Fortino tells the man that he has no money, it is obvious that regardless of his choice he would have to trust Fortino. Since the amount of money involved would have been small, the man prefers to cast the transaction into the realm of generalized reciprocities and obligate Fortino to do him a favor in the future.

8. This narrative illustrates the process of introducing Antonia to his family. Fortino is still a little ashamed of having stolen her and a little reluctant to face his family, who knew nothing of his plans. By introducing her gradually to niece, aunt, and uncle, who accept her, he not only builds family support to face his mother and sister, whom he still fears might disapprove, but in effect will present them with a fait accompli.

9. Fortino tells his mother of his elopement. Although the narrative does not dwell on it, his mother did not approve of his actions. Since he presented her with a fait accompli, however, all she could do was to accept what had happened and say, "All right, there's nothing more to be said."

10. Another indication of the family friction that Fortino's elopement caused is evident in his account of returning to Juquila. While Fortino says he went to live with his aunt to avoid gossip, the real reason that Fortino turned to his aunt was that his mother and sister were none too happy about his marriage.

11. Reconciliation with Antonia's family was possible for two reasons: first, because Antonia had gone with Fortino voluntarily, and second, because some members of Antonia's family were in favor of the union.

Chapter 3. The Beginnings of Factionalism

1. Although Fortino claims in this portion of the narrative that the Cristeros robbed the church, it is apparent from other parts of the narrative that it was the citizens' committees under Calles's mandate that were responsible for the sacking of the church.

2. Under directions from the Calles government, a citizens' committee was established to administer the property of the church.

3. Again, Fortino confuses Calles's supporters with the Cristeros.

4. Fortino's fetishized description that "good" money was wasted on drink has a moral tone to it. Money is wasted when one does not know how to use it, i.e., to invest it to make more money.

5. Entailed in the notion of respect is the concept of worth: a person's worth is measured by the honoring of trusts, not only with respect to property placed in one's care but also with respect to confidential information imparted to him or her. Alfonso violated both of these forms of trust.

6. Fortino notes that before the Revolution, violence was a rare occurrence. The one case he remembers, in which Edmundo Muñoz killed Blas Ramírez, apparently led to a blood feud between the two families. It is interesting that Blas Ramírez's daughter, Eva, married Lázaro Sánchez, who as a cacique was backed by the Muñoz family.

7. The intensity of these conflicts has led to the actual splitting of communities into separate villages along barrio lines. He blames mestizos for the splitting of San Juan Lachao into two villages. The split allowed the mestizos to dominate the new town. The economic effect of the partitioning of San Juan Lachao has been to significantly reduce Indian access to land. As an aside, Fortino's description of bribery, "money talked," is one more example of commodity fetishism.

8. Fortino details the factionalism that led to the partitioning of Teotepec into two towns. According to his account, coffee and "outsiders" again played a major role. Prior to the Revolution, Nicolás Valencia (Florencio Valencia's uncle and a priest) had leased a large tract of land that sprawled over communal lands in Teotepec, Temaxcaltepec, and Yaitepec. He had leased the land because constitutional provisions barred priests from owning property. After the Revolution, the Indians of Teotepec attempted to recover this land. The interesting aspects of this account are: (1) the conflict initially pitted the Indian community against the finqueros through relations of patronage but became a factional struggle between mestizo elites, finquero against finquero; (2) although partially successful, the community is then exploited by their "patron"; (3) this gives rise to another factional struggle between priest and finqueros, which is fought out at the state level; (4) when the finqueros are triumphant, the conflict returns to the level of the community and they are killed.

9. The aftermath of the Chico murder illustrates the tendency of personal conflicts to expand. What began as a conflict between two individuals soon pitted families against one another and finally divided the community, causing a section of it to split off from Teotepec. Teotepec reacted violently to the killing of Chico Rodríguez Aguilar. The townspeople rebelled against the Valencias, and things got very confused. The murders split the community, and the conflict that had originally been limited to the Valencia and Aguilar families expanded. The supporters and opponents of the Valencias began to fight among themselves. The Valencias called in the federales, and what had been a local matter moved into a larger political arena. The turmoil eventually led to the partitioning of the community: the supporters of the Valencias remained in Teotepec, and the opposition moved down the mountain to establish the community of Cerro del Aire. The state government, to reestablish its authority and to punish the community for "rebelling," demoted Teotepec from a municipio to an agencia and made both towns agencias of Nopala. The upshot of this division was to increase Florencio Valencia's power as a cacique and give him a free hand in Teotepec.

10. Fortino indicates that it was common practice for priests to have mistresses and children and to have businesses on the side.

11. Don Saúl León Villanueva was an "outsider" who came to Juquila in the wave of migration from Miahuatlán between 1880 and 1890 to grab Indian lands and impose a plantation economy. Fortino's account of his background makes it clear that he had all the makings of a cacique: education, business interests, and a network of friends among the elite.

12. After Sánchez's power waned, his cousin Florencio Valencia, the owner of a large coffee plantation, succeeded him as leader of the faction. Like Sánchez, Florencio Valencia enjoyed the support of the Muñoz family.

13. Fortino implies that the presidente did not grant him a lot because he was a poor Indian. His suspicions underline the class and ethnic dimensions of the conflict. "Outsiders" with money had more influence than native sons.

14. Fortino calls him Uncle Ricardo not because he was a kinsman but out of respect for the Chatino elder.

15. The dimension of ethnic conflict here is interesting. Juquila's town government was dominated by Chatino Indians until the 1920s. The mestizos, who had come to Juquila during the Revolution, soon took over political leadership—the last Chatino presidente held office in the 1930s—but at the time that Fortino made his petition the Chatino still had a strong influence in the council and in local affairs.

16. This confrontation underlines the growing conflict between outside money and power and the traditional norms of authority.

17. Fortino's building of his shop illustrates the various modes of exchange. Some of the materials he purchased outright, others he obtained as gifts through relations of reciprocity, and some he bought on credit from a compadre. In the last case, the credit was based on relations of reciprocity and trust entailed in compadrazgo.

18. In the idiom of local land tenure, by erecting a fence Fortino had laid a de facto claim to the land as his property. Actually, Fortino's field was fairly large, covering some forty hectares. Invading the land and cutting down the fence is a classic means of defense used by the pueblo to protect the status of communal lands.

19. When Fortino's compadre wrote a letter of complaint to the president of Mex-

ico, the conflict was elevated to a national level. Making peace with Fortino, from this perspective, was an attempt to contain the conflict and prevent it from expanding into long, costly court battles.

20. What is notable in this incident is that other than Fortino's protest, no one seems to have been concerned, probably because few realized the archive's value or importance.

21. Because of the obvious similarities between the pueblo's reactions to Fortino's field and their actions in defending the communal lands of Rancho Viejo, Fortino feels called upon to distinguish his case from that of Don Esteban's. In his defense that, unlike Don Esteban, he never used "false documents" to make his claim but was legally granted his land by the authorities, he also implies that there is a contrast between his land use and Don Esteban's. Fortino obtained his land to plant corn for subsistence; Don Esteban uses his land for commercial purposes, as a coffee plantation.

22. Fortino's description of the violence in Nopala that broke out in 1937 suggests it was very much of a piece with the factional fighting that was occurring in Juquila, and it seems also to have been linked to the introduction of coffee growing by peasants on communal lands.

23. Apparently, after Angel's band fled to San Gabriel Mixtepec, what had been an internal factional conflict expanded into a conflict between Nopala and San Gabriel Mixtepec.

24. Although Fortino does not tell us why Nicolás Pérez wanted to shoot him, if one remembers that as a judge Fortino had sent Perez's kinsmen, Abdón and Gregorio Pérez, to prison in the Sánchez affair just a few years before, it is easy to see why Fortino felt threatened.

Chapter 5. Affairs

1. Fortino's calling Esperanza a bitch who was going to lead him God knows where is the expression of a double standard in which any woman who enters into an elicit relationship is a "fallen" woman and is blamed by the man if the family is broken up.

2. Sending a girl away is a common defense against unwanted suitors when parents cannot control their offspring.

3. The metaphor used in this account bears closer examination. On the one hand, Fortino uses the language of commodity fetishism to compare love to an "old account," to a bill, and he comes as a bill collector. Talia's language, on the other hand, compares love to a wild animal; she is the huntress who traps her prey. Perhaps the most interesting of all is her use of the word cure. When women are pregnant they are said to be ill, and when they give birth, they are cured. When she says that if there is another woman, she will cure him, she implies that the other woman is a disease and her own sexuality is the cure.

4. Although he does not explain why it was not safe, there are at least two possibilities: (1) because her father knew Fortino was married, or (2) because his rival, Alfonso, whom he had sent to jail, was an old enemy.

Chapter 6. Brujos and Curing

1. The Chatino use two hallucinogens: morning glory seeds and mushrooms, which they call the saints. These may be taken only on certain days of the week (Cordero Avendaño de Durand 1986:145–160).

2. Although Fortino clearly has disdain for the brujo's trickery and sucking, he has a little more respect for the psychic powers that come from taking the "saint." Chatino belief holds that in diseases that are the result of witchcraft, illness is caused either by magically projecting objects into one's body or by burying images (Cordero Avendaño de Durand 1986:152–160).

3. Fortino gained his knowledge of folk medicine in part from his mother and in part, as he puts it, from experimenting. The interesting part of this discussion is not his testimony about effectiveness but his statements about when he charges for medicine and when he does not. Generally, Fortino does not charge people for treating them, because if they were desperate and he is successful, they are forever in his debt, which means he can count on them to do him favors. He does, however, charge them for treating animals—cows, mules, etc. He justifies this in two ways: first, because of the animal's worth, and second, because of the cost of the herbs, which he must bring from Mexico City. The point is that while animal life may have a price, one cannot put a price on human life.

Chapter 7. I Stop Drinking and Get Ahead

1. As this incident shows, there is enormous social pressure from his friends to continue drinking despite family pressures to stop. From the family's perspective, such behavior is egotistical or selfish, since it consumes money and time that could be spent on the family. However, the social pressure to drink—refusing is considered antisocial —is also phrased in terms of egoism. Hence, men find it hard to strike a balance between the demands of the two spheres.

2. His daughter's action symbolizes the conflict women feel about their men drinking. It is tolerated up to a point, but it is threatening to them, not only economically but also physically.

3. To stop drinking, Fortino was forced to become antisocial, an aberrant member of his society.

4. Fortino's recipe for handling drunks allows him to avoid being accused of egoism, of being selfish or antisocial, without having to drink himself.

5. Fortino explains his overcoming his fear of credit in terms of a macho ideology, which includes as ingredients self-confidence and risk taking. Since one of its basic tenets is to be in no man's debt, however, Fortino boasts that what is in the store now is his own. He considers being dependent on credit to be a *compromiso*. For Fortino, credit was a stepping-stone to independence.

6. As Fortino began to accumulate capital, he continued to follow a strategy of diversification. His use of personal relations in the process is interesting. These are as important as capital because they provide not only good buys but also reliable labor, the other essential ingredient for capital accumulation.

7. Fortino's total holdings, 5,700 trees, classifies him as small peasant farmer. The

large plantations in the region, by way of comparison, typically have more than 100,000 trees. If his coffee holdings had been properly cared for, Fortino could have expected to get seventeen sacks of coffee, worth some 34,000 pesos, or about 1,360 dollars at the time. But he got only about half this, partly because of his arrangement with Ricardo and partly because his other cafetal was old and not very productive. He made up for this somewhat, however, by working as a small-scale coffee buyer. He bought three sacks from Ricardo for 3,000 pesos and four sacks from an Indian in Panixtlahuaca for 3,200 pesos, clearing a profit of 7,800 pesos (about 312 dollars). Although the share-cropping arrangement with Heraclio meant less money per tree, it was money he did not have to work for—pure surplus value—and in the end he bought Heraclio's sacks for half their market value anyway.

Chapter 8. Conflict With Kinsmen

1. Agustino probably earned his keep. Throughout his life, Fortino took in (though he did not actually adopt) several children. Many, like Agustino, had living parents who were too poor to provide for them. They were a source of cheap and obedient labor.

2. Apparently Fortino's mother gave Rutilo a lot on which to build a house. It is Fortino's position that his mother gave Rutilo only usufruct rights—that is, the land is still part of his dead mother's and deceased grandfather's estate.

Chapter 9. My Young Son's Death and My Wife's Ingratitude

1. The death of their son put an enormous strain on their marriage and led to a semiseparation in which they lived under the same roof but had little to do with one another.

2. The interesting feature of this marital conflict is that the couple is being kept together by social pressures from their children. If Fortino were to throw out their mother and "remarry," her children might lose their inheritance rights, so they oppose their father's wishes to be rid of his wife.

3. Since separating from his wife, Fortino recounts how he has entered into arrangements with other women for sex. These are not prostitutes but simply women in need of money—widows, for example. On a more general level one might note that many women are put into difficult circumstances when widowed or abandoned because most resources are controlled by men, so women are easy victims of such offers of "help."

4. Although Fortino insists that the problems in their marriage were not his fault, he turns a blind eye to his history of drinking, adultery, and semisupport. But then, some self-delusion is unavoidable.

Chapter 10. Nico's Courtship and Marriage

1. This warning is the most important aspect of this story. Nico's situation was potentially dangerous. Fortino feared that his son's jealousy might get him into trouble or that there might be a rival, hence he cautioned him to act decently.

Chapter 11. Political Factionalism in Juquila

1. As Fortino points out, strong ties draw people into conflicts and lead to compromisos that can get one killed. Given the violent nature of village society, the only way to survive, Fortino argues, is to remain uninvolved.

2. Fortino observes that if one consistently stays out of these conflicts, people know what to expect and leave one alone. The latter point is especially important. People are often killed because they cannot be trusted to remain uninvolved.

3. The killing of members of one's nuclear family or close kin is rare. As almost everyone in the village is at least distantly related, however, killings almost inevitably involve kin.

4. Apparently Nico, under the influence of his cousin Diego, had gotten into a fistfight with Tomás shortly before he was killed. So when Tomás Muñoz was murdered, public gossip and rumor placed the blame on Nico.

5. Attributing the attack on his son to their envy of his work, to his success as a coffee buyer, shows that Fortino understands that there are economic factors behind the attack on his son. At the same time, by explaining the attempt to kill Nico as envy, he reduces this economic dimension to human passion.

Chapter 12. Land Conflicts

1. Although president Cárdenas's land reform program began in 1934, it did not reach the district of Juquila until 1935.

2. Such disputes are one of the instruments of domination used, just as they were used throughout the colonial period, to provide a steady source of revenue to government bureaucrats and to maintain political control of the hinterland.

3. Fortino lists the towns and areas in which coffee is grown in the region. Not all the towns in the district, however, produce coffee. Coffee is best grown in a temperate climate. Little is grown in the hot lowlands or in the cold highlands.

4. Much of what Fortino says is collaborated by a study by sociologist Hernández-Díaz (1982:33–59). In 1973 two presidentes were killed. One of them, as Fortino tells us, was named Saúl Olivera. In all probability he was a backer of Don Pepe Flores, who had been named when the former presidente, who had been backed by the Franciscan priest, was forced out of office.

5. Fortino's account of the battle in Panixtlahuaca between the Franciscan priest and his compadre, the cacique, accords well with Hernández-Díaz's accounts (1982, 1987). As Hernández-Díaz notes, the conflict was over the cacique's land. The priest pushed for its expropriation and redivision among the people, but the cacique appealed to the government, which gave him authorization to continue working these lands.

6. The interesting feature of this conflict is that it was directed not against the seller of the land, Saúl Amado's aunt, but against the buyer. Although Saúl Amado undoubtedly questioned her right to sell the land, the conflict was directed at Emiliano, since he had possession.

7. In arguing that the foundation of all these killings is coffee, Fortino confirms my own perception that the feud between Emiliano and Saúl Amado was also a struggle

for political power. Although the root of the hatred may have been jealousy and a conflict over the coffee parcel, the battle was fought out on the political field, with Saúl Amado accusing Emiliano of usurping power, of being a cacique, because he refused to hand over the official seal to the presidente.

8. I have legal documents that confirm Fortino's allegations on this matter.

9. Emiliano's son Salomón did not leave the village but managed to avoid the conflict by showing no interest in it. This shows that feuds do not simply follow kinship lines but also take account of a person's "position" on the conflict. By not attending his father's funeral, Salomón signaled to the community that he was interested neither in the conflict nor in revenge.

10. Fortino tried to warn Emiliano not to go walking around with so much confidence, to hide himself, first because in Yaitepec when people are mad they continue to kill members of a family until they have wiped out the men. Now that they had killed his son, people distrusted him and might kill him out of distrust. Second, charges of homicide had been brought against Emiliano when Govino Valencia was killed during the land invasion in 1974, and Fortino suggested that there might still be a warrant out for his arrest and that the police might put him in jail.

11. Since Emiliano's exile in Zacatepec deprived him of access to his lands, money, and work, he began a gradual process of going back and forth between Yaitepec and Zacatepec to attend to business. The fact that he was unmolested during this period gave him a false sense of security and confidence and led him to decide to return to Yaitepec.

12. Fortino's narrative of the death of Emiliano's son, Valeriano, is particularly interesting because it illustrates revenge, betrayal, and the ideology of the *valiente*. As a valiente Valeriano was a marked man. Fortino offers the opinion that when his supporters realized what the issues in the land conflict were, they turned on him. Although this seems plausible, doubtless his murder spree earned him new enemies.

Chapter 13. Explanations of Violence

1. In 1981 the homicide rate in Mexico was 17.7 per 100,000 population (United Nations 1985:Table 31).

2. Fortino's memory of relative peace is not just a remembrance of a "golden age"; it is supported by court documents. In Yaitepec, for instance, while court documents for the period 1909 to 1929 record many incidents of violence—drunken brawls, machete fights—no homicides were recorded in this period.

3. Between harvests, peasant producers often need credit. Coffee buyers are willing to extend them credit for the overpriced merchandise they carry in their stores or to make loans at high rates of interest in return for an agreement to sell their coffee crop at a price fixed well below its true market value. Further, the profits made at the local level are but the first in a series as local coffee buyers, middlemen, and retailers move the coffee into the world market.

4. For discussions of the interface between state and indigenous legal systems in Mexico, see Nader 1967, Collier 1973, and Parnell 1988.

5. The evidence for Yaitepec suggests that the rate of incidents of violence is proba-

bly decreasing over this period, but because the proportion of incidents that end in homicide has increased, homicide rates have risen.

6. In the literature on violence in rural Mexico, the following factors have been proposed as contributing to bloodshed: problems of land tenure and distribution, including conflicts over boundaries between communities (Dennis 1976; Flanet 1977; Friedrich 1977; Taylor 1972; Wolf 1969); alcohol (Kappel 1978; Nash 1967; Romanucci-Ross 1973; Sumner 1978; Taylor 1979); genetic factors (Augur 1954); guns, which usually lead the list when the weapon used has been recorded (Kappel 1978; Nash 1967; Romanucci-Ross 1973); outsiders and caciques, who have been implicated in political violence (Flanet 1977; Hernández-Díaz 1982, 1987; Friedrich 1977); injustice, abuse of power, fear of reprisal (Flanet 1977; Nader 1964; Parnell 1988; Taylor 1979); penetration of capitalism and class conflict (Flanet 1977; Friedrich 1977; Wolf 1969).

7. Although there is an enormous literature on aggression, crime, and warfare in complex industrial societies, little of it is directly relevant to rural Mexico. For example, a long debate has raged in the literature between sociobiologists, who argue that violence is genetically determined, and cultural anthropologists, who argue that it is a learned cultural response. This debate, however, is of little relevance to the problem of violence in rural Mexico. Even if it could be proved that there is a genetic component to violence, it would tell us little about the form violence takes in a specific instance.

8. The characterization of this approach has been drawn from Paddock 1975, 1978, and 1982. Several other authors are also associated with this approach (Fry 1986; Hauer 1978; Kappel 1978; O'Nell 1979, 1981; Sumner 1978), but there are subtle differences among them. Fry, for instance, recognizes that man-land differences are probably an underlying factor in violence in the two communities he contrasted, but he nonetheless focuses on child socialization.

9. Although this social structure approach has been applied most frequently to explanations of witchcraft (Firth 1936; Leach 1961; Nadel 1952; Rattray 1923), some authors have also used it to explain violence in rural Mexico (Nash 1967; Romanucci-Ross 1973).

10. Since Foster confounds individualism with egalitarian aspects of behavior intended as defenses against capitalism, he argues that "two theoretical avenues of action are open to people who see themselves in threatened circumstances, which the Image of Limited Good implies. They may exhibit cooperation, to as pronounced degrees as Communism, burying personal differences and placing sanctions against individualism, or they may follow the opposite road of unbridled individualism, in which everyone is on his own" (1967:133). His lack of appreciation that these opposite choices represent the clash of two economic orders is then made abundantly clear. Foster argues that "Tzintzuntzenos, like other peasants, have chosen—or had forced upon them—the second alternative. The reasons are not entirely clear, but two factors seem significant" (1967:133). He goes on to argue that they have chosen the path of extreme individualism because "cooperation requires leadership," but strong leadership "produces *caciques*" who are easily coopted (1967:133–134).

11. Foster is not alone as a cultural idealist. Much the same approach has been used by Romanucci-Ross who, for example, uses the concept of *machismo* in her explanation of the moral codes of violence and the emotional tone of the culture (1973:93–155).

12. Most of the writers who have used historical approaches that emphasize the penetration of capitalism have focused on collective forms of violence, such as agrarian revolts or the Mexican Revolution (Buve 1971; Casarrubias 1945; Friedrich 1977; Huitzer and Stavenhagen 1974; Taylor 1979; Wolf 1969; Womack 1969), rather than on the persistent and unremitting violence of blood feuding and factionalism in the country. Among the few studies that address homicide from this perspective are Flanet 1977, Hernández-Díaz 1982 and 1987, and Bartolomé and Barabas 1982.

13. The notion of the disorganization of society under the impact of Western society has its roots in the works of Durkheim (1951) and Merton (1957). Merton, using Durkheim's concept of *anomie*, proposed that social conflict and disintegration may be analyzed in terms of the discrepancies between a culture's goals and its institutionalized means of satisfying them. As the cleavage between goals and means increases, several adaptations may be made: conformity, innovation, ritualism, retreat, and rebellion. Levy and Kunitz 1971 employed this model of means-goal disjunction in the analysis of homicides and social deviance on American Indian reservations.

14. As Taylor notes (1979:131), this kind of explanation places the causes of revolt (and for that matter, violence) completely outside the villages themselves.

15. These authors use dualist models of the economy, with modern and archaic sectors in which development flows from the modern capitalist sector and transforms a backward subsistence economy (assumed to be the traditional or original state). This notion of "regions of refuge"—developed by Aguirre Beltrán (1973), the former Director of the National Indian Institute—has guided indigenous development policy in Mexico.

Chapter 14. The Historical Dimensions of Conflict

1. This type of social organization still forms the basis of production in Chatino communities (Greenberg 1981:63). Farriss provides an excellent description of the functioning of such extended family units in colonial Yucatan (1984:132–139).

2. This point has been made by Farriss (1984:274–275). The evidence from Tututepec seems to confirm her argument (Martínez-Gracida 1907:100).

3. The crown's decision to reassign this encomienda to Don Luis, one may speculate, was probably due to its declining value as European diseases decimated the native population.

4. The *repartimiento de comercio* system worked as follows: "The alcaldes mayores, who were poorly paid and nearly always recruited from less wealthy Spanish families, had sole authority to administer the *repartimiento*. A wealthy merchant, usually a member of the *consulado de Mexico* (the merchants' guild based in Mexico City), who often worked through a Oaxaca City intermediary merchant, became the *aviador* or financial backer of an alcalde mayor. The merchant paid the substantial cash bond required of the alcalde mayor by the government and then supplied him (or his legal assistant, who was sometimes actually an agent of the merchant) with the funds or goods with which the Indians were 'compensated' beforehand for the products they were required to turn over in compliance with their *repartimiento* obligations. In return the merchant received a trade monopoly over one or more communities in the alcalde mayor's district. As

further remuneration the alcalde mayor received a percentage of the take" (Waterbury 1975:420).

Chapter 15. The Ideology of Conflict and Violence

1. The norms of this moral geography correspond closely with the generalized, balanced, and negative forms of reciprocity found as kinship distance increases (see Sahlins 1972).

2. The notion that the nahual is a demon and that the brujo (witch) or the curandero has a pact with the mountain god is an interesting piece of religious syncretism between Catholic and native interpretations of this relationship. We should not conclude, however, that brujos are always evil. Because witchcraft may be undone by witchcraft, the difference between a brujo and a curandero is slight. In the native notion of this relation, the curandero is a ne' ho'o, a "person saint," and his nahual, ho'o kwichi, is a "holy tiger." In orthodox Catholicism, however, the mountain god can only be a devil, the curandero a witch, and his holy tiger a demon.

3. Anthropologists have explained witchcraft in several ways, all of which seem at least partially applicable to the Chatino case. Beatlie 1963, Honigman 1947, Spindler 1952, Walker 1967, and Whiting 1950 all argue that witchcraft accusations are part of the sanctioning apparatus of society and are a mechanism of behavioral control. Evans-Prichard 1937, Hallowell 1940, and Opler 1946 and 1947 contend that these charges deflect antisocial aggressiveness away from the inner group. Bohannan 1958 and Douglas 1963 argue that in times of rapid social change, or social disequilibrium, witchcraft accusations arise as a result of individual tensions and anxieties. Such has certainly been the case with the peasants' adoption of coffee as a cash crop. Similarly, Leach 1961, Firth 1936, Nadel 1952, and Wilson 1951 maintain that witchcraft accusations, which generate tensions and conflicts, are rooted in contradictions in the social structure. As Selby notes, in this view "society is seen as the 'villain' in the sense that it is set up so as to produce conflicts between certain categories of people" (1974:96).

Chapter 16. Disputing and Forms of Conflict

1. As Romanucci-Ross points out, groups may be informal or formal (1973:30–31). Informal groups, like mobs or factions, tend to be generated in response to specific issues and tend to be highly unstable and subject to schism. Formal groups, like families involved in blood feuds or communities engaged in land disputes, not only have a separate basis for organization apart from particular conflicts but also tend to be both more effective in battles and more likely to engage in protracted struggles.

2. Hernández-Díaz describes these incidents as well (1982:33–59; 1987:47–72).

3. Like witchcraft accusations, gossip is a labeling process; see Selby 1974:92.

4. As O'Nell observes, "the requirements of reciprocity and the need for cooperation from others serve fundamentally to inhibit expressed hostility.... If hostilities do arise, continuing interdependence will force some readjustment in their relationship which normally seems to minimize the significance of hostility as an interpersonal problem" (1981:359).

5. See Greenberg 1981:71–72. As O'Nell notes, this kind of "hostility management
... permit[s] people to express hostility toward others in front of community authorities" (1981:357).

6. In the district jail, prisoners are not fed but must buy their own food.

7. Like fiesta systems, as Dennis observes, litigation serves "to siphon off surplus
wealth, but with the important difference that none is redistributed among community
members for consumption" (1976:182).

Afterword

1. The following account of incidents in Yaitepec is based largely on a remarkable
article written by a Chatino man, Tomás Cruz Lorenzo (1987). A native of San Juan
Quiahije, the author, who drives a truck for the Compañía Nacional de Subsistencias
Populares (CONASUPO), was so inspired by the events in Yaitepec and so anxious
to learn from their example that he went to Yaitepec to interview the principals involved in the movement and then spent nearly a year doing documentary background
research about the land conflicts in Yaitepec.

Glossary

Spanish Terms

Adobe. Sun-baked mud brick.

Agencia. A township subordinate to a *municipio*, which is equivalent to a county.

Alcalde. A judge on the *municipio*'s council.

Alcaldía. The jurisdiction of an alcalde.

Almud. A dry measure of approximately 5 liters in volume.

Arroyo. A small river or stream, or a ravine.

Atole. Corn gruel.

Audiencia. A viceregal court and governing body.

Aviador. A backer or supplier.

Barrio. A ward or neighborhood of the village.

Brujo. A witch or sorcerer.

Cabecera. The capital of a county, district, or province.

Cabildo. The municipal government.

Cacicazgo. The Spanish term for a chiefdomship or the jurisdiction of a cacique; also, the estate of a cacique.

Cacique. During the colonial period the term referred to the native ruler of a community. In modern times the term is applied to the political boss of a community.

Caciquismo. Political boss rule.

Cafetal. Coffee plantation.

Caja de communidad. Municipal treasury, literally community chest.

Cargo. Burden, or office in the civil-religious hierarchy.

Caudillo. Military leader or chief.

Cerro. Mountain.

Che. A Chatino word meaning male friend; also used by local mestizos to mean a Chatino man.

Chisme. Malicious gossip or a tale.

Chismoso. A person who spreads gossip or malicious rumors.

Cofradía. A lay organization of the Catholic church dedicated to the cult of one or more saints.

Comadre. Literally a co-mother, a fictive kinship relation between a child's parents and the woman who sponsors the child's Catholic life-cycle rituals.

Compadrazgo. Co-parenthood established through Catholic ritual.

Compadre. Literally a co-father, a fictive kinship relation between a child's parents and the man who sponsors the child's Catholic life-cycle rituals.

Compromiso. A difficulty or embarrassment that compromises one's position or ability to do something.

Confianza. A trust or a confidence.

Corregidor. The Spanish magistrate in charge of a local Indian district.

Corregimento. The district of jurisdiction of a corregidor.

Curandero. Healer or curer.

Curato. Rectory or parsonage.

Ejido. Land returned to a community as part of a land reform and administered under a national ejido program through specifically elected local officials.

Empacho. A folk concept that undigested food causes stomach infections and indigestion.

Encomendero. Spanish colonizer appointed by the Crown with the right to collect tribute and exact labor services from Indians, presumably in exchange for seeing to their spiritual welfare.

Encomienda. The grant of an Indian town or towns held by an encomendero.

Envidia. Envy or jealousy.

Finca. A plantation.

Finquero. The owner of a finca.

Fundo legal. The communal lands of an Indian community.

Grana. Cochineal.

Hacendado. The owner of a hacienda.

Jefe político. Political boss or chief of a district.

Juzgado de Indios. A special court for Indians under Spanish colonial rule.

Lepero. A base or vile person.

Loma. A hill.

Lucha. A struggle or conflict.

Maguey. A century plant.

Maquila. A dry measure equivalent to about two kilograms.

Mayor. A minor official in the town government, a steward.

Mayordomía. A fiesta held for a village saint.

Mayordomo. The sponsor of a feast for a village saint or an officer of a *cofradía*; also, the foreman of an estate.

Mescal. A liquor distilled from the maguey plant.

Mestizo. A racial term used to designate a descendant of mixed Indian-white parentage, used more generally to refer to the Mexican population, which culturally does not identify itself as Indian.

Meterse. To become involved.

Metiche. A person who sticks his nose in other people's business.

Mole. A Mexican stew with a special hot chile sauce.

Mozo. A hand or a man servant.

Muina. A bitter anger believed to affect one's bile.

Municipio. A county unit of government.

Nahual. The animal form taken by a transforming witch.

Nana. Grandmother.

Padrino. Godfather.

Padrino de evangelio. A godfather for a small book containing the first chapters of St. John and other evangelists, worn around the neck of children.

Paisano. Countryman; refers to someone from one's home community.

Palacio municipal. Town hall.

Petate. Woven straw mat.

Pistolero. A gunfighter or assassin.

Pleitista. A litigious person who encourages disputes.

Principal. High-ranking Indian, nobleman.

Rajarse. To break or crack.

Regidor. A councilman or alderman on the town council.

Repartimiento. Labor draft.

Repartimiento de comercio. Forced distribution of goods or money by a Spanish official to be repaid with tribute goods.

Revoltoso. An agitator, rebel, or troublemaker.

Robo. A robbery or theft; also, an elopement.

Ruda. Rue, a medicinal herb used for stomach pain.

Rurales. Rural police force.

Síndico. A trustee for the municipio who supervises public works and who represents the municipio in fiscal, administrative, and judicial matters.

Tepache. A fermented alcohol made from pineapples.

Tequío. Collective labor on public works required by the community as a form of taxation.

Tequitlato. An officer in the civil hierarchy of Indian communities whose duties may include acting as overseer of tequío service.

Tonal. An animal spirit companion.

Topil. An unarmed policeman or errand boy for the town council.

Valiente. A person who has reckless or suicidal courage.

Significant Individuals Mentioned by Don Fortino

Aguilar, Benjamin. Don Fortino's cousin.

Aguilar, Euladia. The mother of Don Fortino's girlfriend Natalia Vasilides Aguilar.

Aguilar, Juana. Don Fortino's niece, living in Temaxcaltepec.

Aguilar, Santos. A kinsman of Don Fortino.

Aguilar González, Carmen de Dolores. Don Fortino's mother.

Aguilar González, Dominga. Don Fortino's mother's sister.

Aguilar González, Martina. Don Fortino's mother's sister.

Aguilar González, Modesta. Don Fortino's mother's sister.

Aguilar González, Sabino. Don Fortino's mother's brother.

Aguilar Suárez, León. Don Fortino's maternal grandfather.

Aguirre, Angel. Succeeded his father as leader of one faction in the Nopala when he was killed in about 1937 in a feud.

Aguirre, Diego. Father of Angel Aguirre, leader of one faction in Nopala; killed in a feud.

Allende, Carlos. Don Fortino's brother-in-law, married to Magdalena Aguilar.

Amado, Saúl. A presidente of Yaitepec; feuded with Emiliano.

Ayuzo, Berta. Nicknamed Bertita, daughter of Genaro Ayuzo and wife of Don Fortino's son, Nicolás Santiago.

Ayuzo, Genaro. A wealthy finquero and coffee buyer–exporter.

Ayuzo, Genaro. Son of Genaro Ayuzo, killed in a plane crash.

Ayuzo, Rodrigo. Finquero, brother of Genaro Ayuzo, member of the Carranzista detachment in Juquila.

Ayuzo, Rosabla. Daughter of Genaro Ayuzo.

Baños, Juan José. The general of the Carranzistas along the coast of Oaxaca.

Castellanos, Andrés. Owner of the finca San Rafael and a first cousin of Don Fortino's uncle Vicente.

Castellanos, Hortencia. Daughter of Andrés Castellanos, married Don Fortino's brother Francisco Santiago.

Castellanos, Virginia. Daughter of Andrés Castellanos.

Castillo, Isreal del. A colonel of federal troops who came in the early 1920s to wipe out the remaining Zapatista forces in the region; killed in an ambush.

Cervin, Colonel. A Zapatista colonel in Juquila killed by his own men during the Revolution.

Comas, Luis. A telegraph lineman in Juquila; friend of Don Fortino's.

Cortez de Ayuzo, Rosabla. Mother of Don Fortino's daughter-in-law, Berta Ayuzo.

Cruz, León. A Chatino man from Ixtapan; head of Cruz family in Yaitepec.

Cruz, Sabino. A Chatino resident of Yaitepec and son of León Cruz; killed in a feud with the Saldivars.

Cuevas Aguilar, Bartolo. A cousin of Don Fortino.

Cuevas, Enriqueta de. The wife of Don Fortino's cousin Bartolo Cuevas Aguilar.

Dávila, José Luis. A governor of Oaxaca during the Revolution.

Díaz, Saúl. A friend in Juchatengo who helped Don Fortino elope with his wife, Antonia Vargas.

Dominga. A woman from Ocotlán and a girlfriend of Don Fortino.

Emiliano. A Chatino leader in Yaitepec, compadre of Don Fortino, and husband of his half sister, Chica Santiago; killed in a feud.

Esteban, Don. Resident of Juquila, owner of Rancho Viejo, and son-in-law of Lázaro Sánchez.

Flores, Ausencia. A teacher who lived in Juquila; lived with Don Fortino's son Nicolás before he married Bertita Ayuzo; had two children by him.

Flores, Pepe. Don Fortino's compadre, a mestizo resident of Panixtlahauca, finquero, coffee buyer, and cacique.

Franco, Jerónimo. A resident of Juquila who lived in the church with Don Fortino during the revolution.

González, Cornelio. Don Fortino's father's foreman and a Zapatista killed by his own men in Juquila during the Revolution.

González, Lázaro. A Zapatista comandante in Juquila during the Revolution.

González, Sofía. Don Fortino's maternal grandmother and a Chatino resident of Juquila.

Guzmán, Arturo. A Chatino resident of Panixtlahuaca killed in its feuds.

Guzmán, Rebecca. A Chatino resident of Panixtlahuaca.

Hernández, Antonio. The Chatino secretary of Yaitepec and Don Fortino's godson.

Jijón, Federico. The jefe político in Juquila at the beginning of the Revolution.

Labastida, Gustavo. A Carranzista colonel who captured Juquila during the Revolution.

Mauleón Pantoja, Maximina. Don Fortino's mother-in-law, nicknamed Nana.

Mendosa, Antonio. Zapatista who led Colonel Isreal del Castillo into an ambush.

Mendosa, Ausencia. Nicknamed Chencha, her sons whose last name is Ramos are referred to as the Chenchos.

Micaela, Doña. Mother of Don Fortino's girlfriend Dominga, the woman from Ocotlán.

Miguel. Don Fortino's compadre in Panixtlahuaca; killed in a feud.

Morales Guzmán, Joel. A man killed by Abdón and Gregorio Pérez in Juquila in 1935 on the orders of Lázaro Sánchez.

Muñoz, Amado. Resident of Juquila, son of Edmundo Muñoz, behind the attempt on the life of Timoteo Santiago (Don Fortino's half brother); killed in a feud.

Muñoz, Bartolo. Grandson of Leonor Muñoz; killed by his uncle Dario Muñoz.

Muñoz, Dario. Son of Leonor Muñoz.

Muñoz, Diego. Son of Amado Muñoz; killed in a feud.

Muñoz, Edmundo. Father of Amado Muñoz.

Muñoz, Ezequiel. Son of Amado Muñoz; killed by state police.

Muñoz, León. Son of Amado Muñoz.

Muñoz, Leonor. Son of Amado Muñoz.

Muñoz, Ramona de. Wife of Leonor Muñoz.

Muñoz, Tomás. Son of Amado Muñoz; killed in a feud.

Núñez, Alfonso. Brother of Urbano Núñez and a Serrano during the Revolution.

Núñez, Urbano. A Serrano during the Revolution and brother of Alfonso and Diego Núñez.

Olivera, Delfino. Killed by Abdón and Gregorio Pérez in 1935 in Juquila on orders of Lázaro Sánchez.

Ortiz, Raimundo. Nicknamed the Otter, a cousin of Don Fortino's girlfriend Natalia Vasilides Aguilar.

Palacios, Rosabla de. The aunt of Colonel Gustavo Labastida and Urbano Núñez; mediated the conflict between them.

Palacios, Sabina. Daughter of Arnulfo Palacios and mistress of Padre Modesto Valerina.

Palacios Guiterrez, Arnulfo. Father of Sabina Palacios; referred to by Don Fortino as Padre Modesto's father-in-law.

Pérez, Abdón. An assassin working for Lázaro Sánchez; sent to prison by Don Fortino.

Pérez, Esperanza. A girlfriend of Don Fortino.

Pérez, Gregorio. An assassin working for Lázaro Sánchez; sent to prison by Don Fortino.

Pérez, Lauro. A former Zapatista and a resident of Juquila.

Pérez, Nicolás. Son of Lauro Pérez, who threatened to shoot Don Fortino in Nopala.

Ponchito. A Chatino Indian from Ixpantepec.

Pozas, Valeriano. Presidente in Juquila during the Cristero Rebellion.

Próspero, José. Zapatista leader killed in Teotepec in about 1927.

Ramírez, Blas. Father of Eva Ramírez; killed by Edmundo Muñoz during the Revolution.

Ramírez, Eva. Daughter of Blas Ramírez and wife of Lázaro Sánchez.

Ramírez, Melquiades. Brother of the comandante Leonardo Ramírez; tried to kill Don Fortino during the Revolution.

Ramos, Los Chenchos. The name that refers to the sons of Ausencia Mendosa de Ramos; feuded with the Muñoz family.

Ramos, Genaro. General of the Cuerudos of Miahuatlán, a Zapatista division.

Ricardo, Uncle. A Chatino man who held the post of first regidor during the early 1930s in Juquila.

Ríos, Benjamin. A compadre of Don Fortino in Juquila.

Ríos, Nicolás. Brother of Rodolfo and member of a Carranzista detachment in Juquila.

Ríos, Rodolfo. Brother of Fernando, Nicolás, and Patricio, and member of a Carranzista detachment in Juquila.

Ríos Villavicencio, Catalina. Was engaged to marry Don Fortino's son, Nicolás Santiago.

Rodríguez Aguilar, Francisco. Nicknamed Chico, a distant kinsman of Don Fortino; killed by Gilberto Valencia in Teotepec.

Rodríguez, Juan. A general of the Zapatistas in the district.

Rojas, Elizido. A brujo and friend of Don Fortino.

Salazar, Basilio. A beltmaker in Juquila and friend of Don Fortino.

Salazar, Olga. The owner of a cantina in Juquila.

Saldivar, Fidel. A son of Samuel Saldivar and a musician; killed in a feud in Yaitepec.

Saldivar, Samuel. A resident of Yaitepec; killed in a feud.

Salinas, Maximilliano. A shop owner in Juquila.

Salomón. A Chatino resident of Yaitepec, Emiliano's eldest son by a previous marriage, and Don Fortino's godson.

Sánchez Pantoja, Lázaro. A merchant and cacique in Juquila and a son of Nicolás Valencia.

Santiago, Adriana. One of Don Fortino's daughters.

Santiago, Agustino. A son of Serafín Santiago (Don Fortino's nephew).

Santiago, Amalia. Daughter of Serafín Santiago (Don Fortino's nephew).

Santiago, Andrés. A mestizo from Miahuatlán and Don Fortino's grandfather.

Santiago, Berto. A mestizo from Miahuatlán and Don Fortino's father.

Santiago, Berto. Born in Juquila, Don Fortino's half brother; nicknamed Beto.

Santiago, Chica. Don Fortino's Chatino half sister in Yaitepec and wife of Emiliano.

Santiago, Claudia. A daughter of Rutilo Santiago (Don Fortino's nephew).

Santiago, Concepción. Nicknamed Concho Biche, a cousin of Don Fortino from Miahuatlán and a Zapatista; assassinated on the order of General Genaro Ramos.

Santiago, Diego. Cacique in Juquila and a son of Don Fortino's half brother Timoteo Santiago.

Santiago, Felicitas. Don Fortino's eldest daughter; nicknamed Licha.

Santiago, Francisco. Don Fortino's half brother.

Santiago, Juliana de. Wife of Diego Santiago (Don Fortino's nephew).

Santiago, Nicolás. Nicknamed Nico, Don Fortino's son and husband of Berta Ayuzo.

Santiago, Rutilo. A son of Teófilo Santiago Aguilar (Don Fortino's brother).

Santiago, Serafín. Don Fortino's nephew, his brother Teófilo's son.

Santiago, Silvia. A daughter of Timoteo Santiago, Don Fortino's half brother.

Santiago, Timoteo. Merchant and cacique in Juquila and Don Fortino's half brother.

Santiago Aguilar, Fortino. Nicknamed Tino, the narrator of the book and a Chatino resident of Juquila, 1901–1986.

Santiago Aguilar, Magdalena. Don Fortino's sister and wife of Carlos Allende.

Santiago Aguilar, Serafina. A sister of Don Fortino who died at age four before he was born.

Santiago Aguilar, Teófilo. Don Fortino's elder brother, who lived in Río Grande; killed in a feud in 1945.

Siriaco. Don Fortino's nephew and Emiliano's son; killed in Yaitepec.

Soreano, Rosalino. A priest in Juquila, Don Fortino's godfather.

Torres Rojas, Enrique. Ex-Proferista soldier and jailer in Juquila.

Valencia, Arnulfo. Son of Florencio Valencia, finquero in Yaitepec, and member of a provisional detachment captured by Gustavo Labastida during the Revolution.

Valencia, Florencio. A finquero and cacique in Juquila and Teotepec.

Valencia, Gilberto. Florencio Valencia's brother and a resident of Teotepec.

Valencia, Nicolás. Brother of Padre Valencia and father of Lázaro Sánchez.

Valencia, Padre. A priest who established the finca La Constancia in Yaitepec and a brother of Nicolás Valencia.

Valentín, Anselmo. Don Fortino's nephew.

Valentín, Darío, of Juquila. Father of León Valentín.

Valentín, León. Don Fortino's brother-in-law, from Juquila; killed in Yaitepec at a fiesta.

Valentín, Micaela de. Wife of Darío Valentín.

Valeriano. Don Fortino's nephew in Yaitepec, Emiliano's son; killed in a feud.

Valerina, Modesto. A priest and cacique in Juquila.

Varela Villavicencio, Felipe. Don Fortino's compadre and uncle of his half brother Timoteo Santiago.

Vargas, Efren. Don Fortino's father-in-law.

Vargas, Emiliano. Eldest brother of Don Fortino's father-in-law, Efren Vargas.

Vargas, Irinia. A sister of Don Fortino's wife, Antonia.

Vargas, Manuel. A brother of Don Fortino's father-in-law, Efren Vargas.

Vargas, Sidronia. Don Fortino's wife's eldest sister.

Vargas Pantoja, Antonia. Don Fortino's wife, from Juchatengo.

Vasilides Aguilar, Natalia. Don Fortino's girlfriend; nicknamed Talia.

Vásquez, Nicolás. Don Fortino's teacher.

Velasco, Heraclio. A distant cousin of Don Fortino.

Venegas, Gustavo. Nicknamed Tavo, a foreman on the finca Las Delicias and the leader who drove Angel Aguirre from power in Nopala; killed in a feud.

Villanueva, Audifas. A brother of Alfonso Zárate Pérez, who also went to prison for stealing from the church.

Villanueva, Saúl León. A merchant in Juquila, Don Fortino's godfather, and a cacique in Juquila.

Villavicencio, Viviana. Mother of Catalina Ríos Villavicencio.

Zárate Pérez, Alfonso. Served as church sacristan with Don Fortino in Juquila; later stole the Virgin's crown and was sent to prison.

Place-Names Not Shown on the Maps

Note: Because Don Fortino generally refers to places without using their saint's name, these have been omitted except where they are necessary to distinguish between two localities.

Agua de Encino. A place in the municipio of Panixtlahuaca.
Alhaja. A place in the municipio of Juchatengo.
Arroyo de Abajo. A stream that runs through the Barrio de Jesús in Juquila.
Barrio Abajo. A barrio in Yaitepec.
Barrio Arriba. A barrio in Yaitepec.
Chiapas. A state in Mexico.
Chilillo. A village between Nopala and Lachao.
Choro Conejo. A waterfall near the town of Juquila.
Ciruelo, El. A finca near Nopala.
Ciudad Obregón. A city in the state of Sonora.
Guerrero. A state in Mexico.
Hornos de Cal. Site of a battle near Tataltepec.
Jazmín, El. A finca in the municipio of San Gabriel Mixtepec.
Miramar. A rancho near Río Grande.
Mixteca Alta. A region in northwestern Oaxaca composed of the districts of Huajuapam de León, Silacayoapan, Juxtlahuaca, Coixtlahuaca, Teposcolula, and Nochixtlán.
Navajoa. A city in the state of Sonora.
Petén. A region in Yucatán.
Petra, La. A finca in the municipio of Nopala.
Pila, La. A field in Juquila in the Barrio de San Nicolás.
Profeta, La. A finca in the municipio of Nopala.
Puebla. A state in Mexico.
Queretaro. A state in Mexico.
Río Concha. A river in the district of Juquila.
Río Grande. A river near the town of Río Grande.
Río Mano. A river near Panixtlahuaca.
San Jerónimo Coatlán. A town in the district of Miahuatlán.
Santa Mariana. A finca in the municipio of San Gabriel Mixtepec.
Santo Domingo Coatlán. A town in the district of Miahuatlán.
Tampico. A city in the state of Veracruz.
Tierra Colorada. A place on the outskirts of Juquila.
Veracruz. A state in Mexico.
Virgen, La. A finca in the municipio of San Gabriel Mixtepec.

Bibliography

Aberle, David F.
1966 *The Peyote Religion Among the Navaho*. Viking Fund Publications in Anthropology, 42. New York: Wenner Gren Foundation for Anthropological Research.

Augur, H.
1954 *Zapotec*. New York: Doubleday.

Bacon, M. K., H. Barry, and I. L. Child
1963 A Cross-Cultural Study of Correlates of Crime. *Journal of Abnormal and Social Pathology* 66:291–300.

Bartolomé, Miguel Alberto, and Alicia Mabel Barabas
1982 *Tierra de la palabra: Historia y etnografía de los Chatinos de Oaxaca*. Centro Regional de Oaxaca, Etnología, Colección Científica, 108. Mexico City: Instituto Nacional de Antropología e Historia.

Basauri, Carlos
1940 Tribu Chatinos. In *La población indígena de México*. Vol. 2. Mexico City: Secretaría de Educación Pública.

Beatlie, John
1963 Sorcery in Bunyoro. In *Witchcraft and Sorcery in East Africa*, ed. John Middleton and Edward Winter. London: Routledge and Kegan Paul.

Beltrán, Gonzalo Aguirre
1973 *Regiones de refugio: El desarrollo de la comunidad y el proceso dominical en mestizo America*. Serie de Antropología Social, no. 17. Mexico City: Instituto Nacional Indigenista.

Berlin, Heinrich
1947 *Fragmentos desconocidos del códice de Yanhuitlán y otros investigaciones mixtecas*. Mexico City: Porrúa, S. A.

Bohannan, Paul
1958 Extra-Processual Events in Tiv Political Institutions. *American Anthropologist* 60: 1–12.

Brading, David A.
1971 *Miners and Merchants in Bourbon Mexico, 1763–1810*. Cambridge: Cambridge University Press.

Brand, Donald D.
   1966   Cochineal: Aboriginal Dyestuff from Nueva España. *XXXVI Congreso Interna-cional de Americanistas, Proceedings*, 2:77–91. Seville: Congreso Internacional de Americanistas.
Buve, Raymond, Th. J.
   1971   Movimientos campesinos mexicanos: Algunos apuntes e interrogantes sobre sus orígenes en la sociedad virreinal. *Anuario de Estudios Americanos* 28:423–457.
Carrasco, Pedro
   1949   Chatino Fieldnotes. MS.
   1961   The Civil-Religious Hierarchy in Mesoamerican Communities: Pre-Hispanic Background and Colonial Development. *American Anthropologist* 63:483–497.
Casarrubias, Vicente
   1963   *Rebeliones indígenas de la Nueva España.* Mexico City: Secretaría de Educación Pública.
Chance, John K.
   1978   *Race and Class in Colonial Oaxaca.* Stanford, Calif.: Stanford University Press.
Cheetham, Nicolas
   1971   *A History of Mexico.* London: Rupert Hart-Davis.
Cinquemani, Dorothy K.
   1975   Drinking and Violence Among Middle American Indians. Ph.D. dissertation, Columbia University.
Collier, Jane F.
   1973   *Law and Social Change in Zinacantan.* Stanford, Calif.: Stanford University Press.
Cordero Avendaño de Durand, Carmen
   1986   *Stina jo'o kucha, el santo padre sol: Contribucion al conocimiento socio-religioso del grupo etnico Chatino.* Oaxaca, Mexico: Biblioteca Publica de Oaxaca, Cultura y Re-creación, Estado de Oaxaca.
Cortés, Hernando
   1942   *Cartas de relación de la conquista de Mejico.* Vols. 1 and 2. Madrid: Espasa-Calpe.
Cruz Lorenzo, Tomás
   1987   De porque las flores nunca se doblegan con el aguacero. *El Medio Milenio* (Oaxaca, Mexico) No. 1, April, pp. 28–49.
Dahlgren de Jordán, Barbro
   1954   *La Mixteca: Su cultura e historia pre-hispanica.* Mexico City: Cultura Mexicana.
DeCicco, Gabriel
   1969   The Chatino. In *Handbook of Middle American Indians*, vol. 7, ed. Robert Wauchope and Evon Z. Vogt. Austin: University of Texas Press.
Dennis, Phillip
   1976   The Uses of Inter-Village Feuding. *Anthropological Quarterly* 49:174–184.
Douglas, Mary
   1963   Techniques of Sorcery Control in Central Africa. In *Witchcraft and Sorcery in East Africa*, ed. John Middleton and Edward Winter. London: Routledge and Kegan Paul.
Durkheim, Emile
   1951   *Suicide.* Trans. John A. Spaulding and George Simpson. Glencoe, Ill.: Free Press.

Esteva, Cayetano
1913   *Geografía del Estado de Oaxaca*. Oaxaca: San German Hros.
Evans-Prichard, E. E.
1937   *Witchcraft, Oracles and Magic Among the Zande*. Oxford: Clarendon Press.
Farriss, Nancy
1984   *Maya Society Under Colonial Rule: The Collective Enterprise of Survival*. Princeton, N.J.:
        Princeton University Press.
Firth, Raymond
1936   *We, the Tikopia*. New York: American Book Co.
Flanet, Véronique
1977   *Viviré si dios quiere: Un estudio de la violencia en la Mixteca de la costa*. Mexico City:
        Instituto Nacional Indigenista.
Flannery, Kent, and Joyce Marcus, eds.
1983   *The Cloud People: Divergent Evolution of the Zapotec and Mixtec Civilizations*. New York:
        Academic Press.
Florescano, Enrique, and Isabel Gil Sánchez
1976   *Descripciones economicas regionales de Nueva España: Provincias del Centro y Sur, 1766–
        1827*. Mexico City: Instituto Nacional de Antropología e Historia, SEP-INAH.
Foster, George
1967   *Tzintzuntzan: Mexican Peasants in a Changing World*. Boston: Little, Brown.
Frank, Andre Gunder
1969   *Capitalism and Underdevelopment in Latin America: Historical Studies of Chile and Brazil*.
        2d rev. ed. New York: Monthly Review Press.
1978   *World Accumulation, 1492–1789*. New York: Monthly Review Press.
Friedrich, Paul
1977   *Agrarian Revolt in a Mexican Village*. 2d rev. ed. Chicago: University of Chicago
        Press.
Fromm, Eric, and Michael Maccoby
1970   *Social Character in a Mexican Village*. Englewood Cliffs, N.J.: Prentice-Hall.
Fry, Douglas P.
1986   An Ethnological Study of Aggression and Aggression Socialization Among
        Zapotec Children of Oaxaca, Mexico. Ph.D. dissertation, University of Indi-
        ana.
Gay, J. A.
1881   *Historia de Oaxaca*. Vols. 1 and 2. Mexico City: Telleres Venero.
Gerhard, Peter
1960   *Pirates on the West Coast of New Spain, 1575–1742*. Glendale, Calif.: Arthur H. Clark.
1972   *A Guide to the Historical Geography of New Spain*. Cambridge: Cambridge University
        Press.
Greenberg, James B.
1981   *Santiago's Sword: Chatino Peasant Economics and Religion*. Berkeley and Los Angeles:
        University of California Press.
Gregory, James R.
1975   Image of Limited Good, or Expectation of Reciprocity. *Current Anthropology*
        16(1): 73–92.

Hallowell, A. Irving
    1940   Aggression in Salteaux Society. *Psychiatry* 13:404–415.
Harris, Marvin
    1964   *Patterns of Race in the Americas.* New York: Walker.
Hauer, Rose W.
    1978   Learning to Be Violent versus Learning to be Antiviolent. Paper presented at
           the meetings of the International Society for Research on Aggression, Wash-
           ington, D.C.
Helms, Mary W.
    1975   *Middle America: A Cultural History of Heartland and Frontiers.* Englewood Cliffs, N.J.:
           Prentice-Hall.
Hernández-Díaz, Jorge
    1982   Panixtlahuaca: El café como agente de diferenciación social. In *Sociedad y po-
           litica en Oaxaca, 1980: 15 estudios de caso,* ed. Raul Benítez Zenteno. Oaxaca,
           Mexico: Instituto de Investigaciones Sociológicas, Universidad Autónoma
           Benito Juárez de Oaxaca.
    1987   *El café amargo: Diferenciación y cambio social entre los Chatinos.* Oaxaca, Mexico: In-
           stituto de Investigaciones Sociologicas, Universidad Autónoma Benito Juárez
           de Oaxaca.
Herrera y Tordesillas, Antonio de
    1726– *Historia general de los hechos castellanos en las islas y tierra firma de el mar océano.* Madrid:
    1729   Nicolás Rodríguez-Franco.
Hobsbawm, Eric
    1959   *Primitive Rebels: Studies in Archaic Forms of Social Movement in the 19th and 20th Centuries.*
           17 vols. New York: W. W. Norton.
Honigman, John
    1947   Witch-fear in post-contact Kaska Society. *American Anthropologist* 49:222–242.
Huerta, María Teresa, and Patricia Palacios, eds.
    1976   *Rebeliones indígenas de la época colonial.* Mexico City: Instituto Nacional de Antro-
           pología e Historia, SEP-INAH.
Huitzer, Gerrit, and Rodolfo Stavenhagen
    1974   Peasant Movements and Land Reform in Latin America: Mexico and Bolivia.
           In *Rural Protest, Peasant Movements and Social Change,* ed. Henry A. Landsberger.
           London: International Institute of Labour Studies.
Jayawardena, Chandra
    1968   Ideology and Conflict in Lower-Class Communities. *Comparative Studies in Soci-
           ety and History* 10:413–446.
Jijón, Octaviano
    1883   Cuadro Sinóptico y Estadístico del Distrito de Juquila. In *Colección de "cuadros
           sinópticos" de los pueblos, haciendas y ranchos del Estado libre y soberano de Oaxaca.* Vol. II.
           Ed. Martínez Gracida. Oaxaca, Mexico: Impresador del Estado.
Kappel, Wayne
    1978   The Biological Face of Antiviolence. Paper presented at the meetings of the
           International Society for Research on Aggression, Washington, D.C.
Lameiras, Brigitte B. De
    1973   *Indios de México y viajeros extranjeros: Siglo XIX.* Sep-setentas No. 74. Mexico City:
           Secretaría de Educación Pública.

Leach, Edmond R.
  1961 *Rethinking Anthropology*. London: Athlone Press.
Levy, Jerrold E., and Stephen J. Kunitz
  1971 Indian Reservations, Anomie, and Social Pathologies. *Southwestern Journal of Anthropology* 27(2): 97–128.
Lewis, Oscar
  1951 *Life in a Mexican Village: Tepoztlán Restudied*. Urbana: University of Illinois Press.
McCord, William, and Joan McCord
  1959 *Origins of Crime*. New York: Columbia University Press.
McHenry, J. Patrick
  1962 *A Short History of Mexico*. Garden City, N.J.: Doubleday.
Martínez Gracida, Manuel
  1907 Reseña histórica del antiguo reino de Tututepec. Colección Martínez Gracida, Archivo de la Casa de la Cultura de Oaxaca, Mexico. MS.
Merton, Robert K.
  1957 *Social Theory and Social Structure*. 2d rev. ed. New York: Free Press.
Nadel, Siegfried
  1952 Witchcraft in Four African Societies: An Essay in Comparison. *American Anthropologist* 54:18–29.
Nader, Laura
  1964 *Talea and Juquila: A Comparison of Zapotec Social Organization*. Los Angeles and Berkeley: University of California Press.
  1967 An Analysis of Zapotec Law Cases. In *Law and Warfare: Studies in the Anthropology of Conflict*, ed. Paul Bohannan. Garden City, N.J.: Natural History Press.
Nash, June
  1967 Death as a Way of Life: The Increasing Resort to Homicide in a Mexican Indian Town. *American Anthropologist* 69:455–470.
O'Nell, Carl W.
  1979 Nonviolence and Personality Dispositions Among the Zapotec: A Paradox Within an Enigma. *Journal of Psychological Anthropology* 2:301–322.
  1981 Hostility Management and the Control of Aggression in a Zapotec Community. *Aggressive Behavior* 7:351–366.
Opler, Morris
  1946 Chiricahua Apache Materials Relating to Sorcery. *Primitive Man* vol. 19, nos. 3–4:82–92.
  1947 Notes on Chiricahua Apache Culture: Supernatural Power and the Shaman. *Primitive Man* vol. 20, nos. 1–2:1–14.
Paddock, John
  1975 Studies on Antiviolent and 'Normal' Communities. *Aggressive Behavior* 1:217–233.
  1978 Faces of Antiviolence Symposium Introduction: The Study as Science. Paper presented at the meetings of the International Society for Research on Aggression, Washington, D.C.
  1982 Anti-violence in Oaxaca, Mexico: Archive Research. Paper presented at the meetings of the American Society for Ethnohistory, Nashville, Tennessee.

Parnell, Philip C.
  1988 *Escalating Disputes: Social Participation and Change in the Oaxacan Highlands.* Tucson: University of Arizona Press.
Paso y Troncoso, Francisco del, ed.
  1905– *Papeles de Nueva España* (PNE). 2d ser., vol. 1–6. Madrid: Sucesores de Revade-
  1906 neyra.
  1939– *Epistolario de Nueva España* (ENE). 2d ser. Mexico City: Biblioteca Historia Mexi-
  1942 cana de Obras Inéditas.
Paz, Octavio
  1961 *The Labyrinth of Solitude.* New York: Grove Press.
Pérez, Jiménez Gustavo
  1968 *La institución del municipio libre en Oaxaca: Protuario de legislación orgánica municipal.* Mexico City: Editorial Costa-Amic.
Rattray, A. S.
  1923 *Ashanti.* Oxford: Clarendon Press.
Redfield, Robert
  1930 *Tepoztlán, a Mexican Village: A Study of Folk Life.* Chicago: University of Chicago Press.
Restrepo, Camilo Torres
  1970 Social Change and Rural Violence in Colombia. In *Masses and Mobilization,* ed. Irving Louis Horowitz. New York: Oxford University Press.
Riding, Alan
  1986 *Distant Neighbors: A Portrait of the Mexicans.* New York: Vintage Press.
Rojas, Basilio
  1964 *El café.* Mexico City: Instituto Mexicano del Café.
Romanucci-Ross, Lola
  1973 *Conflict, Violence, and Morality in a Mexican Village.* Palo Alto, Calif.: National Press.
Romero-Frizzi, María de los Angeles, and Mercedes Olivera B. de Vásquez.
  1973 La estructura política de Oaxaca en el siglo XVI. *Revista Mexicana de Sociología* 35(2): 227–287.
Ruiz y Cervántez, José Manuel
  1786 *Memorias de la portentosa imagen de Nuestra Señora de Juquila.* Juquila, Oaxaca: La Iglesia Cathólica.
Sahlins, Marshall
  1972 *Stone Age Economics.* Chicago: Aldine.
Secretaría de Programación y Presupuesto
  1983 *X Censo General de Población y Vivienda, 1980, Estado de Oaxaca.* Vol. 20. Mexico City: Instituto Nacional de Estadística, Geografía e Informatica.
Selby, Henry A.
  1974 *Zapotec Deviance: The Convergence of Folk and Modern Sociology.* Austin: University of Texas Press.
Smith, Mary Elizabeth
  1973 *Picture Writing from Ancient Southern Mexico: Mixtec Place Signs and Maps.* Norman: University of Oklahoma Press.
Spindler, Louis
  1952 Witchcraft in Menominee Acculturation. *American Anthropologist* 54:393–403.

Spores, Ronald
1967 *The Mixtec Kings and Their People*. Norman: University of Oklahoma Press.
1975 Regional Systems and Sociopolitical Domains in the Mixteca of Oaxaca. Paper presented at the annual meeting of the American Anthropological Association, San Francisco.
1984 Multi-Level Government in Nineteenth-Century Oaxaca. In *Five Centuries of Law and Politics in Central Mexico*, ed. Ronald Spores and Ross Hassig. Publications in Anthropology. Nashville: Vanderbilt University.

Spores, Ronald, and M. Saldaña
1975 *Documentos para la etnohistoria del Estado de Oaxaca. Indice del ramo de indios del Archivo General de la Nación*. Vanderbilt University Publications in Anthropology, no. 5. Nashville: Vanderbilt University.

Sumner, M. L.
1978 The Social Face of Antiviolence. Paper presented at the meetings of the International Society for Research on Aggression, Washington, D.C.

Takahashi, Hitoshi
1981 De la huerta a la hacienda: El orígen de la producción agropecuaria en la Mixteca Costera. *Historia Mexicana*. 3(1): 1–78.

Taussig, Michael
1978 The Devil and Commodity Fetishism in Colombia and Bolivia. Ms.
1980 *The Devil and Commodity Fetishism in South America*. Chapel Hill: University of North Carolina Press.

Taylor, William B.
1972 *Landlord and Peasant in Colonial Oaxaca*. Stanford: Stanford University Press.
1979 *Drinking, Homicide, and Rebellion in Colonial Mexican Villages*. Stanford, Calif.: Stanford University Press.

United Nations. Department of Economic and Social Affairs. Statistical Office
1985 *Demographic Yearbook*. New York: United Nations.

Vélez-Ibáñez, Carlos
1983 *Bonds of Mutual Trust: The Cultural Systems of Rotating Credit Associations Among Urban Mexicans and Chicanos*. New Brunswick, N.J.: Rutgers University Press.

Vogt, Evon Z.
1969 *Zinacantan: A Maya Community in the Highlands of Chiapas*. Cambridge, Mass: Harvard University Press.

Walker, Deward D.
1967 Nez Perce Sorcery. *Ethnology* 6:66–96.

Wallerstein, Immanuel
1974 *The Modern World-System: Capitalist Agriculture and the Origins of the European World-Economy in the Sixteenth Century*. New York: Academic Press.
1979 *The Capitalist World-Economy*. New York: Cambridge University Press.

Waterbury, Ronald
1975 Non-Revolutionary Peasants: Oaxaca Compared to Morelos in the Mexican Revolution. *Comparative Studies in Sociology and History* 17(4): 410–442.

Whitecotton, Joseph
1977 *The Zapotecs: Princes, Priests, and Peasants*. Norman: University of Oklahoma Press.

Whiting, B.
   1950   *Paiute Sorcery.* Viking Fund Publications in Anthropology, no. 15. New York: Wenner Gren Foundation for Anthropological Research.
Wilson, Monica
   1951   Witch Beliefs and Social Structure. *American Journal of Sociology* 56:307–313.
Wolf, Eric
   1955   Types of Latin American Peasantry: A Preliminary Discussion. *American Anthropologist* 57:452–471.
   1957   Closed Corporate Peasant Communities in Mesoamerica and Java. *Southwestern Journal of Anthropology* 13:1–18.
   1959   *Sons of the Shaking Earth: The People of Mexico and Guatemala—Their Land, History, and Culture.* Chicago: University of Chicago Press.
   1969   *Peasant Wars of the Twentieth Century.* New York: Harper and Row.
Womack, John, Jr.
   1969   *Zapata and the Mexican Revolution.* New York: Alfred A. Knopf.
Zavala, Silvio, and José Miranda
   1973   Instituciones indígenas en la colonia. In *La política indigenista en México: Metodos y resultados,* ed. Alfonso Caso. 2d ed. Mexico City: Instituto Nacional Indigenista.

Index

About the Author

James B. Greenberg is the head of the borderlands section of the Bureau of Applied Research in Anthropology at the University of Arizona. He received his doctorate from the University of Michigan and has worked among the Chatino since 1973. He is the author of *Santiago's Sword: Chatino Peasant Religion and Economics*, which was published by the University of California Press in 1981.